Becoming a Critical Thinker

A User-Friendly Manual

Sherry Diestler
Contra Costa College

Macmillan Publishing Company
NEW YORK
Maxwell Macmillan Canada
TORONTO
Maxwell Macmillan International
NEW YORK • OXFORD • SINGAPORE • SYDNEY

For John
and for Zachary, Jenna, and Laura

Editor: Maggie Barbieri
Production Editor: Ann-Marie WongSam
Art Coordinator: Lorraine Woost
Cover Designer: Robert Vega
Production Manager: Jeanie Berke
Artist: Jane Lopez
Electronic Text Management: Ben Ko, Marilyn Wilson Phelps

This book was set in Garamond and Avant Garde Gothic by Macmillan Publishing Company and was printed and bound by R. R. Donnelley & Sons Company. The cover was printed by Phoenix Color Corp.

Macmillan Publishing Company
866 Third Avenue
New York, New York 10022

Macmillan Publishing Company is part of the
Maxwell Communication Group of Companies.

Maxwell Macmillan Canada, Inc.
1200 Eglinton Avenue East, Suite 200
Don Mills, Ontario M3C 3N1

Library of Congress Cataloging-in-Publication Data
Diestler, Sherry.
    Becoming a critical thinker : a user-friendly manual / Sherry
Diestler.
        p.   cm.
    Includes index.
    ISBN 0-02-328772-1 (pbk.)
    1. Critical thinking.   I. Title.
BF441.D54   1994
160—dc20   92-40153
        CIP
Printing: 1 2 3 4 5 6 7   Year: 4 5 6 7 8 9 0

Foreword

This book is fresh air. Consider the title. Consider the word "Becoming." The word is a reminder. It is a reminder that the tasks, skills, mind sets, ways of life, involved in thinking critically are ongoing. Someone with whom I spent a quarter century inclined to end a conversation, "And you call yourself a critical thinker!" Half the time she was right. Everyone can get better. The state indeed is one of "becoming."

What is this "it," this state? It's the art of asking right questions, including right questions about one's own thoughts. It's the art of mustering reasons. Accordingly, it's the art of obtaining the right facts—knowing where to look for them and of measuring to what degrees they count. It's the art of pinpointing the real issue and of noticing when an arguer evades it.

The "it" is not just an art, it's a disposition and a commitment. In their place tantrums may be fine, but not usually. Judiciously employed logic, cool thinking, gentle persuasion, are normally superior by far.

What passes for this book's field—what is variously called argumentation, informal logic, critical thinking, argument rhetoric—has until recently to an extent been clogged—with legalese and Latin, with philosophical and sciences theory. Of it could be said what one Victorian said of the Common Room at Balliol College, Oxford, that it "stank of logic."

Not anymore. This book is nearly devoid of clogs. It's indeed, as its title proclaims, "user friendly."

Perry Weddle
Center for Reasoning Arts
Editor, CT News
CSU-Sacramento

Preface

Everyone thinks. If you ask people where they stand on a particular issue, they will usually tell you what they believe and give reasons to support their beliefs. Many people, however, find it difficult to evaluate a written or spoken commentary on a controversial issue because both sides of the controversy seem to have good arguments.

The *critical* thinker is able to distinguish high-quality, well-supported arguments from arguments with little or no evidence to back them. This text is meant to train students to evaluate the many claims facing them as citizens, learners, consumers, and human beings, and also to be effective advocates for their beliefs.

Becoming a Critical Thinker is designed to be interdisciplinary and to be useful in courses in critical thinking and informal logic, English, speech, journalism, and the social sciences. The skills that distinguish critical thinkers across the curriculum are presented in a clear and comprehensible manner.

Unique Features

Many elements of this text have been chosen because of their practical application for the student:

1. Each concept is explained with examples, and the examples often proceed from the personal to the social or political. In this way, students can see that the same skills used in understanding arguments in daily life are used in analyzing political and commercial rhetoric.

2. Graphic illustrations help students visualize important concepts.

3. Exercises of varying levels of difficulty are given throughout the chapters to help students practice critical thinking skills.

4. Students are taught to construct and present arguments so that they can gain skill and confidence as advocates.

5. There is an early and primary emphasis on understanding conflicting value systems and on ethics in argumentation and decision-making.

6. Students are given practical methods for overcoming egocentrism and sociocentrism.

7. Emphasis is placed on understanding and analyzing the impact of print and electronic media on arguments.

8. The articles selected for use in the text are contemporary and express a variety of political viewpoints and ethical concerns.

9. Multicultural perspectives are presented throughout, in examples and articles. Many exercises and assignments encourage students to understand the perspectives of others and to broaden their own perspectives.

10. There is a variety of writing and speaking assignments at the end of each chapter.

Acknowledgments

My husband, John Diestler, has been an invaluable help in many ways. He provided expertise on the "user-friendly" format; he worked out preliminary designs for the logos and figures in the text; and he made useful suggestions on the manuscript throughout its production.

I want to thank Maggie Barbieri, editor of Philosophy and Religion at Macmillan, for her enthusiasm and encouragement throughout this project; her belief in the importance of the concepts covered in this text and her succinct suggestions for improving the manuscript inspired me to complete the book in a timely manner. I am appreciative of Barbara Duffy for bringing the book to Macmillan's attention and to Helen McInnis for initially expressing interest in it. I also want to thank Ann-Marie WongSam and her supportive staff for their highly skillful and professional supervision of the text's production.

I am grateful to the instructors who used material from this text for their critical thinking classes. Linda Berry, English instructor at College of Alameda, helped create some of the exercises that are in the text. Connie Anderson, Candy Rose, Lee Loots, Sandy Ruliffson, and Barbara Jackowski used material from the book in their courses in critical thinking in the Contra Costa Community College district; all of the instructors provided constructive suggestions and gathered student papers to use as samples for the text. Bruce Reeves of Diablo Valley College also gave generously of his time and advice on effective writing assignments. Several presenters and participants from the annual Conference on Critical Thinking at Sonoma State University, including Betty Duffey, Connie Missimer, Marlys Mayfield, and John Splaine, kindly shared a variety of relevant research material. Beth Dubberley did an excellent job of copy editing the text and provided many helpful suggestions. Patti Preut was a dedicated and resourceful research assistant.

In addition, I wish to thank the following reviewers for their invaluable advice and encouragement: Mark Weinstein, Montclair State; David Seiple, Columbia University; Jarrett Leplin, University of North Carolina; Janet Maddeu, El Camino College; Sahotra Sarkar, Boston University; Lynn Phelps, Ohio University; Connie Anderson, Diablo Valley College; Donna Bestock, Skyline College; and Perry Weddle, CSU-Sacramento.

I am appreciative of the students who have taken my critical thinking classes and have let me know what worked well and what needed improvement in the course, and of my own mentors, Gerald Phillips, Joseph DeVito, and Parke Burgess.

For their practical help that allowed me the time and energy to write the text, I have many friends to thank, but in the interest of space will limit these to my parents, Anne and Al Goldstein, and to Kathleen and Hugo Santucci, and John, Zachary, Jenna, and Laura Diestler.

Above all, I am grateful to the Creator of the human mind.

Contents

x   Contents

CHAPTER ONE

Foundations of Arguments

What Is a Critical Thinker and When Do You Need to Be One?

A critical thinker understands the structure of an argument, whether that argument is presented by a politician, a salesperson, a friend, a spouse, or a child.

This chapter will cover:

◆ The structure of an argument
◆ The three parts of an argument: issues, reasons, and conclusions

We live in what has been called the Age of Information because of the many messages that we receive daily from newspapers, magazines, radio, television, and books.

Sometimes we turn to this information for its entertainment value, such as when we watch a situation comedy, listen to music, or read the sports page. But in a democratic society, in which the people are asked to vote on candidates and political propositions, we also need to use print and electronic sources to help us make decisions about the direction our community, state, and nation will take.

We need to know how to understand and evaluate the information that comes our way. This book will give you tools for coming to rational conclusions and making responsible choices.

A critical thinker is someone who uses careful and objective reasoning to evaluate claims and make decisions.

When you learn to communicate well in a formal situation, your skill usually transfers to informal situations as well. For example, if you learn to make an effective informative speech in the classroom, you will also feel better about introducing yourself at parties or making a spontaneous toast at your brother's wedding. The same principle applies to critical thinking skills.

When you can listen to a presidential debate and make good judgments about what each candidate has to offer, you may also be more thoughtful about less formal arguments that are presented, such as which breakfast cereal is best for you or which car you should buy. You will be better prepared to deal with sales pitches, whether written, televised, or personal.

The methods of decision-making that you learn will apply to choosing a viewpoint on a political issue or to choosing a career, a place to live, or a mate.

In short, critical thinkers do not just drift through life subject to every message that they hear; they think through their choices and make conscious decisions. They also understand the basics of both creating and presenting credible arguments.

The Structure of Argument

"The aim of argument, or of discussion, should not be victory, but progress."

Joseph Joubert, *Pensees* (1842)

When most people hear the word *argument,* they think of a disagreement between two or more people that may escalate into name-calling, angry words, or even physical violence.

Our definition of argument is different. When critical thinkers speak about an argument, we are referring to a **conclusion** that someone has (often called a claim or position) about a particular **issue**. This conclusion is supported with **reasons** (often called premises). If an individual has a conclusion but offers no reasons why he has come to that conclusion, then he has only made a statement, not an argument.

Political slogans, often found on billboards or in television advertisements, are good examples of conclusions (opinions) that should not be relied upon because supporting reasons are not offered. If you see a billboard that proclaims, "A vote for Johnson is a vote for the right choice," you are encountering a conclusion with no evidence, which does not constitute an argument.

Critical thinkers withhold judgment on such a claim until they have looked at evidence both for and against Johnson as a candidate.

The three parts of an argument are the *issue,* the *conclusion,* and the *reasons.*

The Issue

The issue is the question that is being addressed. It is easiest to put the issue in question form so that you know what is being discussed. When you listen to a discussion of a political or social issue, think of the question being addressed.

Examples of Issues:
- Should North, Central, and South Americans work together to combat acid rain?
- Should air traffic controllers be given periodic drug tests?

The same method of "issue detection" will be useful in understanding commercial appeals (ads) and personal requests.

More Examples of Issues:
- Is Alpo the best food for your dog?
- Should you marry Leslie?
- Should you subscribe to the *Wall Street Journal?*

Another way to isolate the issue is to state, "The issue is whether _____."

- The issue is whether aspirin can prevent heart disease.

Every decision we need to make will be made easier if we can define exactly what we are being asked to believe or do. Public discourse often breaks down when two or more parties get into a heated discussion over different issues. This phenomenon occurs regularly on talk shows.

For example, a recent television talk show featured the general topic of spousal support, and the issue was "Should the salary of a second wife be used in figuring alimony for the first wife?" The lawyer who was being interviewed kept reminding the guests of this issue as they proceeded to argue instead about whether child support should be figured from the second wife's salary, whether the first wife should hold a job, and even whether one first wife was a good person.

A general rule is that the more emotional the reactions to the issue, the more likely the issue will become lost. The real problem here is that the basic issue can become so fragmented into different sub-issues that people are no longer discussing the same question.

SKILL

Understand the issue, make sure everyone is discussing the same issue, and bring the discussion back on target when necessary.

When you listen to televised debates or interviews, note how often a good speaker or interviewer will remind the audience of the issue. Also notice how experienced spokespersons or politicians will often respond to a direct, clearly defined issue with a pre-programmed answer that addresses a *different* issue, one they can discuss more easily.

If a presidential candidate is asked how he is going to balance our federal budget, he might declare passionately that he will never raise taxes. He has thus skillfully accomplished two things: He has avoided the difficult issue, and he has taken a popular, vote-enhancing stand on a separate issue.

EXERCISE

Purpose: To be able to identify issues.

1. Read an essay or an editorial, study an advertisement, listen to a radio talk-show, or watch a television show on a controversial issue. Define the issue and see if the speakers or writers stay with the issue.

   In particular, try to find an example of a person who is asked to respond to one issue and instead gives an answer to a different issue. Check to see if the interviewer reminds the speaker that he or she has not answered the question.

2. By yourself, or as a class, come up with as many current issues as you can. Think of both light and serious issues; consider campus, community, social, national, and international concerns. Now, look at your list of issues and choose three that really concern you. Then, try to choose three about which you are neutral. Finally, answer these questions:
   a. What is it about the first three issues that makes you concerned?
   b. Why are you neutral about some issues?
   c. Do you believe there are issues on the list that should be more important to you? Why or why not?

REMINDER

Whenever you are confronted with an argument, try to define the issue and put the issue in question form.

The Conclusion

Once an issue has been defined, we can state our conclusion about the issue. Using some examples previously mentioned, **we can say yes or no to the issues presented**: yes, I believe air traffic controllers should be tested for drug usage; no, I don't want to subscribe to the *Wall Street Journal;* yes, I will marry Leslie, and so on. We take a stand on the issues given.

The conclusion is the position taken about an issue. It is a claim supported by evidence statements. These evidence statements are called reasons or premises. (For a discussion of premises, see Chapter 3.)

We often hear the cliche "Everyone has a right to his or her opinion." This is true, in the legal sense—North Americans do not have "thought police" who decide what can and cannot be discussed. When you are a critically thinking person, however, your opinion has *substance*. That substance consists of the reasons you give to support your opinion. Conclusions (opinions) with substance are more valuable and credible than conclusions offering no supporting evidence.

The term *conclusion* is used differently in different fields of study. The definition given here applies most correctly to the study of argumentation. In an argumentative essay, the thesis statement will express the conclusion of the writer. In Chapter 3, you will note a related definition of conclusion used by philosophers in the study of deductive and inductive reasoning. In addition, the term *conclusion* is used to describe the final part of an essay or speech.

REMINDER

Conclusions are the positions people take on issues. Other words used to mean conclusions are claims, viewpoints, opinions, and stands. We use the term conclusion because most people who teach argumentation use the term. The other words listed can mean the same thing.

How can we locate the conclusion of an argument? Try the following methods when you have trouble finding the conclusions:

1. Find the issue and ask yourself what position the writer or speaker is taking on the issue.

2. Look at the beginning, or ending of a paragraph or an essay; the conclusion is often found in one of these places.

3. Look for conclusion indicator words: *therefore, so, thus, hence*. Also, look for indicator phrases: *"My point is," "What I am saying is," "What I believe is."* Some indicator words and phrases are selected to imply that the conclusion drawn is the right one. These include: *obviously, it is evident that, there is no doubt (or question) that, certainly,* and *of course*.

4. Ask yourself, "What is being claimed by this writer or speaker?"

5. Look at the title of an essay; sometimes the conclusion is contained within the title. For example, an essay might be called "Why I believe vitamins are essential to health."

SKILL

Find the conclusion or conclusions to an argument. Ask yourself what position the writer or speaker is taking on the issue.

You may hear people discussing an issue, and someone says, "I don't know anything about this, but . . ." and proceeds to give an opinion about the issue. This is usually a non-critical comment made to continue a conversation. A critical thinker takes a stand only when he or she knows something about the issue. This something is expressed in the form of reasons why the critical thinker has come to a certain conclusion. Of course, a critical thinker is open to hearing new evidence and may change his or her opinion on issues as new information becomes available.

EXERCISE

Purpose: To be able to isolate conclusions.

Take your list of issues from Question 2 in the previous exercise. Choose four issues and, in a simple declarative sentence, write your conclusion for each one.

The Reasons

> *Everything reasonable may be supported.*
>
> Epictetus, *Discourses* (2nd century)

Reasons are the statements that provide support for conclusions. Without reasons, you have no argument; you simply have a statement of someone's opinion as evidenced in the following limerick:

> I do not like thee, Doctor Fell
> The reason why I cannot tell
> But this I know, I know full well
> I do not like thee, Doctor Fell.

Reasons are also called *evidence, premises, support,* or *justification*. You will spend most of your time and energy as a critical thinker and responsible writer and speaker looking at the quality of the reasons used to support a conclusion.

Here are some ways to locate the reasons in an argument:

1. Find the conclusion and then apply the "because trick." The writer or speaker believes _____ (conclusion) because _____ . The reasons will naturally follow the word *because*.

2. Look for other indicator words that are similar to *because: since, for, first, second, third, as evidenced by, also, furthermore, in addition*.

3. Look for evidence supporting the conclusion. This support can be in the form of examples, statistics, analogies, reports of studies and expert testimony.

There is a world of difference between supporting a political candidate because his or her policies make sense to you and supporting the same candidate because he or she looks like a good person. Information in the following chapters of this book will give you the skills to help you decide how a reason supports a conclusion.

Critical thinkers focus their attention first on what issue is being discussed, second, on what conclusions are taken, and third, on what reasons are given to support or justify the conclusions.

The Born Loser ® by Art and Chip Sansom
BORN LOSER reprinted by permission of NEA, Inc.

SKILL

Find the reasons that support the conclusion.

REMINDER

Since the reasons answer the question "Why do you believe what you believe?" a good trick in isolating the reasons is to write the conclusion and then add the word because.

Example

I believe student athletes should be paid (conclusion) because:

- they are committed to certain hours and demands on their time
- they are making money for their schools

EXERCISE

Purposes: To be able to use reasons to support a conclusion. To be able to use knowledge gained in this chapter to both analyze and construct basic arguments.

1. Write a short rebuttal to the student athletes example, using reasons to support your conclusion.
2. Take your conclusions from the exercise on conclusions and support each conclusion with at least three reasons. This exercise can be done alone or in classroom groups.
3. Get the editorial page of your favorite newspaper (including your campus paper) and list the issue, conclusion, and reasons given for each editorial. Use this format:

   The issue (question) is:
   The conclusion of this writer is:
   The reasons he/she gives are:

Then evaluate the editorial by answering the questions:
a. Was the writer clear about the reasons given for the conclusion?

      b. Were there other reasons that could have been included in the argument?

      c. Did the writer express any understanding for an opposing viewpoint? If so, how? If not, can you articulate an opposing viewpoint for the editorial?

      d. Were you convinced by the editorial? Why or why not?

4. Read the following editorial essays, letters, and writings. Then, isolate the issues discussed, the conclusions of the writers, and the reasons given for the conclusions. Answer the following questions:

      a. Are the reasons given adequate to support the conclusions? If not, what other reasons could have been given?

      b. Do you agree or disagree with the conclusions? If you disagree, what are your reasons for disagreeing?

Taxpayers' Money Wasted

by Roy H. Wallis
Contra Costa Times, May 25, 1990

The taxpayers of California have paid $600,000 to the Public Health School at UC–Berkeley (where else?) to prepare an 80-page "Wellness Guide" with such advice as: Don't beat, starve or lock up your kids. Don't buy something you can't afford. If you are sexually active and don't want to have a baby, you may want to use birth control.

Not included was: Don't sit down on the street in a busy intersection. But maybe that's being saved for the next edition.

OK, taxpayers, who intends to vote for a tax increase in the upcoming election?

Don't Starve Kids' Nutrition Program

San Diego Union–Tribune, July 31, 1990

Thousands of toddlers and infants in poor families across the nation will soon find less cereal in their breakfast bowls, less orange juice or formula in their bottles. They may not understand that the program that helped nourish them was hurt by rising food prices and a deficit-ridden federal government pleading its own poverty case.

But some are sure to feel the effects of government stinginess—hunger, malnutrition and preventable disease. Studies have shown that Special Supplemental 39 Food Program for Women, Infants and Children, a welfare service for poor pregnant women and new mothers, is an effective program.

It has a record of reducing infant mortality, increasing birth weights and improving the health of mothers and their young offspring.

Now, the whims of the dairy, orange and grain market have dictated an 8 percent increase in the price of the government's basic nutritional package, and states are scrambling to figure out how to stretch their food dollars. In California, a poor child's monthly juice allotment will drop from 288 ounces to 144 ounces.

In Missouri, officials have decided to suspend food benefits for children that look healthy—until they show signs of malnutrition.

The foolish policy of underfunding a vital nutrition program not only threatens more hardships for the poor. It's likely to backfire on the taxpayers. More low birth-weight infants and sick children eventually results in higher health-care costs.

Congress is only proposing a $150 million increase in the $2.1 billion program. That's not even enough to keep up with the higher food prices.

Meanwhile, the federal government seems willing to fork over billions more to bail out failing savings and loan companies. Our priorities are out of kilter.

Do we really want to be remembered as the prosperous nation that took bottles out of the mouths of hungry babies?

Reprinted by permission of the *San Diego Union–Tribune*.

Male and Female Olympians

by Tom Callahan
U.S. News & World Report, March 2, 1992

"Unlike the women, we don't train with the full weight of our psyches," said figure skater Paul Wylie, a Harvard man of 27 from whom nothing was expected and to whom a silver medal was delivered. "If he's not in a monied sport—football, baseball or basketball—an American male can get to feeling a little self-conscious when he reaches his upper 20s and he's still on an athletic grant. American men just feel like they should have real jobs. A man's job is supposed to be the most important thing, isn't it? How can he define himself totally as a skater or a luger? He can't help but have some kind of an identity crisis."

And the U.S. woman does not?

"No," Wylie offered, "because athletics might be the only medium open to her where she can perform and be rewarded fairly. For the woman Olympian, this is more of a primary thing. It's a career path. She's not putting off the rest of her life. This is her life . . ."

. . ."In my sport, figure skating, there's no doubt that European women are holding on to old roles. They're better ice dancers and pairs skaters than individuals. To Europeans, sport is still fundamentally a man's thing. The woman still takes the man's arm. Not the Americans, though. Not anymore. Our women are going to be the greatest athletes in the world. They're pretty great now."

Reprinted by permission of the publisher.

Chapter Highlights

1. Critical thinking about information is necessary for us to make clear decisions as citizens, consumers, and human beings.
2. An argument consists of issues, conclusions, and reasons.
3. The issue is the question that is raised; our decisions are made easier if we can define the issues on which we are asked to comment or act.
4. The conclusion is the position a person takes on an issue.
5. Reasons, often called premises, provide support for conclusions; reasons are acceptable or unacceptable on the basis of their relevance and quality.

Articles for Discussion

These two articles give differing viewpoints on the same issue. Read both and then consider the questions that follow.

Talk-show Host Angers Disabled Community

Hand Deformity Inherited from Mom Sparks L.A. Dispute

by Michael Fleeman
Associated Press, September 2, 1991

LOS ANGELES—Aaron James Lampley, all 7 pounds, 14 1/2 ounces of him, was only a few hours old when a local radio station dedicated a show for the second time to the circumstances and controversy surrounding his birth.

In addressing the matter again, KFI-AM last week refueled a dispute that pitted the station against activists for the disabled and raised questions about freedom of speech and society's treatment of the disabled.

Aaron Lampley was born Wednesday morning, with ectodactyly, which leaves the bones in the feet and hands fused. His mother, local TV anchorwoman Bree Walker Lampley, also has the condition and knew the child had a 50 percent chance of inheriting it.

Her other child, a daughter, has the condition as well.

Before the boy's birth, KFI outraged the KCBS-TV anchorwoman and advocates for people with disabilities with a July 22 call-in show in which host Jane Norris asked whether it was fair for Walker Lampley to give birth when the child had a "very good chance of having a disfiguring disease."

Critics of the show said it smacked of bigotry and illustrated societal prejudice and lack of understanding toward the disabled. KFI said the matter was handled properly and that radio talk shows are appropriate forums for controversial issues.

In KFI's second visit to the subject, this time with Norris acting as guest on Tom Leykis' afternoon show, Norris accused Walker Lampley of orchestrating a campaign to discredit her and contended she had a First Amendment right to discuss the matter.

"I was supportive of Bree's decision," Norris said on the show. "All I did, and have done, is voice my opinion of what would be right for me. I thought I handled the topic sensitively, but all [Walker Lampley has] seen fit to do is slander me."

Norris' statements did nothing to cool the situation.

"They came on the air supposedly to set the record straight. In our view, she set the record even more crooked," said Lillabeth Navarro of *American Disabled for Access Power Today*.

"This is like a bunch of thugs ganging up on the disability community. It just rained forth what caused us to be outraged to begin with."

Navarro said activists planned a protest at KFI studios.

The demonstration is part of a grass-roots campaign organized in part by a media consulting firm hired by Walker Lampley and her husband, KCBS anchorman Jim Lampley.

The company, EIN SOF Communications, gives the disability rights community a public voice. The firm has sent tapes of the Norris show to disability rights groups and is helping to file a complaint with the Federal Communications Commission.

In the original show, Norris said she wasn't intending to dictate what Walker Lampley should have done. But she said she couldn't have made the same decision if she were in Walker Lampley's position.

Norris said there were "so many other options available," including adoption and surrogate parenting, and "it would be difficult to bring myself to morally cast my child forever to disfigured hands."

Throughout the show, Norris seemed to take issue with people who disagreed with her.

After a caller named Jennifer from Los Angeles said, "I don't really see why it's your business," Norris responded, "Well, I think it's everybody's business. This is life. These things happen in life. What's your problem? Do you have a problem talking about deformities?"

Norris also repeatedly referred to Walker Lampley's condition, ectodactyly, as a disease, even though it is a genetically caused disability.

Walker Lampley and her husband, in interviews before their child was born, said Norris' first program was an attack on the handicapped and Walker Lampley personally, and was full of errors and poorly chosen remarks.

"I felt assaulted and terrorized," Walker Lampley said. "I felt like my pregnancy had been robbed of some of its joy."

She added, "I felt disappointed that someone would be so insensitive."

Reprinted by permission of the Associated Press.

Radio Show on Rights of Disabled Defended

Crippled Woman's Pregnancy Debated

San Francisco Examiner, December 15, 1991

LOS ANGELES—The chairman of the Equal Employment Opportunity Commission said a local radio station shouldn't be disciplined for a talk show that debated whether a disabled TV anchorwoman should give birth.

Chairman Evan J. Kemp, who is disabled and confined to a wheelchair, said he was "appalled and sickened" by the majority of callers to the KFI program who said KCBS anchor Bree Walker Lampley had no right to become pregnant and should abort if she did.

However, Kemp said the right of free speech should protect KFI from any Federal Communications Commission action.

Kemp's statements were published in the Los Angeles *Times*.

Lampley, who was pregnant at the time of the July 1991 broadcast, lodged a complaint to the FCC and asked for an investigation. The newswoman, her husband, co-anchor Jim Lampley, and more than 20 organizations for the disabled asked the agency to examine whether the station and its owner, Cox Broadcasting Corp., should lose their license, be fined or reprimanded.

The couple charged the broadcast was not a thorough discussion, but rather an attack on Lampley's integrity without inviting them to appear and harassed callers who attempted to express contrary views.

Lampley gave birth five weeks after the broadcast to a boy who had the same genetic condition as his mother—ectodactylism, in which the bones of the hands and feet are fused. There was a 50 percent chance that the baby would have the condition.

Kemp said he was not speaking out as chairman of the Washington, D.C.-based EEOC, but as a "severely disabled person" with a rare polio-like disease—Kugelberg–Welander—that may be inherited.

He said he plans to write to the FCC to defend grass-roots discussions and radio talk shows such as the KFI program as necessary forums.

Reprinted by permission of the Associated Press.

Questions for Discussion

1. The author of the first article states that this controversy "raised questions about freedom of speech and society's treatment of the disabled." What were the questions—i.e., issues—that were raised?

2. Take one of the issues raised by the talk show controversy and discuss how well it was defended by those mentioned in the articles.

3. Comment on the following excerpt from the first article. What is your opinion of the host's response to the caller?

   After a caller named Jennifer from Los Angeles said, "I don't really see why it's your business," Norris responded, "Well, I think it's everybody's business. This is life. These things happen in life. What's your problem? Do you have a problem talking about deformities?"

4. Are there any issues discussed by radio and television talk shows that you consider inappropriate? Are certain groups targeted for criticism and others left alone, or is every topic fair game? Give examples to support your answer.

5. Each article used a different subheading to explain the controversy. The first article's subheading reads: "Hand Deformity Inherited from Mom Sparks L.A. Dispute." The second article's subheading says: "Crippled Woman's Pregnancy Debated." How do these different subheadings frame the issue? To what extent do you think they are fair and accurate statements about the controversy?

Ideas for Writing or Speaking

1. Consider the following quote from the first article: "Critics of the show said it smacked of bigotry and illustrated societal prejudice and lack of understanding toward the disabled. KFI said the matter was handled properly and that radio talk shows are appropriate forums for controversial issues." The framers of our Bill of Rights did not anticipate the phenomenon of broadcast media. Based on your understanding of the freedom of speech, are there any issues that should not be discussed in a public forum? Does the sensitivity to the feelings of a particular group make some topics less desirable for public discussion? State your conclusion and support it with reasons.

2. Take a stand on one of the issues involved in these articles. Write an essay or give a short speech, expressing your viewpoint and supporting it with reasons.

3. Imagine that you are a program director for a radio talk show. What guidelines would you give your talk show hosts? Give reasons for each guideline. Share your guidelines in a group, or write them in essay form.

4. Write or speak on the following: Given the power of talk show hosts to influence large numbers of people, do you believe there should be stricter licensing requirements for this profession, as there are for doctors, lawyers, and accountants, to ensure a uniform code of journalistic conduct? If so, why? If not, why not?

More Ideas for Writing or Speaking

1. Think about an issue that really interests you; it might be an issue currently being debated on your campus, or a community or national problem. The editorial pages of campus, community, or national newspapers may give you more ideas to help you choose your issue.

   In the form of an essay or a brief speech, state the issue and your conclusion and give at least three reasons to support your conclusion.

   In the classroom, take a few minutes for each person to share his or her speech or essay and see if the rest of the class understands the issue, conclusion, and reasons of the speaker. Don't use this exercise to debate issues (that will come later). At this point, strive only to make yourself clear and to understand the basic arguments of others.

2. Letter or speech of complaint: Practice using your knowledge about the structure of argument by writing a letter of complaint or doing a classroom "complaint speech."

   Constructive complaining is an important life skill. Use this letter or speech to express your dissatisfaction. Choose the most relevant aspects of the problem to discuss. A clear statement of the issue, your conclusion, and reasons distinguishes "whining" from complaining. Whereas whining could be characterized as a long string of feelings expressed vehemently about random aspects of a problem, a true complaint describes the nature of the problem in an organized fashion. Sincerely expressed feelings then add richness to the clear and organized content.

   To make the complaint clear, be sure to support your ideas with examples, illustrations, instances, statistics, testimony, or visual aids. To make your feelings clear, you can use vivid language, humor, sarcasm, understatement, exaggeration, irony, and dramatic emphasis.

   Examples of topics for the complaint speech/essay: a letter or speech to a city planning commission about excessive airport noise, a letter to a supervisor about a change in salary or working conditions, a complaint to neighbors about reckless driving in the neighborhood, a complaint to housemates about sharing the work load, a letter or speech to insurance agents about rates for college students.[1]

---

[1] This assignment was created with help from the Diablo Valley College Speech Department with Lee Loots and additional ideas from English instructor Bruce Reeves.

CHAPTER TWO

Values and Ethics

What Price Ethics and Can You Afford Not to Pay?

A critical thinker understands the value assumptions underlying many arguments, and recognizes that conflicts are often based on differing values.

A critical thinker is aware of his or her standards.

This chapter will cover:

◆ Value assumptions
◆ Conflict between value assumptions
◆ Ethics in argumentation
◆ Ethical decision-making

In the first chapter, we discussed the structure of argument, including issues, conclusions about issues, and evidence to support conclusions. Chapters 4, 5, and 6 will examine the quality of evidence given to support conclusions. This chapter and the next will cover the assumptions underlying arguments that influence all of us as we consider claims and take positions on issues.

Assumptions are ideas we take for granted; as such, they are often left out of a written or spoken argument. Just as we can look at the structure of a house without seeing the foundation, we can look at the structure of an argument without examining the foundational elements. To truly understand the quality of a house or an argument, we need to understand the foundation upon which it is built.

Assumptions made by speakers and writers come in two forms: value assumptions and reality assumptions. *Value assumptions* are beliefs about how the world should be, and *reality assumptions* are beliefs about how the world is. We will look at reality assumptions in Chapter 3. In this chapter, we will focus on value assumptions that form the foundations of conclusions; we will also examine ethics in argumentation and decision-making.

Consider the values expressed in the following newspaper column. Compare the answers given to the question, "What fictional character do you admire most?" What are the different values represented by the choices? Do you think the careers chosen by the respondents reflect their values?

Question Man: Fictional Character You Admire Most?

by Kris Conti
San Francisco Chronicle, January 28, 1990

Female, 23, curatorial assistant:
Howard Roark of *The Fountainhead* for never compromising his standards. His self-centeredness and arrogance was a problem, but I admired the fact that he had standards and lived by them. It seems that standards are fairly loose, sort of ad hoc. People go by the situation they're in rather than a set of standards that they follow. I admire someone who has ideals.

Female, 31, bank teller:
Scrooge. He was a cad but when he had a chance to turn his life around he did. I admire his ability to turn his life around, because it's hard to change. He finally found that being rich is not what makes you

happy. That being a true giver and a caring person are very rich qualities, and you can be happy in spite of poverty and adversity.

Male, 28, office manager:
Bugs Bunny. I admire the way he outsmarts his rivals and talks his way out of adverse situations. He always gets the best of any situation. Of course, in the cartoon universe, it doesn't matter how, so it's not applicable in the nonanimated universe. Who's going to discuss morals once you throw the law of physics and gravity out the window?

Male, 38, nuclear industry engineer:
Mr. Spock. He always has the answer. Whatever the problem is, he's always got the solution. He's witty. He's got a great sense of humor. It's just a subtle-type humor. I love that his character is very intelligent. Everything to him has a logic. It has to be logical. It has to click for him in a logical, rational way or it isn't happening.

Female, 25, Salvation Army program assistant:
Cinderella. She overcame through all the hardships she had to face and kept that spirit of endurance and forgiveness. She just kept plugging away and was humble. She served her stepsisters and stepmother and didn't gripe. We could all be a little more serving. Not to the point of being oppressed, but be more serving like she was.

© *San Francisco Chronicle*. Reprinted by permission.

STOP AND THINK

What fictional character do you admire most? What does your answer reveal about your values?

Value Assumptions

Have you ever noticed how some issues are really interesting to you while others are not? Your interest in a particular question and your opinion about the question are often influenced by your **values**, those ideals, people, or things you believe are important and that you hold dear.

Value assumptions are those beliefs held by individuals that form the basis of their opinions on issues.

These assumptions are important for the critical thinker because:

1. Many arguments between individuals and groups are primarily based on strongly held values that need to be understood, and, if possible, respected.
2. An issue that continues to be unresolved or bitterly contested often involves cherished values on both sides. These value conflicts can be *between* groups or individuals or *within* an individual.

Almost everyone in a civilized society believes that its members, especially young and defenseless members, should be protected. That's why we never hear a debate on the pros and cons of child abuse—most of us agree that there are no "pros" to this issue. Similarly, we don't hear people arguing about the virtues of mass murder, rape, or burglary.

Our values, however, do come into the discussion when we are asked to decide how to treat the people who engage in these acts. Some issues having a value component would be:

> Should we have and enforce the death penalty?
>
> Should rapists receive the death penalty?
>
> Should we allow for plea bargaining?

Although most of us value order and justice, we often disagree on how justice is best administered, on what should be done to those who break the law.

REMINDER

When you read or hear the words should *or* ought to, *you are probably being addressed on a question of value.*

You can see that the question of the death penalty centers on a conflict between justice and mercy, two values cherished by many. Of course, a good debate on this issue will discuss such factual (not value-based) issues as whether the death penalty is a deterrent to crimes and whether the penalty is fairly administered throughout the country.

Keep in mind, however, that most people who argue passionately about this issue are motivated by their values and beliefs concerning justice and mercy. In fact, we generally hear arguments involving values by persons who are highly motivated about their side of an issue. Both sides of arguments involving values are likely to be persuasive because of the conviction of their advocates.

In coming to thoughtful conclusions on value-based arguments, the critical thinker needs to decide which of two or more (often reasonable) values is best. In other words, the thinker must give one value or set of values a higher priority than the other.

Examples

We often hear arguments about the legalization of drugs, gambling, or prostitution. People may claim that legalizing these activities would lessen crime, improve public health, and direct large sums of money to the government and out of the hands of dealers, bookies, and pimps.

Those who oppose legalization of these activities may have equally impressive arguments about the problems the community would face if these activities were legalized. We need to understand the root of this argument as a disagreement about which is more important:

1. Cleaning up the crime problem caused by underground activities linked to illegal vices, i.e., the value of taking care of the immediate problem, or

2. Maintaining our standards of healthy living by discouraging and making it a crime to engage in activities that we as a culture deem inappropriate and harmful, i.e., the value of honoring cultural standards and long-term societal goals.

If most people in our society believe that taking drugs, gambling, and prostitution are morally wrong, then no list of advantages of legalizing them would be meaningful. Thus, the argument starts with understanding whether the conclusion is based upon values; relative societal benefits have a much lower priority for those who believe we cannot condone harmful activities.

SKILL

Understand that different values form the basis of many arguments and that conflicts are often based on differing values.

Think of a decision you might be facing now or in the future, such as whether you should work (or continue working) while attending school, which career you should choose, or which person you should marry. An internal conflict about a decision often involves an impasse (being stuck) between two or more values.

Let's say you are undecided about continuing to work. You want to devote yourself to school because in the long run you can get a better job (long-term goal). On the other hand, you'd really like the money for an upgraded life-style—a car or a better car, money to eat out, and nicer clothes.

Your career decision may involve a conflict between the value of serving others in a field such as nursing or teaching and the value of a secure and substantial salary (such as you might find in a business career) that would help you to provide better for your future family.

You might think of getting serious with one person because he or she has good prospects for the future and is ambitious, but another person is more honest and seems to care about you more. In this case, the conflict is between security (or materialism) and loyalty.

EXERCISE

Purpose: To isolate value conflicts and to understand how different conclusions can be based on conflicting values.

Try to isolate the various value conflicts in these personal and social problems. You can do this on your own, with others, or as a classroom exercise. Some of the issues may involve more than one set of conflicting values.

Note especially how sometimes both values are important and we as persons or as citizens need to make tough decisions for which there are no easy answers. Creating policies for difficult problems means giving one value a higher priority than another.

The first one is done for you as an example.

1. Should teenagers be required to obtain the approval of their parents before they receive birth control pills or other forms of contraception?

    The conflict in this issue is between the value of individual freedom and privacy on one side and parental responsibility and guidance on the other.

2. Should you take a low-priced trip to Greece or stay home to be in your best friend's wedding?

3. Should you give your last $40.00 of the month to a charity that feeds famine-stricken families or use it for some new jeans you've wanted?

4. Should air-traffic controllers be given tests for drug usage?

5. Should persons be hired for jobs without regard to maintaining an ethnic mix?

6. Should prisoners on death row be allowed to father children?

7. Should superior athletes receive admission to colleges regardless of their grades or SAT scores?

8. Should criminals be allowed to accept royalties on books they've written about the crimes they committed?

Read the following articles and isolate the conflicting values. State your conclusions about the issues discussed and the related value assumptions you hold.

Dress Codes Back in Style

Contra Costa Times, September 13, 1989

Students returning to class this fall are being sent home if their hair's too long or skirts are too short, as more high schools across the country enact new hair and dress codes to impose official ideas of fashion.

But some parents and students say there's too much ado about hair-dos and the clothes kids wear. They argue that long hair or tattered jeans tell little about how a student will do in class . . .

Several Texas school systems have new dress codes, mostly aimed at offensive or suggestive T-shirts, and Baltimore schools banned furs, costly jewelry and leather coats. Dozens of other systems, including some in Michigan, New York and Louisiana, adopted voluntary dress codes for schools to consider.

A Houston father filed a lawsuit Tuesday against school officials, accusing them of sexual discrimination and civil rights violations for barring his two sons, Travis and Brian Wilkinson, from class for a second consecutive year because of their long hair.

Laurence Tribe, a Harvard University law professor who specializes in First Amendment issues, said the Supreme Court has never dealt directly with the issue and the lower federal courts have ruled both ways. Still, he said, the high court would likely side with school boards if it ruled today.

In California, the state Administrative Code prohibits schools from imposing blanket dress codes. That law grew out of parents' legal challenges upheld by the state courts.

Reprinted by permission.

Questions for Discussion

1. What values are reflected in a dress code?
2. Do you believe that dress codes are valuable? Why or why not?
3. If you were to establish a dress code, what would it include?

Do Colleges Treat Asian-American Applicants Fairly?

by Joan Beck
Chicago Tribune, August 24, 1989

It almost sounds like a replay of 1970s affirmative action battles. But it has an Oriental twist.

This time, it's Asian-Americans complaining that they aren't getting a fair deal in admissions to top-level colleges, even though their share of student slots far exceeds their percentage in the population.

The case they make is opening up old conflicts about quotas and goals, about affirmative action and excellence, about whites versus minorities, and about racism and equal opportunity in America.

The uneasy accommodations of the '80s in college admissions may be coming apart at the top, for the curious reason that too many Asian-Americans are—or are perceived to be—too smart.

Rep. Dana Rohrabacher (R-Calif.) and Patricia Saiki (R-Hawaii) are collecting support for a resolution they have introduced in Congress comparing "restrictive quotas" on Asian-Americans to those imposed in the 1920s against Jews and asking for a Justice Department investigation.

The Office of Civil Rights of the Department of Education is holding compliance reviews at Harvard and the University of California at Los Angeles to check for violations of the Civil Rights Act of 1964. Several other highly selective colleges have promised to make sure Asian-American applicants get a fair chance at admission without tacitly saying they haven't had it in recent years.

The University of California at Berkeley is the most obvious case in point. The popular, prestigious school must turn down far more applicants than it has room to accept; it had 21,301 applicants for 3,500 freshman places this fall, for example. More than 25 percent of the entering class will be Asian-Americans, although that minority makes up only 7 percent of California's population.

But Berkeley, which has been extremely aggressive—and successful— in recruiting minority students, has been under fire for several years for discriminating against Asian-Americans in its admissions choices. The university has used slightly higher standards for them than for other applicants and turned down some who would have gotten in had they been white or members of another minority.

Blacks, Hispanics and other minorities must meet basic requirements for admission but are essentially accepted under different standards.

One controversial study released last February by a panel set up by the school's academic senate found no systematic bias against Asian-Americans but suggested admissions policies may have kept an estimated 18 to 50 well-qualified Asian students out in each of the years between 1981 and 1987.

The Berkeley chancellor has apologized publicly and promised to correct the problem. Another committee has recommended two important changes: that the percentage of students admitted solely on the basis of academic criteria be raised from 40 percent to 50 percent and that students who are disadvantaged socioeconomically get a secondary review, regardless of their race. Both proposals should help Asian-Americans.

What few people are saying out loud is that increasing the number of Asian-Americans in the most selective schools will necessarily come at the expense of white students. Berkeley's student body is now 48.5 percent white—giving whites less representation on campus than in the population of the state as a whole.

The real problem is not racism, but the convoluted, complex policies most colleges have adopted to avoid it. They're trying to remedy centuries-old problems with preferential treatment for some minorities that, in effect, penalizes whites and now Asian-Americans.

Colleges are essentially attempting to reconcile competing values: Academic excellence, affirmative action and a diverse student body. The results, inevitably, are controversial admissions decisions.

Neither grades nor test scores are completely reliable measures of academic ability, for example. "Diversity" is difficult to define, requires flexible admissions standards and hurts the well-qualified students who are left out in the process.

(Colleges traditionally have bent admission standards for promising athletes, children of alumni and well-connected families, perhaps even a trombone player needed by the marching band, and for other reasons.)

If racial and ethnic "diversity" in the student body of a prestigious college is an acceptable goal, then Asian-Americans don't have a legitimate complaint; they are very well represented, indeed.

But by traditional standards of academic merit, they do have a justifiable case—even if the criteria are expanded to include such qualities as leadership, extracurricular activities and volunteer work. So does every applicant who loses out to a candidate who brings nontraditional qualifications such as the ability to overcome racial, cultural, physical or economic disadvantage and whose admission to college can be seen as furthering vital national goals.

There is no easy resolution to these issues. And there won't be until race and ethnicity are no longer so divisive.

Questions for Discussion

1. What are the competing values colleges are attempting to reconcile with their admissions policies? How can these values be reconciled?
2. What values are most important, in your mind, when considering college admissions policies? Should these values be the same for private as for state-supported universities?

Ideas for Writing or Speaking

Part A: List some values you hold. These can be character traits, such as honesty, fairness, and compassion. You can also list such concerns as peace, freedom of speech, family ties, ethnic identity, health, wealth, competition, or cooperation.

To isolate some of your values, consider the professions that interest you. If you want to be a high school coach, you may value sports, young people, and education. If you want to be an artist, you may value beauty and creativity.

Also, consider how you spend your free time. Different values may be expressed by those who spend time reading science fiction, shopping, volunteering at a nursing home, socializing, or working on a political campaign.

Try to list at least three values reflected in your life.

Part B: Choose a controversial issue and take a position on this issue; your position should reflect a value you hold. Examples of controversial topics with a value dimension include capital punishment, surrogate parenting, affirmative action, nuclear power, active and passive euthanasia, socialized medicine, welfare, immigration, and environmental policies.

After you have chosen an issue and taken a position reflecting your value, arrange your ideas in the following manner:

1. Give several reasons to support your position. Give both moral and fact-based reasons. Use examples and evidence to strengthen your reasons.
2. State some good reasons why you think a person might believe the opposite of what you believe. For example, if you are against compulsory drug testing for athletes, state why someone might argue in favor of it.
3. Conclude by indicating if and how your initial belief was changed by considering the opposite viewpoint. Or conclude by stating why your initial belief was not changed, despite your fair consideration of the arguments against your belief.

Ethics—An Important Dimension of Values

> *"Without civic morality, communities perish; without personal morality, their survival has no value."*
>
> Bertrand Russell, "Individual and Social Ethics,"
> *Authority and the Individual* (1949)

For our purposes, we will examine ethics as one dimension of values. **Ethics**, sometimes called morals, are standards of conduct reflecting what we consider to be right or wrong behavior. Many conflicts about values involve an ethical dimension; i.e., we are asked to choose whether one action or policy is more ethical than another.

Look at the differences in the following value conflicts:

Should you take a job that pays more but has evening hours you value for studying, or should you take a job that pays less but gives you the hours that you want?

If you arrive home and notice that a cashier at a store gave you too much change, should you go back to the store and return the money?

Note that in the first example you need to decide what you value more—the extra money or the working hours you want. There is no ethical (good–bad) dimension to this decision; you can still study even if you take the job with the less desirable hours.

The second dilemma is about your personal standards of right and wrong, or good and evil. Do you inconvenience yourself by making a trip to the store or sending the money back because you believe it is wrong to take what does not belong to you? Or do you believe that if you didn't intend to take the money, you are not responsible? What are your standards of right and wrong, especially regarding relationships with others?

Philosophers and theologians have grappled with theories of ethical behavior for centuries. Several schools of thought about ethics have emerged. Some of the more common are listed below. Note the substantial similarity among the principles listed.

LIBERTARIANISM

Value Assumption:
The highest value is to promote the liberty of all.

Principles:
Behavior is considered ethical when it both allows for one's individual freedom and does not restrict the freedom of others.

Examples:
Honesty is important because dishonesty restricts the freedom of others. Education is good because it increases personal freedom.

Violence, oppression, and poverty are bad because they restrict freedom.

Freedom of speech and assembly are important; restrictions on the right of any group to speak and assemble threaten the rights of other groups.

Reporters should not have to reveal sources of information because that would restrict the freedom of the press.

UTILITARIANISM

Value Assumption:

The highest value is that which promotes the greatest general happiness and minimizes unhappiness.

Principles:

Behavior is judged according to its utility (usefulness) in creating the greatest human well-being. Actions are considered in terms of "happiness" consequences.

Examples:

Giving to others is good when it makes people, including the giver, happy. Giving would be discouraged if it caused greater unhappiness in the long run, as in the case of giving treats to children who throw tantrums.

National policies should consider the happiness consequences for the majority of the people affected by the policy. Taxing the rich might be better than taxing the middle-class, since more people are middle-class and would feel the pinch of taxes to a greater degree.

Societal rules which maximize the possibilities of individuals flourishing and prospering involve all of our "enlightened self-interest." Selfishness and greed are bad when they don't make it probable for most people to be happy.

Freedom of assembly for "hate groups" might be restricted because of the strife and unhappiness they would cause to a larger number of citizens.

Happiness in humans is different from happiness in the animal kingdom; humans may derive happiness from labor, as when a sports team trains and works for an ultimate victory.

EGALITARIANISM

Value Assumption:

The highest value is equality. Justice and fairness are synonymous with equality.

Principles:

Behavior is ethical when the same opportunities and consequences apply to all people. We should treat others as we wish to be treated.

Examples:

Since people are equal, discrimination of any kind is unethical.

People should not take more than their fair share; they should give to those who have not received their fair share.

Punishment for crimes should be exacted in a fair manner; the poor and unknown should not be given harsher sentencing than the rich and famous.

If the justice system allows for unequal or unfair treatment of certain individuals or groups, then the system needs to be changed to ensure fairness for all citizens.

JUDEO-CHRISTIAN PRINCIPLES

Value Assumption:

The highest values are to love God and to love one's neighbor.

Principles:

Ethical behavior is based on biblical principles found in the Ten Commandments and other prescriptions and on the desire to please and honor God.

Examples:

Since all people are created by God, all should be treated with love and respect.

People should not steal, cheat, lie, or envy because these acts are contrary to biblical principles; they are not loving to others and they dishonor God.

When values conflict, resolution comes by doing the most loving, God-honoring act. For example, some Christians lied to SS officers about hiding Jews during the Nazi occupation; had they told the truth, the Jews would have been sent to concentration camps or killed.

UNIVERSAL ETHICAL NORMS OR
UNIVERSAL ACTION-GUIDING PRINCIPLES

Value Assumption:

Universal ethical principles exist and are self-evident (prima facie) and obvious to rational individuals of every culture.

Principles:

Individuals should act in accordance with these principles for the betterment of the individual and the society.

Examples:

A modern system of prima facie principles has been developed by Michael Josephson, of the Josephson Institute. His list includes honesty, integrity, fidelity, fairness, caring and respect for others, accountability, and responsible citizenship. Implications of these values are that individuals should not steal, should be responsible enough to avoid drinking when working or driving, and should be informed voters and contributors to the larger society.

Values cited above are to be honored and values such as materialism and self-centeredness are to be discouraged.

SKILL

A critical thinker is aware of his or her standards and knows the reason a certain decision has been made.

One Bandit's Ethic

Harper's Magazine, January 1992

We all have personal standards. Consider this list of personal rules that Dennis Lee Curtis, an armed robber in Rapid City, South Dakota, was carrying in his wallet when he was arrested in June of 1991.

1. I will not kill anyone unless I have to.
2. I will take cash and food stamps—no checks.
3. I will rob only at night.
4. I will not wear a mask.
5. I will not rob minimarts or 7-Eleven stores.
6. If chased by cops on foot I will get away. If chased by a vehicle I will not put the lives of innocent citizens on the line.

7. I will rob only seven months out of the year.

8. I will enjoy robbing from the poor to give to the poor.

STOP AND THINK

Look at the standards given by Dennis Lee Curtis; what general principles are revealed by this list? Do these principles fit into any of the schools of thought covered in the previous section?

EXERCISES

Purposes: To discover personal standards and principles that determine how ethical dilemmas are resolved.

1. Consider your own definition of ethical behavior; it may fit into one of the schools of thought outlined in this chapter, or it may be a combination of several approaches. Then, using your own principles, try to be completely "ethical" for one week. As often as possible, ask yourself, "What is the best way to respond to this situation?" Keep a daily record of your ethical challenges. Then, report your successes and failures in dealing with these situations.

    Here are some examples of common ethical dilemmas: Should you defend a friend who is being criticized by another friend? Should you give to a homeless person who approaches you? Should you tell the truth to someone even if it hurts their feelings? Should you tell your instructor that several students cheated when she answered a knock at the classroom door? Should you tell callers your roommate isn't home if she asks you to? Should you complain about rude treatment in a store? Should you copy a friend's tape of your favorite music rather than buying your own copy?

    Your own situations will be unique. If time permits, share some ethical dilemmas that you encountered with the rest of the class.

2. Consider the following situations alone or with a group:

    a. You and your friend are taking the same required history class; you are taking it on Mondays and Wednesdays and your friend is taking it Tuesday evening. You have given up much of your social life to study for this class because the tests are hard. One Monday after the midterm, your friend calls you and wants to know what was on the test since he partied too hard over the weekend and didn't study. You have a good memory and could tell him many of the questions. Do you tell him what was on the test?

b. You go to a garage sale and notice a diamond ring that is being sold for $10.00. You know that the ring is worth far more than that. What do you do?

c. The manager of the fast-food restaurant where you work is selling food that is not fresh or prepared according to the standards of the company. You have complained to him but he has done nothing despite your complaints. You need this job and the location, hours, and pay are perfect for you; in fact, this boss has tailored your working hours to your class schedule. Nevertheless, you are concerned about public safety. What do you do?

d. You are a member of a town council and you have a serious problem of homelessness in your city. An executive offers you $100,000 in aid for the homeless if you will let him or her build an office building over a popular park. How do you vote?

Ideal Values versus Real Values

If you completed the last exercises, you may have realized that ethical behavior is easier to discuss than it is to carry out. We have complex needs and emotions, and situations are also complicated. Even with good intentions, we sometimes find it difficult to choose ethical behavior.

Because of the difficulty of living up to our standards, most of us can make a distinction between our ideal values and our real values. An **ideal value** can be considered a value that you believe to be right and good. A **real value** is a value that you consider to be right and good and actually act upon in your life. As critical thinkers, it is important for us to understand and be honest about our own behavior and to distinguish our words from our actions.

People may say they value good citizenship; they believe people should be informed about candidates and issues and express their viewpoints by voting, but they may continue to vote without studying issues and candidates. In some cases, the value of citizenship is only an ideal. For the value to be real, it must be carried out in the life of the individual claiming that value.

EXERCISE

Purpose: To understand the difference between real and ideal values.

List five of your real values and five of your ideal values.

1. Describe what it would take for these ideal values to become real values for you. Think about why you have not made these ideal values real in your life.

2. Then explain what changes in your habits and your priorities would be involved for these values to be real for you.

Example:

"One of my ideal values is physical fitness. I believe it is important for everyone to keep their bodies strong through exercise and good eating habits.

"As a student, I don't take the time to exercise every day or even every other day. Since I quit the swim team, I hardly exercise at all. When I do have spare time, I sleep or go out with my girlfriend. Also, I eat a lot of fast foods or canned foods because I don't cook.

"For this ideal value to become real for me, I would have to graduate and have more time. Or I would have to make the time to exercise. The best way would be to combine going out with my girlfriend with exercising. She likes to skate and play basketball, so we could do that together. Getting more exercise is a real possibility.

"Eating right is probably not going to happen soon. I would have to learn to cook or to marry someone who would cook for me. At this point in my life, I can't see how I could have a healthier diet, even though it is an ideal for me. But it's just not important enough for me to learn at this time."

Ethics in Argumentation

"It is terrible to speak well and be wrong."

Sophocles, *Electra* (c. 418–14 B.C.)

Ethical concerns are central to any message. Those who seek to influence votes, sales, or the personal decisions of others need to:

- be honest about their conclusions and reasons
- not leave out or distort important information
- have thoroughly researched any claims they make
- listen with respect, if not agreement, to opposing viewpoints
- be willing to revise a position when better information becomes available
- give credit to secondary sources of information.

EXERCISE

Purpose: To examine the ethical dimensions of an argument.

Listen to a political speech or a sales pitch or read an editorial essay. Then evaluate the message, stating if the writer or speaker met the criteria given for ethical argumentation.

You might also use one of your own essays or speeches; analyze it to see whether you were as honest as you could have been and whether you credited secondary sources of information.

Ethical Decision-Making

> *"Every man takes care that his neighbor shall not cheat him. But a day comes when he begins to care that he does not cheat his neighbor. Then all goes well."*
>
> Ralph Waldo Emerson, "Worship," *The Conduct of Life* (1860)

The first step in clear-headed decision-making is knowing your principles and standards. In considering difficult decisions, there are several "tests" that can be useful to apply to your known principles. These tests can help you to assess how well your decision adheres to your standards.

1. **The Role Exchange Test.** This test asks you to empathize with the people who will be affected by the action you take. You try to see the situation from their point of view. You ask yourself how the others affected by your decision would feel and what consequences they would face.

You also ask whether it would be right for the other person to take the action if you were going to be the one experiencing the consequences of the decision. Using your imagination, you change places with the person or persons who would receive the effects of your decision. In short, you decide to treat the other person as you would want to be treated in his or her place.

For example, you see your brother's girlfriend out with other men. You hesitate to tell him because of the hurt it would cause and because you feel it's not really your business to interfere. However, when you do the role exchange test, you decide to tell him because you realize you would want to know if you were in his situation.

2.   **The Universal Consequences Test**. This test focuses on the general results (consequences) of an action you might take. You imagine what would happen if everyone in a situation similar to yours took this action—would the results be acceptable?

Under the universal consequences test, if you would find it unacceptable for everyone in a similar situation to take this action, then you would reject the action.

For example, imagine that you are asked to join a community program for recycling cans, bottles, and paper. You enjoy the freedom of just throwing everything together in the trash, but you stop and assess the consequences of everyone refusing to recycle. Your assessment causes you to join the program.

3.   **The New Cases Test**. This test asks you to consider whether your action is consistent with other actions that are in the same category. You choose the hardest case you can and see if you would act the same way in that case as you plan to act in this case. If you would, then your decision is consistent with your principles.

For example, you are deciding whether to vote to continue experiments that may be successful in finding a cure for AIDS but involve injecting animals with the HIV virus. Your principle is that cruelty to animals is not justified in any circumstance. To formulate a new, harder case you might ask yourself if you would allow the research to be conducted if it would save your life or the life of your child. If you would, then you might reconsider your voting decision and reassess your principles.

4.   **The Higher Principles Test**. This test asks you to determine if the principle on which you are basing your action is consistent with a higher or more general principle you accept.

For example, let's say your roommates are not doing their share of the housework so you are considering not doing your own share. However, because you value promise-keeping and integrity, you realize that it is important to keep your part of the bargain regardless of what they are doing with their part. You decide to keep doing your share and to talk with them about keeping their part of the agreement.

EXERCISE

Purpose: To be able to utilize tests for ethical decision-making.

  Option one: Think about an ethical dilemma you have faced. If you did the exercise on being ethical for a week, you may have a recent example. You may also use the examples given in that exercise. In addition, you might consider a difficult ethical dilemma from your past. Then, follow the directions given below.

  Option two: Think about an ethical dilemma your community or nation is facing; you might also consider an international ethical dilemma. Some examples include the use of scientific information gained by Nazi experimentation on Holocaust victims, the apportionment of funds to poverty-stricken nations, the exporting of cigarettes to other nations, the reporting of names of rape victims. Then, follow the directions.

Directions:
1. On your own or in class groups, take the dilemma through each of the four tests. Write about what each test tells you about the course your decision should take.
2. Come to a conclusion about the decision. Justify your conclusion by referring to the cumulative results of the tests.

Example:
  My friend helped me to get a job at his company and, after only a few months, I was told that he and I were both being considered for a promotion to management. He worked at the job for a year and he's getting married soon, so he really needs this job. I wouldn't even have known about the possibility of working there if he hadn't told me about it and arranged an interview for me. The dilemma is, should I take the promotion if it's offered to me or refuse it, knowing that it will then go to him?

  The role exchange test asks me to look at the situation from his point of view. It would hurt him in two ways if I took this promotion: mainly, he would lose the income and the chances for advancement that go with this position. Also, he would be hurt because he helped me to get this job and then I took a promotion he might have had. There's nothing wrong with my looking out for my own future, but in this case, it would be at his expense.

The universal consequences test asks me to look at general consequences of my decision and determine if it would be acceptable for everyone in this situation to take a similar action. A positive general consequence might be that all of the best people would be given promotions regardless of who needs the promotion most; but being offered a promotion does not necessarily mean that I am the best person for the job. The negative general consequence would be that people would routinely put their own desires ahead of what might be more fair and what might be best for other people, a "me-first" mentality.

The new cases test asks me to pick the hardest case I can and see if I would act the same way in that case, to determine whether I am consistent. To me, the hardest case would be if my parent would be given the promotion if I didn't take it. I don't live with my parents anymore, but I would step down if it meant that either of them could have the promotion.

The higher principles test asks me to look at my own ethical standards to see if my actions fit into these standards. This test is hard to use, because I value both my own advancement and my friend's welfare. But I can find the higher principle of fairness; I don't feel that it would be fair for me to take a job that he would have had since he is the person responsible for my being in the position to take it.

In conclusion, I won't take this job if it is offered to me. It would be hurtful to my friend who cared enough about me to help me get a job. Also, I wouldn't want to live in a world where people always climbed over one another to achieve success. If it were my parents, I wouldn't take a job that they wanted, even if it would benefit me personally. Finally, I believe in the principle of fairness, and I don't think it would be fair to take a promotion from a friend who gave me the opportunity to work for his company.

When we make ethical decisions, it is important that the actions taken are congruent with our values. When our actions go against what we believe is right, we are prone to rationalize our behavior rather than to admit we are not always ethical. Consider this list of common rationalizations used to justify unethical conduct.

Common Rationalizations

Ethics in Action, January–February 1991

I. "If It's Necessary, It's Ethical."

Based on the false assumption that necessity breeds propriety. Necessity is an interpretation not a fact. But even actual necessity does not justify unethical conduct. Leads to ends-justify-the-means reasoning and treating assigned tasks or desired goals as moral imperatives.

II. "If It's Legal and Permissible, It's Proper."

Substitutes legal requirements (which establish minimal standards of behavior) for personal moral judgment. Does not embrace full range of ethical obligations, especially for those involved in upholding the public trust. Ethical people often choose to do less than they are allowed to do and more than they are required to do.

III. "I Was Just Doing It For You."

Primary justification of "white lies" or withholding important information in personal or professional relationships, especially performance reviews. Dilemma: honesty and respect vs. caring. Dangers: Violates principle of respect for others (implies a moral right to make decisions about one's own life based on true information), ignores underlying self-interest of liar, and underestimates uncertainty about other person's desires to be "protected" (most people would rather have unpleasant information than be deluded into believing something that isn't so). Consider perspective of persons lied to: if they discovered the lie, would they thank you for being considerate or feel betrayed, patronized or manipulated?

IV. "I'm Just Fighting Fire With Fire."

Based on false assumption that deceit, lying, promise-breaking, etc. are justified if they are the same sort engaged in by those you are dealing with.

V. "It Doesn't Hurt Anyone."

Rationalization used to excuse misconduct based on the false assumption that one can violate ethical principles so long as there is no clear and immediate harm to others. It treats ethical obligations simply as factors to be considered in decision making rather than ground rules. Problem areas: Asking for or giving special favors to family, friends or politicians, disclosing nonpublic information to benefit others, using one's position for personal advantages (e.g., use of official title/letterhead to get special treatment).

"Wait a minute, Stan. ... These are good hubcaps. If we don't take 'em, it's a cinch some other bears will."

The Far Side by Gary Larson
The Far Side © 1985 Farworks Inc. Reprinted by permission of Universal Press Syndicate. All rights reserved.

VI. "It Can't Be Wrong, Everyone's Doing It."
A false "safety in numbers" rationale fed by the tendency to uncritically adopt cultural, organizational or occupational behavior systems as if they were ethical.

VII. "It's OK If I Don't Gain Personally."
Justifies improper conduct done for others or for institutional purposes on the false assumption that personal gain is the only test of impropriety. A related more narrow excuse is that only behavior resulting in improper *financial gain* warrants ethical criticism.

VIII. "I've Got It Coming."
Persons who feel they are overworked or underpaid rationalize that minor "perks" or acceptance of favors, discounts, or gratuities are noth-

ing more than fair compensation for services rendered. Also used to excuse all manner of personnel policy abuses (re: sick days, insurance claims, overtime, personal phone calls or photocopying, theft of supplies, etc.).

IX. "I Can Still Be Objective."
Ignores the fact that a loss of objectivity always prevents perception of the loss of objectivity. Also underestimates the subtle ways in which gratitude, friendship, anticipation of future favors and the like affect judgment. Does the person providing you with the benefit believe that it will in no way affect your judgment? Would the benefit still be provided if you were in no position to help the provider in any way?

Reprinted by permission of the Joseph and Edna Josephson Institute of Ethics.

EXERCISE

Purpose: To understand common rationalizations used to excuse unethical behavior and to see how these apply to specific cases.

Give examples for each of the above rationalizations. For example, under I. **"If It's Necessary, It's Ethical."**, you might cite unethical behavior on the part of campaign representatives carried out to ensure the election of their candidate. Try to come up with a variety of situations—personal, social, and political—in which these rationalizations are used. If the class is doing this exercise in groups, the examples can be shared with the entire class.

Consider whether you rationalize any of your behavior in the ways mentioned by the article.

Chapter Highlights

1. Value assumptions are beliefs about what is good and important or bad and unimportant; because these beliefs are taken for granted, they are part of the foundation of a person's argument.
2. Differing value assumptions need to be addressed before fruitful discussion over value-saturated conclusions can take place.

3. Ethics are standards of conduct that reflect values.
4. There are several schools of thought about ethics, including libertarianism, utilitarianism, egalitarianism, Judeo-Christian principles, and universal ethical norms.
5. Ideal values are held by an individual in a theoretical sense; real values are held theoretically and also practiced.
6. Ethics are evident in our behavior as we advocate for ideas and make decisions.
7. Several "tests" have been developed to help people make ethical decisions. These include the role exchange test, the universal consequences test, the new cases test, and the higher principles test.
8. Ethical decision-making is undermined when common rationalizations are used to support unethical practices.

Articles for Discussion

It May Not Be Plagiarism, But It's a Rip-Off

by Howard Rosenberg
Los Angeles Times, July 11, 1990

TV news fibs in so many ways.

If it's not the playacting of ratings sweeps series, it's the false promise made to hold viewers through a commercial, that titillating stories are "coming up next." If it's not on-camera reporters taking bows for the work of off-camera field producers, it's newscasts blending electronic press kits in with staff-gathered news.

These are relatively small deceptions.

As the following episode shows, the more you perpetuate the small lie, the easier it is to step up to the big one.

It was last Thursday and featured on KCAL Channel 9's "Prime 9 News" at 10 P.M. was a breezy story lamenting the decline of that great American institution, the drive-in movie. The tape package was introduced live from the studio and given a voice-over narration by KCAL's hammy entertainment reporter, John Corcoran.

Afterward, anchors Larry Carroll and Kate Sullivan seemed pleased with Corcoran's story.

One problem. A small one, really . . .

It *wasn't* Corcoran's story. It was Gloria Hillard's story.

"I was angry," said Hillard, a CNN reporter covering entertainment from the network's Los Angeles bureau. "One of the most sacred tenets of journalism is that you don't take someone else's words and pass them on as your own."

Not sacred to everyone, obviously.

Hillard's story aired July 4 on CNN, a witty, charming enterprise piece that was shaped in such a personal way that it bore her signature as a reporter. "I guess Corcoran saw my piece, liked it and decided to make it his own," Hillard said.

The story is small, but the principle big, with the terrible P-word looming. "I would be highly offended to be called a plagiarist," Corcoran said later.

Like slapping your own dust jacket on someone else's book, Corcoran gave the drive-in story a brief live intro and close from the anchor desk. Otherwise, the story presented as his on KCAL was virtually a twin of Hillard's—but about a minute shorter.

Gone were a few fleeting sound bites, including Hillard's stand-up in the parking lot of a Culver City drive-in—couldn't have that if it was Corcoran's piece. Gone also was Hillard's voice. But her written words remained with only slight changes, spoken instead by Corcoran as if they were his.

How is it that Hillard's two-minute 40-second story—not only her footage and interviews but also her 226-word script—were at Corcoran's disposal?

Along with KTLA Channel 5 and KTTV Channel 11 in Los Angeles and many other independent stations throughout the nation, KCAL has a reciprocal agreement with CNN for mutual use of stories. Wire services such as the Associated Press have similar agreements with their clients.

In another way that deceit is built into the system, stations don't even have to credit CNN, who thus becomes a party to the deception.

"They are free to use our material in any way they want," said CNN's Los Angeles bureau chief, David Farmer. He said that he'd heard of nothing akin to the Hillard–Corcoran matter previously happening in Los Angeles. "But I feel it must happen quite a bit around the country," he added. "We facilitate it by sending out scripts."

There surely are newspapers, too, that attach their own reporters' bylines to wire stories—but no newspapers with integrity.

Hillard said she knew CNN had agreements with stations for exchanging footage, but didn't know that these agreements provided for verbatim use of scripts without attribution.

Legal it may be.

Ethical it isn't.

Corcoran sounded almost shocked that anyone would think that his usurping Hillard's words without giving credit was either misleading or unethical. "I don't have any problem with it ethics-wise," Corcoran said. "Ninety-nine percent of my stuff I write. I didn't rewrite that one, and part of the reason is that I'm moving my family into a new house." Well, as long as there's a valid reason.

Corcoran noted that using words written by others without attribution "is standard procedure throughout television. When anchors read copy written for them by others," he added, "they don't say, 'written by so-and-so.'"

Because CNN allows its scripts to be used "word-for-word," Corcoran insisted, his voice-over with Hillard's words was not plagiarism. Besides, he added, "I put my own inflections on a story."

Words by Hillard, inflections by Corcoran.

"I'm not the kind of guy who's gonna go out and steal anybody's work," Corcoran said. "Trust me."

Yet the narrations on the CNN and KCAL stories track almost identically, as the following excerpts show.

> *Hillard:* And remember that pizza? It's still here, and of course kids even work up a real good appetite at the drive-in's playground. And the drive-ins are a pretty good bargain at $4.50 for adults, and kids under 12 are free.
>
> *Corcoran:* And remember that pizza? It's still here, and of course kids even work up a real good appetite at the drive-in's playground. And the drive-ins are pretty good bargains. That's $4.50 for adults. Kids under 12 are free.
>
> *Hillard:* And how about a kid's point of view on drive-ins over walk-ins?
>
> *Corcoran:* What about drive-ins over walk-ins?
>
> *Hillard:* But they're disappearing. The Studio Drive-In is one of only a couple dozen left in Southern California. And it's scheduled for the bulldozer. The high cost of land outbid the box office, and soon the condos will be here.
>
> *Corcoran:* But drive-ins are disappearing. The Studio Drive-In is one of only a couple of dozen left here. And it's scheduled for the bulldozer. The high cost of land outbid the box office, and soon the condos will be here.

And so on and so on the two stories went . . .

KCAL news director Bob Henry saw nothing improper in what Corcoran did and, incredibly, refused to discount the possibility that the same thing could happen again with his blessing.

He called this "a non-issue." Making Hillard's work sound almost too trivial to matter, he said that "a feature on drive-ins is sort of a discretionary story."

Yet it was significant enough for KCAL to use in an evening newscast and then repeat the next day in its noon newscast. KCAL, Henry snapped, can "use news from CNN any way we want."

While ethics, like drive-in movies, fade into the sunset.

Questions for Discussion

1. What is the ethical problem discussed by the author of this article?
2. Do you agree with the author's conclusions?
3. Are there situations you can think of in which something may be legal but is not ethical? What about situations in which something is ethical but not legal?

Student Markets Primer on the Art of Cheating

Rutgers Senior Finds His $7 How-To Is in Demand Among College Students

by Anthony Flint
Boston Globe, February 3, 1992

One of the hottest books on college campuses isn't the latest collection of Calvin and Hobbes—it's a book about cheating.

"Cheating 101" is a how-to guide on shortcuts to a degree—effective places to hide crib sheets, systems of foot signals for sharing multiple-choice answers, places to buy term papers and dozens of other tips.

Michael Moore, 24, a Rutgers University senior and author of the book, has sold 5,000 copies, mostly at Rutgers, Ohio State and the University of Maryland. He recently returned from a marketing road trip to Penn State. And he plans to go to Boston, home to 11 colleges and universities, to hawk the $7 book around spring break.

"We're going to hit Boston right after we hit Daytona Beach in March."

Moore, a journalism major, contracts with a printer to produce the 86-page book and sells it mostly out of his home in Hopewell, N.J. But because of the book's popularity, he takes sales operations on the road from time to time. Sometimes aided by a pre-visit article in a student newspaper, he sets up a table in a fraternity house or a room on campus and watches the money roll in.

"Students love it," said Moore, who described his weekend selling session at Penn State University and St. Francis College as "a mob scene." The trip was good for 1,150 copies.

Moore said that in addition to students snapping up the guide, several college administrators, lawyers and clinical psychologists have ordered it too—presumably as a form of counterintelligence.

Moore makes no excuses about the profits he reaps from the book, and acknowledges that he set out to make money. But he also considers "Cheating 101" to be a commentary on the shortcomings of higher education: ill-prepared professors more concerned with research, dreary required courses and the lack of training for real-world applications.

"I thought it would be a good opportunity to point out what I believe are the permanent problems in education," said Moore, who said his experience in college has been sour. "It's an indictment of the system. Maybe somebody will make some changes, to curb cheating and make college a better place."

Cheating, Moore said, is a response to the shortcomings that students see. It flourishes because often professors are not interested or look the other way, he said.

"Students just don't cheat because they're lazy or hung over," he said. "They see a professor who's not interested in what they're doing, so students aren't going to be interested in learning. That's a natural defense mechanism."

Rutgers officials, while praising Moore's entrepreneurial skills, have sharply criticized "Cheating 101" as a blatant violation of academic ethics. Some have drawn parallels to Michael Milken and Ivan Boesky, describing the book as the scholar's quick-and-dishonest route to success.

The penalties for cheating vary from school to school, but frequently include suspension or expulsion. Most colleges spell out the rules against cheating or plagiarizing in student codes provided to all freshmen.

Some educators are using the book as an opportunity to teach about ethics. Carol Oppenheim, a communications professor at Boston's Emerson College, recently led a discussion with students on whether a student newspaper should run an advertisement for the book.

"It's an interesting teaching opportunity about a real ethical dilemma," Oppenheim said.

Moore said the wrath of college administrators is to be expected. "It's a manual about their mistakes, their shortcomings and failures. It's like a bad audit."

But he denies that he is engaging in anything dishonest or unethical.

"I don't think people that are buying the book have never cheated before. They already know a lot of the methods. I'm not making a cheater out of anybody," he said.

"There's 'Final Exit,' a book on how to get out of drunk driving, a book on how to get out of speeding tickets," Moore said. "I'm making an honest living. I'm not dealing drugs. I'm just exercising my First Amendment rights."

Reprinted courtesy of the *Boston Globe*.

Questions for Discussion

1. Comment on Moore's statements:

   "They see a professor who's not interested in what they're doing, so students aren't going to be interested in learning. That's a natural defense mechanism. . . . I don't think people that are buying the book have never cheated before. They already know a lot of the methods. I'm not making a cheater out of anybody. . . . I'm making an honest living. I'm not dealing drugs. I'm just exercising my First Amendment rights."

2. If your professor for a particular course looked the other way when students cheated, would you feel justified in cheating? Why or why not?

3. Do you find that the discussion of this book and its popularity by the *Boston Globe* and in student newspapers gives the book a legitimacy that it might not otherwise have? Would it make students feel more or less inclined to read it? On what do you base your answer?

4. Should Moore be allowed to advertise in student newspapers and to sell his book on campus? Why or why not?

5. What is the "real ethical dilemma" concerning this book that is mentioned by Professor Oppenheim?

6. Is it OK to cheat if you feel that the system is cheating you?

Ideas for Writing or Speaking

1. Take a position on Moore's criticisms of "ill-prepared professors more concerned with research, dreary required courses and the lack of training for real-world applications." To what extent, if any, is Moore's perception valid? If not, why not? If so, what should be done about these problems? Give reasons for your conclusion.

2. Consider Moore's comment that the book "Cheating 101" is an effective "commentary on the shortcomings of higher education." Write on either the shortcomings or benefits of higher education as if you were trying to convince someone who was considering going to college. Use your own experience as support, but include objective sources of evidence as well.

3. See if your college has a code of ethics about cheating and plagiarizing. If so, write about this code; take a position on the principles given (agree or disagree with them) and give support for your conclusions. If your college does not have a code of ethics, write one and justify (give reasons for) each of the principles you include.

4. **"The Legacy I'd Like to Leave"**

   Imagine that you are 80 years old. Your son, daughter, niece, nephew, husband, wife, friend, or co-worker is making a speech about you at a party held in your honor. In this speech, he or she mentions your fine qualities and the things you have accomplished in your life. He or she talks about the special traits you have that are treasured by those who know and love you.

   Write the speech, using this format:

   a. List the personal qualities and how they have been specifically evidenced in your life.

   b. List the accomplishments you will have achieved. Again, be specific in your descriptions.

   c. Then, analyze what you would need to do (either internally or externally, or both) to merit that kind of tribute in your old age. What ideal values would have to become real for you? What choices would you have to make about your career, your personal life, and your priorities?

5. Write an essay in which you take a position (agree or disagree) on one of the following quotes. Support your conclusion about the quote with specific reasons.

   a. "Uncle Sam has no conscience. They don't know what morals are. They don't try to eliminate an evil because it's evil, or

because it's illegal, or because it's immoral; they eliminate it only when it threatens their existence."
Malcolm X, *Malcolm X Speaks* (1965), p. 3

b. "The difference between a moral man and a man of honor is that the latter regrets a discreditable act, even when it has worked and he has not been caught."
H. L. Mencken, *Prejudices: Fourth Series* (1924), p.11

c. "The great secret of morals is love."
Percy Bysshe Shelley, *A Defence of Poetry* (1821)

d. "We must never delude ourselves into thinking that physical power is a substitute for moral power, which is the true sign of national greatness."
Adlai Stevenson, speech, Hartford, Connecticut,
September 18, 1952

CHAPTER THREE

Reality Assumptions

It's Eleven O'Clock: Do You Know Where Your Assumptions Are?

A critical thinker understands that people have different assumptions about the world that form the basis for their opinions; he or she also examines these assumptions.

A critical thinker is able to distinguish facts from inferences and to make responsible interpretations.

This chapter will cover:

◆ Reality assumptions

◆ Avoiding untrue assumptions

◆ Deductive and inductive reasoning

◆ The distinction between facts and inferences

We learned in the last chapter that when an issue involves a conflict of values, we need to examine those values foundational to the argument under consideration; in other words, there is no point in bringing in evidence to support a point of view until we address the issue of the clashing values.

For example, it doesn't matter how many statistics a speaker can produce to attempt to prove that we would save money and cut down on crime if we would legalize drugs if the audience believes that legalizing drugs is wrong. When a discussion neglects to consider conflicting value assumptions on both sides of an issue, stalemates occur, and new and improved evidence does nothing to help these stalemates.

The critical thinker who wants to argue on a value-saturated issue needs to clearly and directly address the conflict in values and try to persuade the other side to rethink their value assumptions on that issue.

Reality Assumptions

Another foundational aspect to any argument is the underlying assumptions about reality that the various advocates for an issue hold. Conflicts in value assumptions address questions of "What is right?" or "What should we do or be?"; conflicts in reality assumptions address the questions "What is true and factual?" and "What do we take for granted or as a given fact?"

The fascinating element of assumptions is that they are often hidden to the people arguing for different conclusions. Finding hidden assumptions in arguments is like reading or watching mysteries; you accumulate clues from what people say and then make guesses about what important things they *believe* but aren't directly *stating*.

One person may assume the only way to deal with terrorists is through a show of strength, whereas another person assumes the only effective approach is negotiation. Notice that these two individuals probably hold the same values; both believe terrorism is wrong and is a global problem.

They also may share the value of the importance of world peace. Their conflict is about effective methodology; i.e., they have different ideas (assumptions) about what terrorists are like and what works best in dealing with them. They have different views of reality.

REMINDER

An **assumption** can be defined as a *belief, usually taken for granted, that is based on the experience, observations, or desires of an individual or group.*

When two people or two groups hold different assumptions, they need to stop and discuss the assumptions, rather than facts based on those assumptions. As hidden assumptions are brought to the surface, light is shed on the different positions taken on an issue. People then have the opportunity to change or modify assumptions or to see more clearly why they have strong convictions about particular assumptions.

SKILL

A critical thinker examines the assumptions of self and others that form the foundations of arguments.

DETECTING REALITY ASSUMPTIONS

One reason that assumptions are often hidden from us is because they are so deeply ingrained; they may only surface when we come across someone or some group who holds different assumptions. We may be confronted with a different set of assumptions than our own when we are involved in a classroom debate. Or this process of confronting the "facts" that we take for granted may occur when we are in an unfamiliar situation, like when we travel to a new place and are exposed to a different culture.

Most Americans assume if an interview or meeting is set for 1:00, then the arrival time should be slightly before 1:00, but people from other cultures may view time more loosely. The expected arrival time could be anywhere between 1:00 and 3:00 for members of some cultures. Because of the differing assumptions across cultures, North Americans who are sent abroad by their organizations are often given training about the assumptions commonly made in the country they will be visiting.

When traveling to another country, we can be sensitive to what is expected of us as guests. In defending our conclusions on an issue, however, we need to bring the differing assumptions to light so that the discussion is clear and rational.

Examples of Differing Reality Assumptions:

- One person assumes that anyone can change and therefore any prisoner can be rehabilitated. Another person believes there are individuals who are "career criminals" with no hope of being rehabilitated.
- One dentist assumes that wisdom teeth should be removed at an early age to prevent infection. Another dentist assumes that wisdom teeth should only be removed when necessary because of infection.
- One person assumes that the way to increase employment is to lower taxes. Another person assumes that the way to increase employment is to establish more federal programs that would provide jobs for the unemployed.

The key here is to realize that individuals make basic assumptions, whether they (or we) realize it or not. We need to examine the assumptions we make and try to detect the assumptions that others make. When we have a foundational disagreement about assumptions, we should discuss those assumptions before we discuss any arguments built upon them. For example, if we believe that people can be rehabilitated, we must understand why we believe that and be able to defend our basic belief. We also need to understand why someone else would believe that people cannot be rehabilitated.

THE DANGER IN ASSUMPTIONS

There is a danger in making assumptions, in taking things for granted. The danger is that an assumption we make may not be true; it may have been true at one time, or it may never have been true at all. When we build an argument on a foundation of falsehood, we are lost. We may sound logical and reasonable, but we are leading ourselves and others astray.

Father Andrew Greeley discusses this problem in his autobiography, *Confessions of a Parish Priest*. He explains how he wanted to get a Ph.D. in sociology so he could do research for the Catholic church. Father Greeley wanted his doctoral dissertation to be useful:

So I went over to NORC and asked Jim if he needed somebody to analyze something in the sociology of religion. "Funny you should mention that," he said, in his little cubbyhole in an old two-flat converted into a research center. "We're doing this study of career plans of college students and we need somebody to analyze the influence of religion. We'll find you a chair and a desk somewhere and go to work. . . ."

I checked around with various Catholics in education and asked what they thought would be a good focus for my Ph.D. research. We would have thirty thousand June 1961 college graduates with all kinds of information about their education and their career plans. Bill McManus who was superintendent of Catholic schools in the Archdiocese at the time said, "Find out, for the love of God, why our kids don't go to graduate school."[1]

Father Greeley explains that many professors had written extensively about this problem, so he went to work trying to discover why young Catholics were not attending graduate schools.

One Saturday morning in the summer of 1961, as I was finishing my first full year at the university, I stopped by NORC to see if the first run for my doctoral dissertation had come up from the machine room. I was eager to see the extent of Catholic deficiency in graduate school attendance in the 1961 graduates we were studying.

Everyone knew that Catholics were less likely to go on to graduate school. My doctoral challenge was to learn why.

I found a cross-tab. . . . Catholics from the June 1961 class were *more* [my emphasis] likely to attend graduate schools the following autumn than their Protestant classmates. Across the top of the printout, Davis had written, "It looks like Southern Methodist loses this year to Notre Dame!"

It was my first delightful experience of discovering that *what everyone knows to be true is not necessarily true*[2] [my emphasis].

Father Greeley stumbled upon an assumption about Catholic college graduates that was not true, yet was considered true by many

---

1   Father Andrew Greeley, *Confessions of a Parish Priest* (New York: Simon & Schuster, 1986), p. 206. Copyright © 1986 by Andrew M. Greeley. Reprinted by permission of Simon and Schuster, Inc.

2   Ibid, p. 198.

church leaders. Because his research uncovered the faulty assumption, time and energy was not wasted trying to solve a problem that did not exist.

As critical thinkers, we need to actively discover and then question the assumptions underlying arguments so we are not building arguments on a foundation of falsehood. Conversely, when we critically examine what it is we take for granted, we have the advantage of gaining a strong and solid conviction for those ideas and principles we believe to be true. When we clearly understand both the foundation and the structural supports for our arguments, we can be credible and effective.

EXERCISE

Purpose: To detect possible assumptions underlying conclusions.

What are the assumptions?

Look at the comments below and find possible assumptions that are being made by the speaker. Discuss whether you agree with the assumptions. Often, more than one possible assumption can be found.

1. This is a receptionist position, so we need a female for the job. *Most fitting for female*

2. You can't go to the party in that outfit. *inappropriate outfit*

3. We need to make laetrile available for cancer patients in the United States. *laetrile is effective for cancer patient*

4. Air bags are necessary in a car. *seat belts are not being used*

5. Charlene is really successful—she's only 28 and she's making $70,000 a year! *Money is success*

6. You make me so angry!

7. Rape is on the decline in this county—there are 20 percent fewer police reports this year than last year at this time.

8. Trials and executions should be televised—the public has the right to know what's going on in our judicial system.

9. Bolger's coffee is the best—it's grown in the mountains.

10. The people in that town don't care about the homeless—their city council voted against contributing $2,000 to a county fund to help the homeless.

11. They won't trade their lunches if you give them Twinkle cupcakes.

12. You're going to love this blind date—I've known him since fourth grade, and he's a great friend of mine.

13. Let's put the county dump in Smallville—they haven't had a turn as a dump site yet.

14. Let's just live together—why do we need a piece of paper to prove our love?

15. The death penalty is proof that we value revenge more than we value people.

Read the following article about a jury trial, keeping in mind the various assumptions that contribute to the outcome of the trial.

Acquittal Outrages Women

Jury Blames Provocative Miniskirt for Assault

by Brian Murphy
Contra Costa Times, October 6, 1989

Fort Lauderdale, Fla.—Sexual assault counselors and women's groups reacted with anger and disbelief Thursday to a jury's acquittal of a rape suspect on the grounds that the woman wore a lace miniskirt without underwear.

"It's a fairly horrendous verdict," said Ellen Vargyas at the National Women's Law Center in Washington, D.C. "No one, regardless of how they are dressed, should be allowed to be raped under a knife."

The three male and three female Broward Circuit Court jurors publicly justified their verdict Wednesday to acquit a 26-year-old drifter, who then was ordered returned to Georgia to face several other rape and assault charges.

"We felt she asked for it for the way she was dressed," said jury foreman Roy Diamond. "The way she was dressed with that skirt, you could see everything she had. She was advertising for sex."

"She was obviously dressed for a good time, but we felt she may have bit off more than she could chew," said juror Mary Bradshaw.

The 22-year-old woman testified that Steven Lord abducted her at knife-point from a Fort Lauderdale restaurant parking lot in November 1988 and raped her repeatedly during a trip north on Interstate 95. She said she escaped five hours later.

Defense attorney Tim Day told jurors the woman agreed to have sex with Lord in exchange for $100 and cocaine, but later changed her mind.

Jurors said they also were swayed by the woman's calm demeanor in court, compared to the emotional testimony of a 24-year-old Georgia woman who claims Lord raped her at knife-point last year.

"When the Georgia woman testified, my heart sank," said juror Dean Medeiros. "But when the other one testified, she didn't appear to be shaken up. Basically, we didn't believe her story."

"I thought this was 1989," said Alexander Siegel, attorney for the woman, who was jailed six days in June after failing to answer subpoenas for court appearances. "I guess this means every pervert and nut out there has a license to rape any person who dresses in a manner they think is provocative."

"The whole idea that a woman is asking for it is horrendous," said Dorothea Gallagher of the National Organization for Women's Broward County chapter.

Reprinted by permission of the Associated Press.

Questions for Discussion

1. What are the underlying assumptions made by the prosecution, the jurors, and the defense in this case?
2. If the plaintiff (the raped woman) had agreed to sex in exchange for $100 and cocaine but later changed her mind, as stated by the defense, could the defendant have justified or defended his actions? What assumption guides your answer?
3. What assumption underlies the prosecution attorney's statement, "I thought this was 1989"?
4. What assumption underlies the juror's comment, "She didn't appear to be shaken up . . . we didn't believe her story"?

EXERCISE

Purpose: To find assumptions made by professionals in various fields.

Consider your major area of study. What are some assumptions made by people in that field? For example, if you study dance therapy, then you must assume that dance can be psychologically helpful to people. If you study ecology, then you must believe that the environment is a system that needs to be balanced.

Example:

I am studying Early Childhood Education. It's because I assume children need some structured experiences before they get to kindergarten. I also assume they learn best if they have lots of time to be creative and explore. And I assume they need lots of interaction with other kids to learn to share and relate.

I have argued with some of my teachers who assume children should learn to read before kindergarten. We know that children can learn to read early and they can learn some math, but my assumption is they'll burn out if they have to study so young. And I also assume they'll catch up and be happier than kids who had to read so soon.

Consider the following article about a potential change of some basic assumptions in American culture.

America's Addiction to Addictions

by Art Levine
U.S. News and World Report, February 5, 1990

When District of Columbia Mayor Marion Barry tearfully announced that he had "weaknesses" and entered a Florida treatment program recently, he and his aides were also launching a political and legal strategy. Barry wanted to portray his addiction problems as a disease—something beyond his control and thus politically less damaging.

By going into treatment for chemical dependency, he stood to gain public sympathy and, he and his advisers hoped, prosecutorial leniency. But Barry's downfall and speedy resort to treatment also raise basic questions about the nature and causes of addictions and the role of individual willpower in curbing excessive behavior.

Most medical experts today view alcoholism and drug addiction as chronic diseases with biological, and perhaps genetic, underpinnings. But it was not that long ago that even these excesses were seen as evidence of moral turpitude rather than medical conditions.

What worries some addiction experts is society's willingness to expand the definition of addictive behavior beyond substance abuse to include a host of excessive behaviors—ranging from shopping to promiscuity—and clinicians' readiness to treat what may be social and willpower problems as medical disorders instead.

Helpless and sick?

Addiction was once seen primarily as a physical dependence on a drug that created severe physical symptoms when the drug was withdrawn. But that view is changing.

"The drug is necessary but not sufficient to cause addiction," says Jack Henningfield, chief of the clinical pharmacology branch of the National Institute of Drug Abuse. He and others point to the clear effects of social conditions on drug use: for example, the ability of 90 percent of addicted Vietnam veterans to kick their heroin habits once free of the stress of battle. By contrast, three-fourths of other heroin addicts who try to quit fail.

It is this sort of wide variation in addictive patterns that, in part, prompts some critics to question whether substance abuse is truly a disease with an inevitable course if untreated. Furthermore, they argue, the disease model sends a harmful message to abusers. It not only excuses irresponsibility but "indoctrinates them with the idea they're helpless and sick," says Herbert Fingarette, an addiction expert at UC–Santa Barbara.

Medical authorities generally dismiss these criticisms, noting that other well accepted diseases, such as diabetes, lack a simple pattern while still having a physical component. They also argue that disease-oriented treatment programs don't absolve patients of responsibility for their habits, though they have biological roots.

"Once a behavior becomes an addiction, it involves a biological component," points out Dr. Frederick K. Goodwin, a psychiatrist and administrator of the Alcohol, Drug Abuse and Mental Health Administration. But "it starts as a voluntary act, then becomes reflexive and automatic."

Can any behavior become reflexive and automatic—in effect, an addiction? Some experts are inclined to see addiction in any pleasurable behavior that turns compulsive, despite the problems that can cause.

In part because of this looser definition, addiction chic is everywhere: There are now more than 2,000 meetings each week of groups catering to self-styled sex and love addicts, up at least 20 percent in the past year; there are more than 200 national Alcoholics Anonymous-style groups in the country, including Messies Anonymous; and there are inpatient therapy programs and self-help groups for those people—called "codependents"—whose main problem is that they remain with, and worry too much about, destructive mates.

Whether it is excesses in drug taking or even TV watching, Harvey Milkman, a professor of psychology at Metropolitan State College in Denver and co-author of *Craving for Ecstasy*, argues, "The disease concept may be applied to the entire spectrum of compulsive problem behaviors."

But the prospect of less personal responsibility concerns critics of the would-be addictions. "Creating a world of addictive diseases may mean creating a world in which anything is excusable," says psychologist Stanton Peele, author of the new book *Diseasing of America*. Even some addiction researchers are questioning whether the boom in addiction treatments has gone too far.

"It is vogue now to call any excessive behavior an addiction, and, frankly, the professions are too quick to turn a dollar on this," says Howard J. Shaffer, director of the Center for Addiction Studies at Harvard Medical School and Cambridge Hospital. And none of the often expensive treatments offered for the alleged behavioral addictions has proved effective, experts say.

Yet researchers exploring the disease models of addiction are often genuinely seeking to understand the underpinnings of some self-destructive, repetitive behaviors that trouble individuals—and baffle scientists. How do we explain someone who buys more pairs of shoes than could ever possibly be worn or gambles away the family home and life savings?

The idea of an addictive-personality type has been proposed, but the science is inconclusive. "There is no single characteristic or constellation of traits that is inevitably associated with addiction," notes psychologist Alan Lang of Florida State University, who contributed a chapter on personality to a National Research Council report on habitual behavior. At the same time, his research review points to such predisposing traits as a sense of alienation, impulsivity and a need for instant gratification.

Despite the controversies over addictions, they have made their way into the legal system as defenses. Defendants claiming "diminished capacity" because of their addictions sometimes succeed: one Vietnam veteran accused of drug running was acquitted after a defense expert argued that he was a victim of the "action-addict syndrome." "Is every problem a disease?" asks sociologist Martin Levine of Bloomfield College in New Jersey.

It sometimes seems that way. A leading "sex addiction" theorist, Minnesota psychologist Patrick Carnes, has designed the country's first Sexual Dependency Unit at Golden Valley Health Center in Minnesota.

It has offered both inpatient and outpatient treatment to more than 1,000 people since 1984. The roughly four-week, $16,000 treatment includes an AA style 12-step program, group therapy and celibacy pledges. The critics of the sex-addiction movement view it more as a moralistic crusade than as a genuine medical effort.

Biological Hints

But for many who consider themselves sex addicts, the damage in their lives can be quite real, even if there is no agreement on what causes their problems. Jamie, a Minneapolis member of Sex Addicts Anonymous, says he lost a few jobs because of his constant search for new sex partners.

"Everything else got in the way," he says. And there are some hints of a biological basis for such behavior. New York City psychologist William Wedin recalls one patient, a well-paid executive who began spending thousands of dollars a week on prostitutes and joined a 12-step sex-addict program.

It wasn't until he collapsed on the street one day that doctors diagnosed him as a victim of a stroke, suggesting that an organic brain disorder had probably spurred his flings. Other experts are using anti-depressants to successfully treat sexual compulsives.

Compulsive gambling may pose the greatest theoretical challenge for addiction researchers. Unlike alcoholism and drug addiction, it involves no toxic substance that might directly affect brain chemistry and lead to physical craving. Yet it is well accepted by such groups as the American Psychiatric Association as an addictive syndrome.

The Department of Veterans Affairs offers inpatient and outpatient treatment for gambling at four medical centers. And there may even be a biological factor: In 1988, researchers at the National Institute on Alcohol Abuse and Alcoholism found higher levels of the brain chemical norepinephrine in gamblers, that could signal a mood-regulation disturbance that spurs them to seek greater thrills. It is theoretically possible that others seek the same kinds of rewards through compulsive shopping and sex.

For those who work with such troubled people, the causes are still ultimately mysterious, but Dr. Sheila Blume, who heads the alcohol, chemical-dependency and compulsive-gambling programs at South Oaks Hospital in Amityville, N.Y., says, "I'm hopeful a final pathway in the brain will be found." Until the biology of excessiveness is better understood, America's addiction to addiction will no doubt continue.

Copyright, February 5, 1990, *U.S. News & World Report*.

Questions for Discussion

1. What are some contrasting assumptions made by the experts who are quoted in this article?
2. Do you make different assumptions about addiction to alcohol versus addiction to sex, gambling, or shopping? If so, what are the different assumptions and what do you base them on? If not, why not?

3. Do you believe addictive behavior can be legitimately used as a defense in a criminal trial? If so, why and how can it be used?

Student Response

by Mitchel Hempstead

I find that the article used on addiction is one-sided, and it does not give a clear message of addiction. I am going to say that this article was chosen because it must express the view of the author of the text.

There is research that shows that children of alcoholics have the same low amounts of brain hormones "met-enkephalin, GABA, seratonin" as their parents do, and that it is this low level of hormones that causes these people to drink or use drugs compulsively "despite negative physical, emotional, or life consequences." These hormones help stimulate the brain and make these addicted people feel good, some for the first time in their lives. If people have a low level of these feel-good hormones, and other things will make them feel good or feel normal, then why not use those other things? The problem happens when these other things—shopping, eating, sex, gambling, and drugs—consume their lives and they are unable to stop despite the negative consequences. That is addiction.

The article says that this is a will-power problem. I do not agree, but let us say it is a will-power problem. Let's say that I am addicted to drugs, shopping, and overeating to a point that my life has fallen apart. I go to a medical facility, and at the facility the doctors introduce me to the will-power theory and to a 12-step program that deals with addiction. These 12-step programs cost next to nothing to attend. I get out of the hospital and start attending these 12-step meetings on my own. There I learn that I used drugs, sex, and overeating to avoid my feelings. I get support from the people at the meetings on how to deal with my feelings without using these avoiding activities. I also get an environment that helps me feel good about myself. This environment helps me with this so-called will-power problem.

Now, you tell me what is wrong with that. I am a critical thinker, and I know that people will misuse anything they can in order to look good. Maybe this Mayor Marion Barry has misused these programs, but let us not say that everybody there has done the same thing.

I felt a need to tell you this about the article chosen. Maybe a more neutral article or two articles, one pro and one con, would be fairer to your readers.

Reprinted by permission of the author.

Questions for Discussion

1. To what extent was the article on addiction one-sided or balanced?
2. How does the article handle both the addictive model and the will-power model of substance use? Can these two models be reconciled?

Reasoning: Deductive and Inductive[3]

One tool for uncovering and examining assumptions is called the *syllogism*. A syllogism is a series of statements (called *premises*) leading to a conclusion. In **deductive reasoning**, the conclusion definitely follows from the premises; that is, if the premises are true, the conclusion will be true. Let's look at the classic example of deduction given by Aristotle over 2,000 years ago:

> All men are mortal. (Major premise)
>
> Socrates is a man. (Minor premise)
>
> Therefore, Socrates is mortal. (Conclusion)

This form of deductive reasoning can be coded in letters as follows:

> All P are Q.
>
> m is P.
>
> Therefore, m is Q.

In this form of deductive argument, the first premise (all P are Q) is an "all-encompassing" or universal statement. This statement is called the *major premise*. The second statement, referring to a *specific P (m)*, is called the *minor premise*. The final statement is the conclusion that logically follows from the major and minor premises. Remember, if the premises of a deductive argument are true, then the conclusion must be true; this rule is called *deductive certainty*.

We can visualize this kind of syllogism with Figure 3.1 and this example.

---

3   The process of understanding and outlining deductive reasoning is more complex than can be represented in this short chapter segment. For further discussion of both deductive and inductive argument forms, read Irving Copi's classic *Introduction to Logic* (New York: Macmillan, 1990), especially parts two and three.

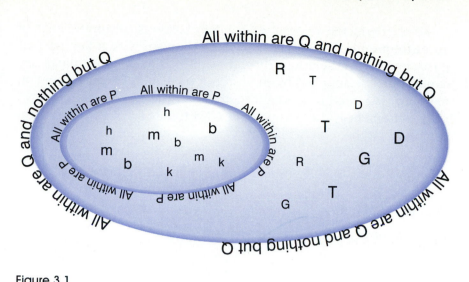

Figure 3.1

All students in this classroom (P) are high school graduates
   (Q).
Marcus (m) is a student in this classroom (P).
Therefore, Marcus (m) is a high school graduate (Q).

Notice that all P's (students in this classroom) are within the circle
of Q (high school graduates). Also, some D's, S's, and T's are in the
circle of Q, but not in the circle of P. In other words, some high
school graduates (Q) are not in this classroom (P). But all students in
this classroom (P) are high school graduates (Q). Because we can
speak with certainty about all of the P's, we can also draw certain
conclusions about any individual that falls within P.
   Here's another commonly used pattern of deductive reasoning:

If A, then B. (Major premise)
A. (Minor premise)
Therefore, B. (Conclusion)

If our team won the playoff game, it will be in the champi-
   onship game.
Our team won the playoff game.
Therefore, it will be in the championship game.

We use deductive reasoning on a daily basis, usually in the form of an **enthymeme**. An enthymeme is a syllogism with a key part or parts implied rather than directly stated. The missing parts are expected to be supplied by the listener or reader. For example, you may say, "We need to stop and get gas on the way to the movies." (This statement is the enthymeme.) Written as a syllogism, the reasoning would be:

> If we want to go to the movies in your car, we need to get gas.
>
> We want to go to the movies in your car.
>
> Therefore, we need to get gas.

Let's say, though, that your friend responds to your "We need to stop and get gas on the way to the movies" by stating "No we don't; we're fine." His reasoning would look like this:

> If we already have enough gas to get to the movies, we don't need to stop for more.
>
> We already have enough gas to get to the movies.
>
> Therefore, we don't need to stop for more.

Validity and Truth

This sample disagreement points out an important element of deductive reasoning; a deductive argument may be *valid* (i.e., fit the correct form) without being *true*. The conclusion may follow from the premises, but one or both of the premises may not be true, and of course the truth factor is essential to argumentation. What happens if you have a perfect syllogism that states the following?

> All students in this classroom are mice.
>
> Marcus is a student in this classroom.
>
> Therefore, Marcus is a mouse.

Because this syllogism follows the correct format, the conclusion does follow logically from the premises. But are the premises true? Obviously not!

REMINDER

Understanding the process of deductive reasoning helps you realize what you are assuming to be true when you state your position on issues.

When you are confronted with an argument to analyze, first try to phrase the argument in the form of a syllogism. If the argument does not fit into a proper syllogistic form, then we say that it is not valid (regardless of whether it is true). If the argument does fit the form (is valid), then we consider the premises to see whether they are true. In the example about getting gas for the movies, we can see that both arguments are valid; they both follow the deductive reasoning pattern correctly. But one of them is not true; either they have enough gas to make it or they don't.

A **prejudicial enthymeme** often involves deductive reasoning that is untrue and unproven, but logically valid. Let's say that you hear someone comment: "Of course Lisa's a terrible driver—she's a woman!" This enthymeme could be placed into a syllogistic format as follows:

> All women are terrible drivers.
>
> Lisa is a woman.
>
> Therefore, Lisa is a terrible driver.

You can see that if the premises of this syllogism are true, then the conclusion would be true. But the major premise given here could never be proven true; we can't know *all* about any group of individuals.

EXERCISE

Purpose: To construct syllogisms from prejudicial enthymemes.

Most prejudicial statements can be unraveled as valid but untrue (unproven) syllogisms. Think of a prejudicial statement that has been directed at you (or a friend) in the past. Reconstruct that statement into syllogistic form.

Example:

My friend is on welfare because her husband left her and her two children. She can't find a job that would make enough money for her to afford childcare. When people find out she is

on welfare, they tell her she should be working and not spong-
ing off of society. Their reasoning is:

> All people on welfare are lazy.
> You are on welfare.
> Therefore, you are lazy.

There might be some people who fit into this description, but
it's unfair to put all people who need welfare into this category. I
think if people understood my friend's situation, they would be
less judgmental and more sympathetic.

All-encompassing syllogisms are most valuable in the realm of
proven fact. There are some P's that do fit into an all-encompassing
category (Q) and give us valuable information. For example, all
women with an HCG (human chorionic gonadotropin) level above 5
are pregnant, and all persons with a blood-alcohol level of .10 in the
state of Illinois are legally drunk. You might discover that all members
of your immediate family have type O blood. Because of these known
"alls," solid conclusions can be drawn: doctors can tell a woman if she
is pregnant, police officers in Illinois can give solid evidence to justify
a drunk driving arrest, and, if you need a blood transfusion, family
members can be approached to volunteer.

However, as soon as we move out of the realm of proven fact,
deductive reasoning can be argued in terms of the *truth* factor. An
issue involves controversy, i.e., more than one plausible side of an
argument. Understanding the process of deduction helps us to outline our own reasoning and the reasoning of others, so that we can
see if it is first of all logical (following correct form) and secondly,
grounded in truth.

The Premise of Contention

> *"What eludes logic is the most precious element in us, and one can
> draw nothing from a syllogism that the mind has not put there
> in advance."*
>
> Andre Gide, *Journals* (June 1927)

Let's look at the reasoning from our previous article; we can use our
understanding of deduction to clearly outline the argument of the
defense attorneys for this case:

All women who dress in a revealing manner are asking to
  be raped.

A Florida woman was dressed in a revealing manner.

Therefore, this woman was asking to be raped.

This syllogism passes the validity test: The conclusion logically follows from the premises. And the woman was dressed in a manner
that revealed her body, so the minor premise is true. But is the major
premise true?

Now consider this syllogism:

All drivers who speed are subject to a fine.

You are speeding.

Therefore, you are subject to a fine.

In this example, you might agree with the major premise, but
question the minor premise.

For our purposes, we will call the questionable premise the
premise of contention. Critical thinkers will argue about the premise
of contention rather than arguing about the conclusion.

When people argue about conclusions, stalemates are inevitable.
Adults end up sounding like children arguing over who left the door
open.

"You did it."

"No, I didn't."

"Yes, you did."

"No, I didn't." etc. etc.

Parents who weren't at the scene of the crime have little basis for a
rational judgment on an issue like this. Only real evidence (finger-
prints, videotapes, or witnesses) would help them get to the truth.

The same frustrating process occurs in some sexual harassment
cases, often called "he said, she said" issues. If there are no witnesses,
tapes, letters, or other forms of evidence, then the accuser has no
proof of being a victim and the accused has no proof of being innocent. Focusing on conclusions without accompanying evidence statements creates no-win arguments.

So what can we reasonably do in arguments that seem to lead to
stalemates? Let's take the highly charged issue of abortion. At demon-
strations, we may witness a scene that is hardly more sophisticated

than the one between children noted previously, as the advocates for both sides focus on conclusions.

"Unborn children are worthy of protection."
"No, they're not."
"Yes, they are."
"No, they're not." etc. etc.

If we can use deductive reasoning to uncover the beliefs of both sides, we can then focus our efforts on fruitful areas of inquiry. For example, we might outline the "pro-life" argument as follows:

All human life is valuable and worthy of protection.
An unborn child is a human life.
Therefore, an unborn child deserves protection.

Those who are "pro-choice" would find the minor premise the premise of contention; the contentious factor is whether or not an unborn child is a human life. In a similar manner, we might outline the "pro-choice" reasoning:

Tissue masses have no civil rights.
A fetus is a tissue mass.
Therefore, a fetus has no civil rights.

Which is the premise of contention in this syllogism?

Both syllogisms are valid in form since the conclusions follow from the premises. But the premise of contention in both cases is the minor one. So, each side needs to focus efforts on proving that their minor premise is true. (Note here that the arguments sound different depending on the terminology used—unborn child, fetus, product of conception. Chapter 8 will focus on the power of words to shape our perceptions of an issue.)

When we argue about a major premise we are questioning whether, in a given case, all P's are Q. When we argue about a minor premise, we are questioning whether something or someone is actually P.

REMINDER

In deductive arguments, a critical thinker will outline his or her argument and the argument of the other person, find the premise(s) of contention, and then argue that his or her premises are correct.

Inductive Reasoning

To prove the truth of a premise, we move to the process of induction. But before we open the door to induction, a qualification should be made. In our human state, there are very few issues that can be proven beyond a shadow of a doubt. Even our court system only asks that a conclusion be proven "beyond a *reasonable* doubt." That means the evidence does point to the conclusion with the reservation that there may be an *unusual* exception.

If we can present evidence to prove that a premise (assertion, statement) is very *likely* to be true, we have valuable information on which to base our decisions. In addition, if we know there can be exceptions, we can understand them when they occur.

The process of **induction** occurs when we look at known facts or research and make inferences about possible conclusions. Stated in coded form, we can say that most P's are Q. Therefore, if I encounter a P, it is probably a Q. However, I realize that there are exceptions. Although the conclusion in a deductive argument *definitely* follows from true and valid premises, the conclusion in a strong inductive argument *probably* follows from the true premises that are given.

Two kinds of logic are used, inductive and deductive. . . . If the cycle goes over a bump and the engine misfires, and then goes over another bump and the engine misfires, and then goes over a long smooth stretch of road and there is no misfiring, and then goes over a fourth bump and the engine misfires again, one can logically conclude that the misfiring is caused by the bumps. That is induction. . . .

If, from reading the hierarchy of facts about the machine, the mechanic knows the horn of the cycle is powered exclusively by electricity from the battery, then he can logically infer that if the battery is dead the horn will not work. That is deduction.

Robert M. Pirsig, *Zen and the Art of Motorcycle Maintenance: An Inquiry into Values.* (New York: William Morrow, 1974), p. 99.

REMINDER

Critical thinkers use the process of induction to draw reasonable conclusions and to make clear decisions.

Inductive reasoning sounds like this:

Researchers claim that most women who have a family history of breast cancer (P) will develop breast cancer (Q). (Most P's are Q.)

My mother (m1) developed breast cancer (Q).

My sister (m2) developed breast cancer (Q).

My two aunts (m3 and m4) died of breast cancer (Q).

Since m1, m2, m3, and m4 are family members, I have a family history (P); I (m5) am P.

Therefore, it is likely that I (m5) will also develop breast cancer (Q). (Conclusion—m5 will probably be Q, because most P's are Q.)

Can you see that the conclusion "It is likely that I will also develop breast cancer" is not a certainty, but a strong possibility? The woman

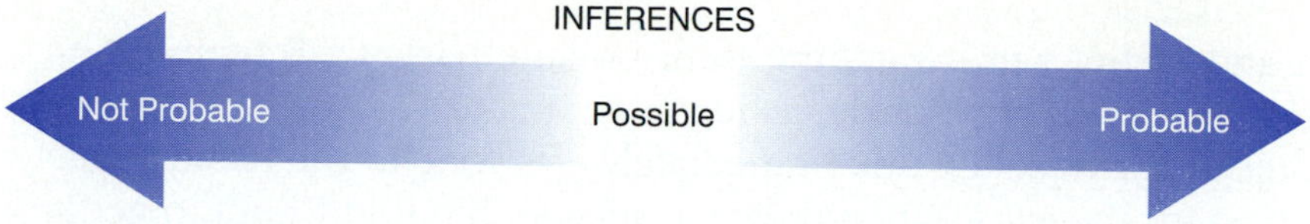

INFERENCES

Not Probable   Possible   Probable

Figure 3.2

who reasons in this way can now examine her choices in a logical manner. She can do a reasonable risk assessment about her chances of developing cancer and also her chances of recovery if she were to develop this form of cancer. Some women faced with this family history have had healthy breasts removed before cancer could develop. These women will never know if they might have "dodged the bullet" and avoided the disease without having taken these measures. But they reasoned that, in their individual cases, the probability was high enough and the consequences grave enough to justify their actions.

When you reason inductively, you go from observations to inferences. You are starting with what is true and proceeding to a reasonable and responsible interpretation of the facts. An inference is a statement about the *unknown* based on the *known*. Good inferences are based upon solid evidence; we can say that they are probable. Poor inferences are not probable (Figure 3.2).

Critical thinkers need to distinguish observations from inferences and then use the inductive reasoning process to draw responsible conclusions that are grounded in evidence. The following chapters of this text will focus on methods of examining and assessing the quality of evidence used to support conclusions.

SKILL

A critical thinker distinguishes observations from inferences and makes responsible interpretations.

Here's a quiz to see if you can distinguish what is definitely true or false (factual) from what is probably true or false (inferential).

Read the story about Jim and Debra and then decide if each statement is true, false, or questionable (that means you don't have enough information to say true or false). Assume that every statement in the story is accurate.

Jim and Debra were watching their college basketball team when suddenly one of the baskets began to shake violently. Someone shouted "Earthquake!" and immediately everyone in the room began running for the exits. When they got outside, Jim told Debra to get in the car and they drove straight home. No injuries were reported after this incident.

1. In brief, this story is about an earthquake that occurred during a college basketball game.	T	F	?
2. One of the baskets was shaking violently.	T	F	?
3. Jim took Debra home in his car.	T	F	?
4. The men on the team were among those who began running for the exits.	T	F	?
5. Jim and Debra drove to a pizza place after they got in the car.	T	F	?
6. There were no injuries as a result of this incident.	T	F	?
7. Someone shouted "Earthquake."	T	F	?
8. One basket did not shake violently.	T	F	?
9. Though Jim and Debra's date was cut short, they did make it out of the building.	T	F	?
10. The earthquake disrupted the college basketball game.	T	F	?

Before reading on, you may want to check your results with others in your class and try to reach a consensus.

Now let's look at the results, keeping a few things in mind. A fact or observation is a statement that can be shown to be true or false—it either did or did not happen according to the information that we are given. An inference is something that *might* be true but has not yet been *proven* to be true.

Anything we say about the future, therefore, is inferential, and so is much of what we say about the past. Observations focus on past or present realities, and they stay with what is known. Inferences go beyond the facts as known; the best inferences are based on many observations.

When we form conclusions by interpreting facts (making inferences), we are engaged in inductive reasoning. Consider, for example, a good weather forecaster who relies on sensitive instruments to give us a picture of what will probably happen in the future. Similarly, an economist can look at certain indicators and make an educated guess about whether the stock market will rise or fall in the coming weeks. Also, a physician can give you a reasonable statement about your chances of recovery from a surgical procedure.

Still, all of these instances are inferences or interpretations. We can say that they are probable inferences, most likely to occur, but as critical thinkers we need to make the distinction between proven fact and probable inference.

Now let's look at our example. We can certainly say that someone shouted "Earthquake" (Question 7) and that one of the baskets was shaking violently (Question 2). Those statements should have been labeled as true. We also can note that since Jim and Debra went straight home, they could not have gone out for pizza after they got in the car. So Question 5 should have been marked false. Every other statement is questionable (inferential) because we do not have enough information to say that those statements are definitely true or false. Let's look at why:

1.   There are two problems with this statement. First, we don't know if there was an earthquake. All we know is that at least one basket was shaking and someone shouted "Earthquake." There is not enough information to make a claim. In addition, although Jim and Debra were watching their team, the story does not say that their team was playing a game. They might have been practicing. Jim and Debra might be cheerleaders. We aren't given enough information to assume a game was being played.

2.   This statement was clearly confirmed by the story.

3.   This statement is questionable. Jim told Debra to get in the car, but whose car was it? It could have been Jim's, but it is also possible that the car belonged to Debra, or that they were getting in a friend's car.

4.   Since everyone began running for the exits that would include team members—but were these members men? How do we know the team was not a women's team? If you missed this one, think about how you would have responded if the question had read, "The women on the team were among those who were running toward the exit."

5.   This statement is clearly false, since Jim and Debra drove home.

6.   There may have been no injuries, but we don't have enough information to draw that conclusion. Even if injuries were not reported, that doesn't mean they didn't occur.

7.   As stated above, this is clearly true.

8.   We are told that one basket was shaking violently. We don't know if any other baskets were shaking, so we can't respond with a true or false answer.

9.   This statement is tricky, because the second half of the statement is true. But the critical thinker needs to look at all of what is said and decide if all of it is true. We don't know if Jim and Debra were on a date—they might have been cousins or twins or just friends sitting together. Also, we don't know that the date, if there was a date, was "cut short"—they might have continued their evening together at home or elsewhere.

10.   Again, we don't know if there was an earthquake, and we also don't know if there was a game, so this statement is questionable.

What are we looking at when we take a test like this, and why is it important for critical thinking? When we make statements, or when we listen to statements made by others, we can classify them in three broad categories (Figure 3.3). We can say:

1. This statement is definitely true (or false).
2. This statement is probably true (or false).
3. This statement is possibly true (or false).

Because we make decisions based on information, we need to know which information is accurate and which, if any, information is

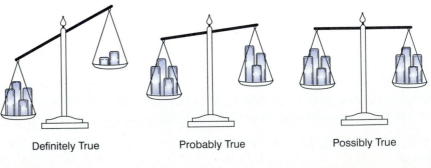

Definitely True   Probably True   Possibly True

Figure 3.3

still missing. Let's say you are planning to go skiing and have a limited budget. You need to know whether you must buy chains for your car. If you hear a report that chains are required on the highway you will be using, then you have clear information with which to make a decision. Note that this information is not set in concrete. It is *probably* true that you will need chains. You may arrive at the highway and find that the requirement has been removed—but you acted as a critical thinker on the information you had at the time you needed to make the decision.

Critical thinkers should recognize facts and observations and use them to make interpretations that are responsible, well-considered inferences. If we waited until we had the absolute facts about every situation, we might never act at all. So we need to get all the information we can, decide what is most likely to be true (probable inferences), and then take calculated risks—risks we have considered—as we live our lives.

Making careful interpretations is more work than simply accepting what friends, politicians, and advertisers tell us to believe. But to the extent that we are careful about basing our conclusions on well-considered inferences, we have more power in our lives. Fewer mistakes are made, and we are in a position to handle situations that don't turn out exactly as we expected.

The Problem of Hasty Conclusions

"Labels are devices for saving talkative persons the trouble of thinking."

John Morley, "Carlyle," *Critical Miscellanies* (1871–1908)

Noncritical thinkers may "jump to conclusions"—that is, they hear a few facts or make a few observations and then draw a hasty conclusion. For example, someone may be treated poorly by a few people in St. Louis and jump to the conclusion that all people in St. Louis are rude. Or someone may have spoken to a Republican who has no sympathy for the homeless and jump to the conclusion that all Republicans are cold and heartless.

Making inferences on a small sample of information—or drawing **hasty conclusions**—is the basis of stereotyping. When we are prejudiced, we are prejudging people and situations instead of taking the responsibility for considering the realities of each situation. The antidote to prejudice is more information and experience, but we sometimes fail to get more information; we draw hasty conclusions because it is the easiest route to take. It's easier to just take someone's word for it when they say "this soup is nutritious" or "this candidate cares about the environment" than it is to do research for ourselves. Other times, we are more comfortable living with our noncritical assumptions because they have become a part of our thinking patterns: If we stereotype people and situations, then we know what we need to do with them.

If we believe that only Republicans or Democrats or Independents can govern the best, then we know who to vote for without having to think about individual qualifications. School teachers sometimes exhibit this uncritical stereotyping by checking a student's past performance and placing him or her in a reading group based on the previous year rather than retesting to see if improvement was made over the summer. You can see how uncritical interpretations can have lasting negative effects for both individuals and society.

Self-Fulfilling Prophecies

One important effect of jumping to conclusions is called the self-fulfilling prophecy. When someone makes a self-fulfilling prophecy, he or she starts with an unproven inference, "I'm no good in math," and then acts as if this inference is a fact (he or she doesn't bother to study math and fails the tests), proving the inference that he or she is poor in math.

There are two types of self-fulfilling prophecies—those that other people make about us, and those we make about ourselves or others. If you think back to labels given to you by teachers, peers, or parents in early years, you may find that they have become fulfilled in your life.

For example, if you were told that you were going to do well in sports, you probably assumed that was true and had the confidence to succeed; on the other hand, if you were told that you were a terrible artist by an art teacher, you probably accepted his evaluation and gave up on art. You assumed that the inference was true and then acted as if it were true. Finally it *became* true.

Examples:

   "You'll never be able to learn geometry."

"I always strike out."

"He's a really selfish guy."

"I'll never learn to swim."

"You can't talk to those Yuppies."

"That textbook is too hard to understand."

"You'll love new Bolger's instant crystals!"

The self-fulfilling prophecy has been operative on a societal level in such forms as bank runs and escalating tensions between ethnic and political groups. On personal levels, self-fulfilling prophecies are responsible for limitations we place on ourselves and our abilities.

As critical thinkers, we are responsible for knowing if personal or group limitations are the results of careless predictions. Then we are empowered to change ourselves or our attitudes.

EXERCISE

Purpose: To analyze the effect of uncritical inferences.

Think of some personal and some cultural self-fulfilling prophecies. How did they come about and how did they become fulfilled? What could be done to change attitudes or actions now?

Example:

During the 1992 Winter Olympics, one of the medal contenders for pairs figure skating fell during a crucial performance. The commentator for CBS said that a reporter had once written that this skater seemed to be having trouble with jumps. The commentator explained that after she read this article, the skater continually had trouble with her jumps.

I noticed that this skater seemed hesitant about her jumps during the Olympics. I wondered if a sports psychologist could help her get over what seemed to be a self-fulfilling prophecy. Her coach and her psychologist could help her to form a positive attitude. She could come to believe she's good at jumping by practicing and watching her jumps. The evidence of many successful jumps completed in practice sessions would change her negative expectation and she would perform better in competition.

EXERCISE

Purpose: To think of ways to respond to situations more critically.

Read each situation, noting what the noncritical thinker would do. Then give an example of what a critical thinker might do.

Example:
A candidate for your state assembly is campaigning door to door and asks for your vote. You tell her that your major concern is waste-water management. She tells you that she is very concerned about this problem also and has given it much consideration.

Noncritical thinker: Votes for the candidate.

Critical thinker: Asks the candidate about her specific concerns and the solutions she proposes; follows up with questions about the details of the candidate's proposal. Asks about the sources of funding for any programs the candidate proposes. May ask her to comment on the proposals of other candidates. Checks out the plans of other candidates and weighs them carefully before voting. Also considers the general platform of other candidates to assess the overall consequences of voting for a given candidate.

1. Your friend from your 10:00 class tells you to meet her at the cafeteria early.

   Noncritical thinker: Arrives at the cafeteria at 9:45, assuming the friend wants to tell her something or to walk to class together.
   Critical thinker:

2. You are depressed because you seem to be balding before your time. While switching channels on your television set one night, you catch a promotional show on anti-balding medication. There are several testimonies in the audience about how well this medication works to restore hair. Also, a famous actor is endorsing the product.

   Noncritical thinker: Dials the 800 number on the screen and charges the product.
   Critical thinker:

3. You are invited to a birthday party at your friend's house. He is a good friend, but each time you have attended a party at his house you have had a bad time. Once, you got food poisoning from the fried chicken; another time, it seemed as though everyone had a date except you. You've started to predict that you'll have a terrible time at his parties. What do you do?

Noncritical thinker: Stays at home.
Critical thinker:

Add any personal situations in which you responded as a non-critical thinker. What could you have done differently?

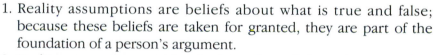

Chapters 4 and 5 will focus on the use of research and expert testimony in helping critical thinkers use induction to make rational decisions about personal, social, and political issues.

Chapter Highlights

1. Reality assumptions are beliefs about what is true and false; because these beliefs are taken for granted, they are part of the foundation of a person's argument.
2. Reality assumptions need to be brought to light and examined so those who make them do not build arguments on untrue or unconsidered premises.
3. In deductive reasoning, the conclusion definitely follows from true premises that are expressed in valid form; syllogisms that use a deductive pattern of reasoning help us to uncover reality assumptions.
4. Critical thinkers argue about premises rather than conclusions.
5. Inductive reasoning proceeds from true premises to a probable conclusion.
6. Inferences are statements about the unknown based on the known; they express inductive conclusions and function on a continuum from improbable to probable.
7. Two effects of drawing hasty inductive conclusions are prejudicial statements and the self-fulfilling prophecy.

Articles for Discussion

Just Walk on By

A Black Man Ponders His Power to Alter Public Space

by Brent Staples
Ms. Magazine, September 1986

My first victim was a woman—white, well dressed, probably in her early twenties. I came upon her late one evening on a deserted street in Hyde Park, a relatively affluent neighborhood in an otherwise mean, impoverished section of Chicago. As I swung onto the avenue behind her, there seemed to be a discreet, uninflammatory distance between us. Not so. She cast back a worried glance. To her, the youngish, black man—a broad six feet two inches with a beard and billowing hair, both hands shoved into the pockets of a bulky military jacket—seemed menacingly close. After a few more quick glimpses, she picked up her pace and was soon running in earnest. Within seconds she disappeared into a cross street.

That was more than a decade ago. I was twenty-two years old, a graduate student newly arrived at the University of Chicago. It was in the echo of that terrified woman's footfalls that I first began to know the unwieldy inheritance I'd come into—the ability to alter public space in ugly ways. It was clear that she thought herself the quarry of a mugger, a rapist, or worse. Suffering a bout of insomnia, however, I was stalking sleep, not defenseless wayfarers. As a softy who is scarcely able to take a knife to a raw chicken—let alone hold it to a person's throat—I was surprised, embarrassed, and dismayed all at once. Her flight made me feel like an accomplice in tyranny. It also made it clear that I was indistinguishable from the muggers who occasionally seeped into the area from the surrounding ghetto. That first encounter, and those that followed, signified that a vast, unnerving gulf lay between nighttime pedestrians—particularly women—and me. And I soon gathered that being perceived as dangerous is a hazard in itself. I only needed to turn a corner into a dicey situation, or crowd some frightened, armed person in a foyer somewhere, or make an errant move after being pulled over by a policeman. Where fear and weapons meet—and they often do in urban America—there is always the possibility of death.

In that first year, my first away from my hometown, I was to become thoroughly familiar with the language of fear. At dark, shadowy intersections in Chicago, I could cross in front of a car stopped at a traffic light and elicit the thunk, thunk, thunk, thunk of the driver—black, white, male, or female—hammering down the door locks. On less traveled streets after dark, I grew accustomed to but never comfortable with people who crossed to the other side of the street rather than pass me. Then there were the standard unpleasantries with police, doormen, bouncers, cabdrivers, and others whose business is to screen out troublesome individuals *before* there is any nastiness.

I moved to New York nearly two years ago and I have remained an avid night walker. In central Manhattan, the near-constant crowd cover minimizes tense one-on-one street encounters. Elsewhere—visiting friends in SoHo, where sidewalks are narrow and tightly spaced buildings shut out the sky—things can get very taut indeed.

Black men have a firm place in New York mugging literature. Norman Podhoretz in his famed (or infamous) 1963 essay, "My Negro Problem— And Ours," recalls growing up in terror of black males; they "were tougher than we were, more ruthless," he writes—and as an adult on the Upper West Side of Manhattan, he continues, he cannot constrain his nervousness when he meets black men on certain streets. Similarly, a decade later, the essayist and novelist Edward Hoagland extols a New York where once "Negro bitterness bore down mainly on other Negroes." Where some see mere panhandlers, Hoagland sees "a mugger who is clearly screwing up his nerve to do more than just *ask* for money." But Hoagland has "the New Yorker's quick-hunch posture for broken-field maneuvering," and the bad guy swerves away.

I often witness that "hunch posture," from women after dark on the warrenlike streets of Brooklyn where I live. They seem to set their faces on neutral and, with their purse straps strung across their chests bandolier style, they forge ahead as though bracing themselves against being tackled. I understand, of course, that the danger they perceive is not a hallucination. Women are particularly vulnerable to street violence, and young black males are drastically overrepresented among the perpetrators of that violence. Yet these truths are no solace against the kind of alienation that comes of being ever the suspect, against being set apart, a fearsome entity with whom pedestrians avoid making eye contact.

It is not altogether clear to me how I reached the ripe old age of twenty-two without being conscious of the lethality nighttime pedestrians attributed to me. Perhaps it was because in Chester, Pennsylvania, the small, angry industrial town where I came of age in the 1960s, I was scarcely noticeable against a backdrop of gang warfare, street knifings, and murders. I grew up one of the good boys, had perhaps a half-dozen fistfights. In retrospect, my shyness of combat has clear sources.

Many things go into the making of a young thug. One of those things is the consummation of the male romance with the power to intimidate. An infant discovers that random flailings send the baby bottle flying out of the crib and crashing to the floor. Delighted, the joyful babe repeats those motions again and again, seeking to duplicate the feat. Just so, I recall the points at which some of my boyhood friends were finally seduced by the perception of themselves as tough guys. When a mark cowered and surrendered his money without resistance, myth and reality merged—and paid off. It is, after all, only manly to embrace the power to frighten and intimidate. We, as men, are not supposed to give an inch of our lane on the highway; we are to seize the fighter's edge in work and in play and even in love; we are to be valiant in the face of hostile forces.

Unfortunately, poor and powerless young men seem to take all this nonsense literally. As a boy, I saw countless tough guys locked away; I have since buried several, too. They were babies, really—a teenage cousin, a brother of twenty-two, a childhood friend in his mid-twenties—all gone down in episodes of bravado played out in the streets. I came to doubt the virtues of intimidation early on. I chose, perhaps even unconsciously, to remain a shadow—timid, but a survivor.

The fearsomeness mistakenly attributed to me in public places often has a perilous flavor. The most frightening of these confusions occurred in the late 1970s and early 1980s when I worked as a journalist in Chicago. One day, rushing into the office of a magazine I was writing for with a deadline story in hand, I was mistaken for a burglar. The office manager called security and, with an ad hoc posse, pursued me through the labyrinthine halls, nearly to my editor's door. I had no way of proving who I was. I could only move briskly toward the company of someone who knew me.

Another time I was on assignment for a local paper and killing time before an interview. I entered a jewelry store on the city's affluent Near North Side. The proprietor excused herself and returned with an enormous red Doberman pinscher straining at the end of a leash. She stood, the dog extended toward me, silent to my questions, her eyes bulging nearly out of her head. I took a cursory look around, nodded, and bade her good night. Relatively speaking, however, I never fared as badly as another black male journalist. He went to nearby Waukegan, Illinois, a couple of summers ago to work on a story about a murderer who was born there. Mistaking the reporter for the killer, police hauled him from his car at gunpoint and but for his press credentials would probably have tried to book him. Such episodes are not uncommon. Black men trade tales like this all the time.

In "My Negro Problem—And Ours," Podhoretz writes that the hatred he feels for blacks makes itself known to him through a variety of avenues—one being his discomfort with that "special brand of paranoid touchiness" to which he says blacks are prone. No doubt he is speaking here of black men. In time, I learned to smother the rage I felt at so often being taken for a criminal. Not to do so would surely have led to madness—via that special "paranoid touchiness" that so annoyed Podhoretz at the time he wrote the essay.

I began to take precautions to make myself less threatening. I move about with care, particularly late in the evening. I give a wide berth to nervous people on subway platforms during the wee hours, particularly when I have exchanged business clothes for jeans. If I happen to be entering a building behind some people who appear skittish, I may walk by, letting them clear the lobby before I return, so as not to seem to be following them. I have been calm and extremely congenial on those rare occasions when I've been pulled over by the police.

And on late-evening constitutionals along streets less traveled by, I employ what has proved to be an excellent tension-reducing measure: I whistle melodies from Beethoven and Vivaldi and the more popular classical composers. Even steely New Yorkers hunching toward nighttime destinations seem to relax, and occasionally they even join in the tune. Virtually everybody seems to sense that a mugger wouldn't be warbling bright, sunny selections from Vivaldi's *Four Seasons*. It is my equivalent of the cowbell that hikers wear when they know they are in bear country.

Reprinted by permission of the author.

Questions for Discussion

1. What reality assumptions were made about the author of this essay that made him uncomfortable? Why were these assumptions made?

2. Brent Staples cites articles written years ago by Norman Podhoretz and Edward Hoagland. Do you believe the comments of these writers would be published today? Do you think the assumptions made years ago by these writers are still widely held?

3. Toward the end of the essay, Staples discusses the method he uses to diffuse anxiety among fellow pedestrians. What assumptions is he hoping they will make about him?

4. All of us have a unique personal appearance. People make assumptions about us because of our race, gender, weight, height, and clothing style. John Molloy, author of *Dress for Success,* and other researchers have discovered that a person is judged on dimensions of competence, authority, and affability based on these superficial characteristics. "Clothing engineers" make a living advising politicians, engineers, and aspiring professionals about how to package themselves for maximum impact on their desired audiences.

   How has your personal appearance been judged by others who do not know you? What assumptions have been made about you because of your race, sex, height, weight, or style? Were these assumptions correct? If not, why do you think they were made?

Is This the Promised Land?

by Hector Martin
A California community college student from Mexico

It was a beautiful evening, that Friday, March 26 in 1985, when I arrived at the Los Angeles Airport. That was when I took my first steps in the United States. From the L.A. airport to my cousin's house, I was admiring the beauty of the city. I was very amused by the magnificent buildings, the beautiful houses and the modern freeways.

A feeling of joy filled my heart. Everything was as great as I had heard from my friends. They said that the United States was one of the most beautiful places on earth, that it was a land of opportunities just waiting to be taken advantage of, and that there I could fulfill all my dreams. Yes, it was beautiful and I was there to conquer that land. I felt a real happiness about being in the United States.

The evening of the next day, my cousin took me to visit some of his friends who were having a party. I was very happy to know, before anything else, what a party was like in this country. Unfortunately, in a few minutes my happiness turned into confusion. At the party, most of the people were celebrating because three of them had just turned eighteen years old, and would be able to leave their parents' homes to go to live with their friends.

I asked my cousin why they were leaving their parents' homes and he told me that it was common in the United States to do so. My mind sought a more logical answer that would excuse their actions, but I could not find one. My mind was struck with a very strong fear, the fear of not being able to understand their customs, and the fear of not fitting into their society.

To become part of a society in a different culture requires much more than the willingness of the individual because of the existence of invisible and unavoidable intercultural barriers. Some of these barriers are discussed by Laray M. Barna in her article *Intercultural Communication Stumbling Blocks*. This article examines the obstacles faced by foreigners in communicating with people from a different culture.

As a person who has experienced the difficulties of adapting to a new culture, I believe that cultural and behavioral differences often create barriers that block the adaptation of foreigners. The first barrier arises when the foreigner faces customs that are strange to him. Since I came from a traditional and conservative family, I found unacceptable the American tradition that after turning eighteen years old, many young Americans leave their parents' homes to live on their own.

Unconsciously, I developed the "tendency to evaluate," a term defined in Barna's article as the tendency to disapprove or approve the actions of others based on one's own culture instead of trying to understand, with an open mind, the thoughts and actions of people in the new culture.

The practice of leaving home at such an age was very strange to me because I never saw that in Mexico, my native country. I felt that the children, who left their parents' homes after all that their parents had done for them, were being ungrateful. In my own mind, because of my experience in Mexico, I could not find an acceptable reason to justify such a decision, so I labeled this action as insensitive.

However, a couple of years after I arrived in the United States, I changed my way of thinking about that custom. I had a conversation with an American girl whose brothers had left their parents' home. She told me that her brothers were attending school out of state and that they had begun to live independently.

In response to my question about her parents' opinion on this matter, she told me that they were very proud of their children because they were not dependent or irresponsible. She said that her parents were actually very happy that their sons were standing on their own two feet and were learning to face life's problems on their own.

Upon hearing these opinions, I realized that the custom which I had labeled as insensitive was actually a reflection of the American value of independence and was not considered an insensitive act by American parents. They perceived that custom as a sign of personal growth and maturity of their children. From that time on, I learned not to evaluate American customs too quickly. I became more aware of the fact that the Mexican and American cultures differ greatly from each other, and I learned to respect and tolerate the factors which make them different.

The difference in the rhythm of life is another factor that can block the adaptation of a foreigner to a new culture. Robert Levine, in his article, *Social Time: The Heartbeat of Culture*, informs us of how the pace of life differs from country to country.

When people from a country with a more relaxed pace of life come to the United States and take notice of the fast rhythm of American life, they may become disconcerted at the difference. Usually foreigners defend themselves against this confusion by using criticism. For example, some Latin people who are not accustomed to living a life which is ruled by the watch do not understand why Americans are always tied to busy schedules and are always answering to their main boss, the clock.

This confusion is revealed in what happened one day when a friend of mine and I were enjoying breakfast in a cafe near the U.C. Berkeley campus. We took notice of the tables around us that were occupied by students from the university. On the tables, the students had their meals, but each had also brought a pile of books. A couple sitting next to us, who had their books open, were writing notes and eating at the same time. The people at the other tables were also reading and eating simultaneously.

My friend wondered why these people did not have enough time to eat normally. He felt that their incredibly rapid way of eating and studying reflected the American saying of "time is money." Then he said to me, "I can't believe these people. Their materialism makes them so obsessed with the idea of succeeding in school, which will prepare them for a job that will help them make a lot of money, that they spend their lives running all the time. These people are so wrapped up in their time limits that they cannot even allow themselves to sit down and enjoy a meal as they should."

I understood my friend's point because I knew that he came from a country ranch where the people's main concern was to finish their daily tasks so that they could spend the rest of the day hunting animals or visiting friends.

Although foreigners use criticism to defend themselves in an unfamiliar environment, they are not the only ones who have the tendency to evaluate. Criticism also comes from the members of the host culture who are unaware of how they are different from the foreigners. As explained earlier, time is a concept that is perceived differently by American and Latin people. Latin people are not very concerned about punctuality, but on the other hand, this is of major importance to Americans. Therefore, when Americans notice the disregard of time by Latin people, they may tend to consider Latins as lazy and irresponsible.

Levine, in his article, provides facts that clearly illustrate the difference of time concepts in different countries. In research which compared Brazilians to Americans regarding their personal sense of "lateness," Levine notes that Brazilians define lateness for a lunch date with a friend as arriving 33.5 minutes after the time arranged, while Americans only allow a 19 minute grace period.

Obviously, this difference in the perception of punctuality as seen from the viewpoint of an American would only reinforce the stereotype that Latin people are lazy and irresponsible. But if judged from a Latin person's point of view, it would only reinforce his belief that Americans are materialistic people who believe that time means money. These differences block the ability of foreigners and Americans to understand each other and this often leads to discomfort between the two groups, which may in turn eventually prevent social interaction between them.

Adaptation to another culture is not an easy task. In many cases, such as my own, it may take several years. I had to learn to break down my old preconceptions about Americans and also to learn to understand others' customs and ways of thinking.

I have come to realize that intercultural differences are easily misunderstood. Does the fast rhythm of American life prove that Americans are materialistic? Does the fact that the Brazilian concept of punctuality, by being not as strict as that of American standards, prove that Brazilians are lazy?

As I think back to the day when I arrived in the United States, I remember how my excitement turned into fear when I was faced with such unexpected intercultural differences. I felt as if a huge ocean was interposed between me and that new and different world. I remember how my dream of conquering that world began to crumble away as I collided with those barriers of misunderstandings, and also how much it hurt to realize that I would be unable to become part of that society.

Fortunately, with the help of day-to-day experiences which have given me insights into this new culture, I have come to understand the world around me and to discover the beauty of its cities, customs, traditions, people, and most importantly, of life.

In order to adjust to a new culture, foreigners should remember that their own flexibility is imperative. They need to accept and respect the customs and ways of living of the culture in which they hope to be integrated. They have to remember that every culture is unique. After all, wouldn't this world be boring if we all thought and acted the same way?

Reprinted by permission of the author.

Questions for Discussion

1. The friend of the author is quoted as saying, "I can't believe these people. Their materialism makes them so obsessed with the idea of succeeding in school, which will prepare them for a job that will help them make a lot of money, that they spend their lives running all the time." To what extent do you believe his assumption is justified? What other interpretations could be made about the behavior of students who are eating and reading or eating and taking notes?

2. In explaining the different interpretations that Americans and Latins make about the others' use of time, Martin states, "These differences block the ability of foreigners and Americans to understand each other and this often leads to discomfort between the two groups, which may in turn eventually prevent social interaction between them." What are some other examples of different interpretations made by members of different cultures or subcultures that prevent or affect social interaction?

3. Martin speaks of the "tendency to evaluate . . . to disapprove or approve the actions of others based on one's own culture instead of trying to understand, with an open mind, the thoughts and

actions of people in the new culture." Can you think of times when you or others have made judgments about the actions of members of other cultures without attempting to understand those actions?

Ideas for Writing or Speaking

1. Explain three or four assumptions made by your culture, subculture, or family. These assumptions can be about use of time and/or resources; holiday traditions; the role of men, women, and/or children; the place of work, family, and citizenship.

   Example:

   > One assumption of my family is that everyone will go to college. My parents were expected to go to college by their parents, even though their parents didn't have the money to go themselves.
   >
   > It was never directly stated that we had to go to college; it was just taken for granted that we would. My parents would start sentences by saying, "When you go to college . . ." or "After you finish college. . . ."
   >
   > When my little brother decided to get a job right after high school, everyone was in shock. It never occurred to us that we wouldn't all go straight to college. After he worked two years in a warehouse, my brother did decide to attend college. Maybe he was living up to the family's expectations, but I think he was hoping for an easier life!

2. Choose a social, political, or religious movement or group and write about three assumptions that guide this group. Take a position, agreeing or disagreeing with the assumptions of this group. Begin with an introductory paragraph that contains your conclusion (thesis statement). Then write a paragraph for each assumption you discuss. End with a paragraph that summarizes your beliefs about the underlying assumptions of this group.

   Some possible topics for this assignment: Greenpeace, the Young Republicans, the Democratic Party, the Libertarian Party, Buddhism, Judaism, Christianity, Islam, Feminism, Action for Children's Television, the National Rifle Association, Mothers Against Drunk Drivers, the Society for the Prevention of Cruelty to Animals.

3. Using the same organizational format as in Question 2, explore the assumptions made by both sides of a controversial issue. For example, you might explore the assumptions of people who support and people who are against tuition for community colleges. One assumption of those who support tuition might be that people work harder when they have to pay for education; an assumption of those against tuition might be that fees are an unnecessary and prohibitive burden on the poor and that they are therefore "classist."

Find several assumptions on both sides of your issue. Then explain which assumptions are the most reasonable and why.

CHAPTER FOUR

Statistics

Prove It to Me.
What Are the Statistics?

A critical thinker understands the basics of polling and the legitimate uses of statistical research in supporting conclusions.

This chapter will cover:

◆ The uses of statistical evidence in arguments
◆ The methods of polling that yield significant data
◆ The reporting of statistical data

In the last two chapters, we focused on the foundations of arguments. In this chapter and from this point on, we will concentrate on the kinds of evidence and the quality of the evidence used to support conclusions.

As mentioned in the first chapter, anyone can have an opinion (conclusion) and give reasons for that opinion. But the critical thinker looks for *solid* reasons that add credibility to the conclusion. Strong reasons are based on good evidence. Let's examine the major types of evidence used to support a conclusion.

Statistical Evidence

The first type of evidence most commonly used to support arguments is evidence gathered from research; this is often called *empirical evidence*. We will divide the discussion of empirical evidence into two categories: **statistical evidence** and **controlled studies**. *Statistical evidence*, the subject of this chapter, refers to data collected by specific methods that have been found to be reliable. We do research to get information to help us make predictions and decisions when situations are uncertain.

Making predictions about the future is a uniquely human trait; we humans tend to live, to varying degrees, in the past, the present, and the future. On the other hand, animals, to the best of our knowledge, live mostly in the present moment. They are attuned to the sights, sounds, smells, and tastes that are around them. Our pets live and react in the present, not planning for the future. If your dog or cat is overweight, he is not likely to be concerned about dieting to enhance future romantic encounters or to prevent premature death. If he's cold or hungry or wants to play, he'll let you know and won't be happy if you pencil him in your calendar for 6:00 this evening—he wants you now. He is blessed with no anxiety about the future: Food shortages, droughts, and impending wars can affect him only if he's neglected in the present. In these ways, animals are like human babies. But as humans begin to grow, they change. They no longer simply move, as animals do; they begin to *act*. Acting means considering options, making choices, and then moving in the direction of those choices.

We like having a sense of control over our individual and collective futures; as critically thinking people, we want to act clearly, deliberately, and responsibly. We want to be prepared for future events. One way we can anticipate the future, which is unknown, is to reason from what is known in the present; in other words, we reason inductively.

For example, you might watch a baseball game and predict that because the batter has a .350 average and has been doing well the last few games, he will make at least a base hit right now. You're surprised if he strikes out. On the other hand, a batter with a .220 average who has just recovered from an injury would not be likely to get a good hit. If he does, you are again surprised. If you've been on three blind dates arranged by your cousin and they have all been terrible, you will probably predict that a fourth date arranged by this person will turn out the same way.

The Use of Statistics

We are constantly using statistics, however small and inadequate, to make predictions and decisions in our personal lives. Polltakers and researchers have used systematic methods to get results with great predictive value; i.e., they can tell us what probably will happen. For example, a Gallup poll or Harris poll generally reflects how people will vote and who will be elected to political office.

Statistics are used in numerous professions in our culture. Lending companies use statistics on interest rates to support their arguments that people should get car and home loans or refinance existing loans. Real estate agents show statistics on public school test scores to clients to convince them to move into a new neighborhood. Weather forecasters use statistics to help them make predictions, and seismologists use statistics about past earthquakes to predict the progression of future earthquakes. Political advisors use statistics to determine the popularity of candidates and policies. Advertisers collect evidence on the size and nature of magazine and newspaper audiences to decide where to place their advertisements. The Nielsen ratings give commercial advertisers a good idea of what channels are being watched for a given period. (For further information on the Nielsen ratings, see "Watching Americans Watch TV" at the end of this chapter.)

New ways to gather statistics are also being discovered. One new method, called a "Q" score, is described in the following excerpt from a daily television column:

The research into who watches television, when and why, has produced an entire sub-industry of pollsters and numbers-crunchers. One of the best-kept secrets, and at the same time one of the most valued tools of network executives, is the so-called "Q" score.

That's short for TvQ, the periodic report's title, with the "Q" standing for qualitative. Essentially, average viewers are asked which stars and shows they recognize, then asked to rate them in terms of best-liked personalities and programs. The results are invariably hush-hush, but they are prized by network execs as a measurement of what shows create audience favorites, even if they're low-rated.[1]

STOP AND THINK

How might advertisers or television or film producers use some of the information gathered from "Q" scores?

How the Research Is Done

In this age of the proliferation of statistical information, most professions are influenced by the findings of research studies. How do we determine the quality of the statistical evidence we hear or read? To answer this question, we need to have a basic understanding of how the research is carried out.

When someone creates a research study, he or she needs to consider three questions:

1. What do I want to find out? This is called the **characteristic of interest**.
2. Who do I want to know about? This is called the **target population**.
3. Who can I study to get accurate answers about my entire target population? This is called the **sample**. We usually can't study everyone in a given target population, so we have to observe some representative members of the population. For polling, the adequate sample size is usually 1,000.

SKILL

Understand the basic structure of statistical research.

---

1 Jonathan Burlingame, "Television," *Contra Costa Times*, January 12, 1990, p. 10-C. Reprinted by permission of the author.

Examples

    Characteristic of interest: What are the most popular television programs during prime time?

    Target population: Americans.

    Sample: At least 1,000 randomly selected Americans.

    Characteristic of interest: Who will win the next gubernatorial election?

    Target population: State residents who are eligible to vote.

    Sample: At least 1,000 randomly selected state residents who are eligible to vote.

    Characteristic of interest: Whether American parents want labels on record albums that warn of violent or sexual content.

    Target population: Americans who are parents.

    Sample: 1,000 randomly selected American parents.

The characteristic of interest and target population are fairly easy to identify. The quality of statistical research depends largely on the sample drawn from the target population. For a study to be accurate and reliable, several things must be true about this sample.

THE SAMPLE MUST BE LARGE ENOUGH

Any sample studied must be sufficiently large to justify the information someone gets from the sample. Otherwise we are dealing in poor experimental design, or even stereotyping. If someone says, "Women are terrible drivers—both my sister and my girlfriend have had two accidents this year," the person is generalizing from a few cases. His outline would look like this:

    Characteristic of interest: Whether women can drive well.

    Target population: One-half of the human race.

    Sample: My girlfriend and my sister.

Sometimes when we stand back and look at what someone is claiming and the evidence they use, we can see how inadequate the argument is. Yet how often do we talk like this or agree when others talk like this?

EXERCISE

Purpose: To assess the adequacy of sample size relative to a target population.

Outline the following claims based on inadequate samples. State the target population, the characteristic of interest, and the sample.

"Asians are so good at math; there are four of them in my algebra class and they have the top scores."

"People who live in that part of town are such freaks—I saw two women with purple hair there last week."

"Men have such a hard time showing their feelings—my dad has never cried in front of us."

There are many theories about why we so easily jump to hasty conclusions about a whole group of people (target population) based on a small sample of people. One theory is that we feel more secure about ourselves and our relations to others when we can place everyone in a neat category.

Another theory is that we are too lazy and/or untrained to be careful about our generalizations. Most of us enjoy giving our opinions, but we're not willing to find the data that is required to prove our opinions. So we "mouth off" about topics we really are just guessing about; other people do the same thing, and we call it *conversing* and *socializing* and everybody's happy. If we happen to hear about a well-done study on a topic of interest to us, we add that to our conversation too.

This author has known only one person who consistently asked people to tell him why they believe the statements they make; he was clear-minded, fair, precise, and extremely unpopular! We get defensive about our pet stereotypes and indefensible positions and don't like people to shake us up. However, as we become critical thinkers, our positions will be taken more carefully and backed up with the kind of evidence that gives us real confidence about the opinions we share with others.

REMINDER

The sample must be large enough—that is, enough people must be studied—to justify the conclusions made by the researchers.

THE SAMPLE MUST REPRESENT THE TARGET AUDIENCE

The people studied must be like the people you are drawing a conclusion about. For example, if you want to study the effects of fluoride on American children, it would not be enough to only study children who live in the northeast. If you draw a conclusion from your research, it must reflect the entire target group about whom you are generalizing.

For a sample to be *representative,* it must have the same significant characteristics in the same proportions as the target group, as illustrated in Figure 4.1. If it does not have these characteristics, then the sample is called *biased*. A biascd sample is not useful as evidence to support a conclusion.

A common problem with modern social science research is that some researchers are college professors who use their students as "volunteers" for their studies. Although some extrapolations from student samples to the general population are reasonable, other findings may relate more specifically to college students on a particular campus rather than to larger segments of the population. For example, students on a given campus may be more politically liberal or conservative than the general population, and student populations generally reflect a limited age grouping.

Figure 4.1

RANDOMNESS IS CLOSELY LINKED TO THE REPRESENTATIVENESS OF A SAMPLE

It has been found that you can draw solid conclusions about a large target population by using a much smaller, but representative and randomly selected, segment of that population. *Randomness* means that every member of the target population has an equal chance of being chosen as part of the sample. For example, pollsters might choose a random method of interviewing residents of a particular city by calling every tenth name in the local directory. Statisticians have discovered that a truly random sample is generally representative of the target population.

Using random samples of the target population makes the results of a study accurate with a small percentage of possible error. Polls could show that a certain candidate will get approximately 25 percent of a vote with a *margin of error* of 5 percent, which means he or she will probably get 20 to 30 percent of the vote. This margin of error will decrease as the random, representative sample increases in size.

Questions to Ask About Statistical Reports

You might think, at this point, that the requirements of a good statistical study are very hard to meet; yet, despite the difficulties in finding random, representative, and sufficiently large samples of a target population, it can be and has been done. You can review polling predictions about election results and find them to be quite accurate.

SKILL

Analyze the quality of statistical evidence by noting the size, representation, and randomness of the sample.

When you need to critically evaluate reports of statistical studies, consider the following questions:

1.   What is the sample size? For national public opinion polls, it is generally considered that at least 1,000 randomly selected individuals who are representative of the target population will give the best results.

When a research study involves carefully supervised testing and training of subjects or expensive material (like the studies discussed in Chapter 5), a much smaller sample might be optimal. For example, it is unreasonable and undesirable to have hundreds of subjects test an experimental drug that may be helpful in treating a particular disease but may also have significant side effects.

2.   Is the sample representative both in all significant characteristics and in the proportion of those characteristics? (If a state has 10 percent of its voters in the age 65 and older range, are 10 percent of the sample voters in this range?) If the sample is not representative, then the study is considered biased.

3.   Have all significant characteristics been considered? Sometimes it is hard to know exactly which factors about the target sample are significant. Does the sex and age of the target matter? What about race and educational level?

4.   If the study is a poll, are the questions biased? In other words, are they slanted to bring about a particular response? For example, consider the following "loaded" questions:

a. Do you believe that the government has a right to invade private lives by taking a census?

b. Do you approve of preventing thousands of senior citizens from enjoying a safe, affordable, and lovely retirement home in order to protect a moth?

Because these questions are biased, the information gathered from them is unreliable.

5.   What is the credibility of the polling organization or research institute? We can look at the characteristics noted above if we have a complete report of the research that was done. In most cases, however, we read about a study in a magazine, newspaper, or textbook. Since we get an abridged version of research from these sources, it is helpful to note whether polls were conducted by credible organizations like Gallup, Harris, and Roper and whether research studies were done under the auspices of universities or reliable "think tanks."

The preceding checklist can be used to help you feel more confident about using statistical evidence to support conclusions. It can also be used to help you refute unreliable and inadequate evidence.

Calvin and Hobbes by Bill Watterson

The Problems with Surveys as Evidence

One method of polling that is not generally considered accurate is the mail-in survey. Let's imagine that a magazine asks its readers to respond to questions about how they spend their money. If the magazine has a circulation of 10,000 and they receive only 2,000 replies (which would be a high response rate), they can't really draw any information from those 2,000 answers because the sample is no longer random. Those who answered are a select group—they have something in common, which is that they are readers of the magazine who had the time and inclination to answer the questions and send them in.

Another problem is that survey questions often do not reflect what people would really do in a given situation; they only reflect what people would like to think they would do. If you ask someone if they use money for necessities first and luxuries second, they might answer yes, but their checkbook could reveal a completely different reality.

In addition, it's possible for someone to send in several surveys to skew the results or just for fun. Survey results can be more controlled than these examples indicate, but you are safe to conclude that most mail-in surveys you read about in magazines and newspapers are not representative and therefore don't provide solid support for your conclusions.

REMINDER

Arguments using statistical evidence need an adequate sample of a target population; the sample must be randomly selected from a representative group in the population. When you find studies like this, you can accept them as accurate and use them for your personal decision-making and argumentation.

Statistical Generalizations

Keep in mind that although you may get information from a well-conducted study, the conclusion will not be true in every case. Statistical evidence reflects only what can *generally* be expected; conclusions about such evidence are called *statistical generalizations*. For example, it can be discovered that most hyperactive children in a study responded well to dietary changes; this finding does not mean that every hyperactive child will respond in the same way. Or, we might read about a study showing that most sports magazine readers are men, but that does not mean every reader is male. Knowing that *most* of the readers are men helps advertisers choose the kinds of messages to put in their ads.

We can get important information from statistical research that helps us make decisions or gain knowledge in a general way. Still, we need to allow room for the complexities of individual people and not expect that what is *generally* true will be true for everyone.

EXERCISE

Purpose: To analyze the quality of one reported study.

Read the following report of a research study, keeping the following questions in mind:

1. What is the conclusion of the researcher?
2. How representative of the target population was his sample? Was the sample size adequate?
3. What methods did he use to gather his data? Are these methods reliable?
4. In the second paragraph the reporter implies that these research results would be duplicated in other classrooms. Do you agree or disagree and why?

At a Lecture—Only 12 Percent Listen

Bright-eyed college students in lecture halls aren't necessarily listening to the professor, the American Psychological Association was told yesterday.

If you shot off a gun at sporadic intervals and asked the students to encode their thoughts and moods at that moment, you would discover that:

- About 20 percent of the students, men and women, are pursuing erotic thoughts.
- Another 20 percent are reminiscing about something.
- Only 20 percent are actually paying attention to the lecture. Twelve percent are actively listening.
- The others are worrying, daydreaming, thinking about lunch or—surprise—religion (8 percent).

This confirmation of the lecturer's worst fears was reported by Paul Cameron, 28, an assistant professor at Wayne State University in Detroit. The annual convention, which ends Tuesday, includes about 2,000 such reports to 10,000 psychologists in a variety of meetings.

Cameron's results were based on a nine-week course in introductory psychology for 85 college sophomores. A gun was fired 21 times at random intervals, usually when Cameron was in the middle of a sentence.

Reprinted from *San Francisco Sunday Examiner and Chronicle* by permission.

The general public does not understand the art of public opinion polling, according to Janice Ballou, who is quoted in the following article. This article provides a good state-of-the-art review of statistical research, giving guidelines for understanding the numbers that are presented to us.

Researchers Practice the Science and Art of Public-Opinion Polling

by Ellen K. Coughlin
The Chronicle of Higher Education, February 7, 1990

Public-opinion polling sometimes appears to be the engine that drives American society. Ever since computers made the juggling of hundreds of numbers the work of an instant, opinion surveys have become ubiquitous, and so influential that they seem to play a part in deciding every-thing from what breakfast cereals we eat to what Presidential candidates we get to vote for.

Yet polling is so little understood by the general public, says Janice Ballou, director of Rutgers University's Eagleton Center for Public Interest Polling, that few people know enough to question the numbers they read. In fact, she adds, "it's actually a little frightening" how easily those numbers can be misleading, even when they are collected and reported in the best of faith.

It's Ms. Ballou's job to question the numbers.

As a researcher, she has taken a particular interest in an area known as "interviewer effects," or the ways in which the interaction between inter-viewer and respondent can influence the answers to questions.

A Little-Understood Tool

Ms. Ballou has spent some 20 years in survey research, working her way up from telephone interviewing to running a polling organization. As an experienced pollster, she will be part of a commission that will travel later this month to investigate public-opinion polls in Nicaragua—where, in anticipation of forthcoming elections, a great deal of polling has been taking place, she says, and "nobody believes the results."

The center Ms. Ballou directs, which is part of the Eagleton Institute of Politics at Rutgers, is both a polling organization and an academic-research center. In addition to running surveys under contract to clients, many of them state agencies in New Jersey, the Eagleton center is part of a national network of more than three dozen "state polls" that regularly canvass residents on issues of public interest. The center is also devoted in part to investigating the methodological problems that can cause error and bias in opinion surveys.

As such a hybrid, encompassing both polling and research on polling, the work of Ms. Ballou and her colleagues at the center illustrates some of the ways in which researchers have been trying to understand and improve what has come to be one of the most important and least understood *tools for designing social policy* [my emphasis].

Laws of Probability

Survey researchers like to say that public-opinion polling is both a sci-ence and an art.

The sampling part—deciding who and how many to survey—falls mostly on the science side.

Laws of probability, for example, have shown that a sample of 1,000 randomly selected respondents, no matter how big the total population, comes close to yielding an ideal balance of precision and economy.

Polls can be costly, and the more respondents, the greater the expense, Ms. Ballou says. Beyond 1,000 respondents, she explains, the precision of the results (or the likelihood that they will match opinion in the general population) usually does not improve enough to warrant the extra cost.

The design and execution of a questionnaire—deciding how to ask the questions and then actually putting them to people—are where most of the art comes in. The human interaction that must take place in any public-opinion poll is probably the area least reducible to rules or theories about how best to conduct a survey.

Something as simple as an introduction or the way in which a person is persuaded to take part in the survey, Ms. Ballou says, can cause error in the responses. Once engaged, most respondents are cooperative, and what researchers call "item nonresponse"—or a person's refusal to answer particular questions—is not a big problem.

"Besides," she says, "you'd be absolutely shocked about the kinds of things people will talk to you about. It's incredible what people will tell you on the phone."

Whether what people tell you is the truth, or whether it's an accurate account of what they believe, is something about which "we all scratch our heads," Ms. Ballou says.

Just last fall, for example, preference polls in elections involving black candidates for Mayor of New York and for Governor of Virginia turned out, when votes were actually cast, to have been significantly wide of the mark. Researchers speculated that white voters might have feared they would appear racist if they admitted to interviewers that they preferred a white candidate.

"It's one of those sources of error that we don't always understand," Ms. Ballou says.

Another example of the problem is a set of polls conducted by the Eagleton center on the subject of abortion.

As a major part of its work, the center runs what is known as the *Star Ledger*/Eagleton Poll, a survey sponsored by the Newark *Star Ledger* on issues of public interest in New Jersey. Established in 1971 as the Eagleton Poll, the survey is well known and highly regarded in the state; the newspaper took over its sponsorship in 1982, when the center became financially strapped. The poll is conducted four times a year; each one covers four or five topics, posing from 5 to 10 questions on each topic. Interviews are conducted over the telephone; that part of the work is subcontracted to a company in New York.

Responses Almost Identical

Twice last year, in March and September, the poll included questions on the subject of abortion. The September poll placed the issue in the context of the race for Governor then taking place in New Jersey. Both polls asked the same basic question: "Do you agree or disagree with the following statement: The decision to have an abortion is a private matter that should be left to the woman to decide without government intervention?"

The two surveys elicited almost identical responses on that key item. In March, 80 percent agreed; in September, 79 percent of all the respondents and 77 percent of the likely voters among them. Other questions that framed the same issue in somewhat different ways showed lower percentages but a similar sentiment—mostly in favor of a woman's right to choose abortion. The September poll revealed that the issue of abortion would probably not be a major factor in most voters' choice for Governor.

Both polls thus showed a decided "pro-choice" sentiment in New Jersey, and researchers at the Eagleton center are confident about that finding. An analysis of the answers that specific respondents gave to specific interviewers, however, revealed an intriguing pattern: Women talking to female interviewers and—oddly enough—men talking to male interviewers tended to give more "pro-choice" responses to the questions than did women talking to men or men talking to women.

So long as such biases are random, Ms. Ballou says, there's no problem. The trick is to keep them from becoming systematic.

In the profession at large, she says, "we're trying to begin to understand where that kind of thing is more likely to happen."

"We're starting to develop a sense of that, but it's far from a theory or a set of rules. But it is important to know that the possibility of that kind of error exists."

A Choice of Answers

Deciding how to word the questions that are asked in a survey is another area of opinion polling that is more art than science. A significant body of research has shown that changes in such things as phrasing, the amount of information offered, and the choice of answers available to respondents can influence the outcome of a survey to a greater or lesser degree.

"One of the rules in this business," says Ms. Ballou, "is that the question determines the answer."

The matter of question wording is particularly tricky on an issue like abortion, which has become so polarized the two sides don't even ask the same questions about it. "Pro-life" adherents think in terms of morality, "pro-choice" people in terms of rights. For one side, abortion is murder; for the other, it is a matter of personal freedom.

For their abortion polls, researchers at the Eagleton center made a difficult decision. None of the questions they asked even suggested that the issue of abortion might have a moral dimension to it, an omission that could have influenced the outcome of the poll.

"That would be a valid criticism," Ms. Ballou says. She says she would have preferred to cover both dimensions of the issue, but she argues that the center made the kind of "trade-off" that survey researchers are often forced to make—a sacrifice of a degree of comprehensiveness in favor of increased economy.

Order Can Affect Responses

"We can't do a whole survey on the abortion issue," Ms. Ballou says. "What do you ask when you can only ask 10 questions?"

By skirting the morality side of the abortion issue, the Eagleton researchers did lessen the possible consequences of another pitfall in polling: the effect that the order in which questions are asked can have on responses.

Studies have shown that the placement of a given question in a survey can change the proportion of people answering it a certain way by as much as 30 percent. That's why, for example, election polls sponsored by a particular candidate will sometimes solicit the respondent's opinion about the candidate at the end of the interview, after having, in effect, primed the respondent with a series of questions on issues the candidate is pushing.

On the issue of abortion, the so-called "personal choice" question—the one posed by the Eagleton center and asked first and in exactly the same way on both its polls—has been shown to elicit a markedly lower "pro-choice" response when it is asked immediately following questions about the morality of abortion.

The Eagleton researchers considered experimenting with the placement of their "personal choice" question between the first and second abortion polls, Ms. Ballou says. But they also wanted to test whatever change in public opinion may have occurred over the six months—in the intervening period, the Supreme Court had issued its decision in Webster v. Reproductive Health Services—and decided that the measurement might be skewed by a change in question order.

The question about a woman's right to make her own decision about abortion has been asked, pretty much in the way the Eagleton poll asked it, in countless surveys since 1973, Ms. Ballou says, and has consistently yielded responses similar to the one Eagleton got.

Such data about trends in public opinion are invaluable to survey researchers, Ms. Ballou says. Any researcher who has done his or her homework, is familiar with the trend data, and understands the issues, generally knows what to expect from the survey.

"You usually aren't surprised," she says. A result that surprises the researcher, she adds, is an indication that something may be wrong.

By the same token, public-opinion surveys rarely hit the nail on the head. In fact, when researchers report, for example, that 80 percent of the people surveyed agree that the decision to abort should be up to the woman, the figure really represents the midpoint on a range that may extend several percentage points in either direction.

Last fall, the Eagleton poll projected the percentage of votes each candidate for Governor of New Jersey would receive—and turned out to be precisely on target.

"We were exactly right, which is unusual," Ms. Ballou says. "There are some cases where you have the opportunity for external validation, but not that often."

Reprinted by permission of the publisher.

Questions for Discussion

1. What are the benefits of a well-done study?
2. What are important characteristics of valid statistical research?
3. What are some obstacles to good statistical research? Identify some sources of research cited in this article.
4. What is the effect of the order and the wording of questions on the results of statistical research?

The Reporting of Research Studies

As previously mentioned, studies are not usually reported in the popular media in their complete context. Instead, excerpts from a study are given, and sometimes the reader or listener gets an incomplete or distorted picture of what was really discovered by the research.

The following article is an example of a study that was reported responsibly. Unfortunately, the headline (which is often the only part noticed by those who scan the news) distorts the information in a dangerous way.

Family Members, Not Strangers, Abduct Most Children

Times wire services, *Contra Costa Times*, May 4, 1990

WASHINGTON—As many as 4,600 children were abducted nationwide by non-family members in 1988, and more than 100,000 were the targets of attempted abductions, primarily by passing motorists, according to the first comprehensive study of the number of children missing in the United States.

The study, released Thursday by the Justice Department, also estimated that more than 350,000 children were abducted by family members during the same time, most often in connection with child-custody cases. The number was at least three times as great as previous estimates, according to the report.

Many of the abductions involving non-family members ended within hours, often after sexual assaults, but 200 to 300 children disappeared for longer periods or were killed, according to the study.

The fact that only 1.4 percent of all abductions of children are committed by strangers should ease parents' fears of strangers, said Ernie Allen, president of the National Center for Missing and Exploited Children.

"We don't want parents to be paralyzed by fear," he said, adding, however, the total still represents "10 elementary school classrooms full. That's a tremendous concern."

Despite widespread publicity about specific child-abduction cases—including the Bay Area kidnappings of Amber Swartz-Garcia of Pinole and Michaela Garecht of Hayward in 1988 and the 1989 abduction of Ilene Misheloff of Dublin—efforts to develop public policy and allocate funds have been severely hampered by a lack of knowledge about the problem.

Police generally do not categorize crimes by the age of the victim, and most nationwide data on child abductions have been compiled by private child-welfare organizations.

The study, called "Missing, Abducted, Runaway, and Thrownaway Children in America," was mandated by Congress in 1984. Prepared by the Office of Juvenile Justice and Delinquency Prevention, it attempted to compile the number of crimes in one year against all children younger than 18.

Although most child abductions involve family members, the estimated 3,200 to 4,600 cases involving non-family members were significant, researchers and child-welfare advocates said.

"That's the size of a small town," said John Walsh, host of the TV show "America's Most Wanted" and father of Adam, a 6-year-old boy abducted from a Florida store and slain. "The Justice Department had some guts to come out and do what they did. It finally puts a handle on the fact that kids are exploited in this country."

Reprinted by permission.

Questions for Discussion

1. What is the difference in your thoughts and feelings when you read "only 1.4 percent of all abductions of children are committed by strangers" versus "as many as 4,600 children were abducted nation-

wide by non-family members in 1988, and more than 100,000 were the targets of attempted abductions"? Why is it important for a report to include both percentages and raw numbers?

2. How does the headline that an editor put on this article summarize the content of the article? Is this summary fair? If so, why? If not, why not?

3. Why do you think that "efforts to develop public policy and allocate funds have been severely hampered by a lack of knowledge about the problem"?

Chapter Highlights

1. The strength of a conclusion is based on the quality of evidence used to support the conclusion.

2. Statistical evidence can be gathered from polling a sample of a target population about a given topic, which is called the characteristic of interest.

3. Samples used to collect data must be sufficiently large, randomly chosen, and representative of the target population.

4. Surveys are usually inadequate sources of statistical evidence because they do not reflect a random and representative sample; when a sample is not representative, the study is biased.

5. Studies reported in both print and electronic media are abridged; critical thinkers will read them carefully and do further investigation of the findings before using them to support conclusions or decisions.

Article for Discussion

Watching Americans Watch TV

by Eric Larson
The Atlantic Monthly, March 1992

A great mystery has gnawed at the hearts of advertisers ever since the Bulova Watch Company paid for the first TV ad, which aired on July 1, 1941: How many people stick around for the commercials? Advertisers have always had to come at the question from an oblique angle, measuring the audiences for the programs surrounding their commercials rather than for the commercials themselves. The A.C. Nielsen Company brought technology to the business of estimating audience size in 1942, with the first mechanical meter, the Audimeter, which used a stylus to scratch out a record of where a radio dial was tuned. The system was crude but once refined proved far faster than the competition's surveys, and Nielsen quickly gained monopoly control over the business of national ratings, at first for radio and later for television. Most viewers know Nielsen as the maker of the bullets that killed *Star Trek* and *Twin Peaks*, but to think of its ratings exclusively in terms of their show-stopping power is to underestimate the depth of Nielsen's influence over the culture, content, and business of television, and thus over the evolution of our consumer culture itself. Nielsen *is* television. Imagine a company like IBM granting to an outside party a decisive say in whether it has a profit or a loss in a given quarter, and you'll begin to understand Nielsen's peculiar hold over broadcasting.

Nielsen kept competitors at bay through the deft and timely use of technology, but each fundamental advance changed the landscape of television. All along, the company's engineers pursued TV's Golden Fleece, the elusive "passive" audience meter, a device capable of recognizing each TV viewer and recording even his briefest exit, without his having to lift a finger. Audience engineers have dreamed of such a device ever since that epiphanic instant in 1952 when a Toledo, Ohio, water commissioner realized that a sudden city-wide drop in pressure coincided exactly with a commercial break in *I Love Lucy*, and joked that someone should invent a "flushometer." The men from Nielsen tried weight-sensing scales and electric eyes and even sophisticated military technology of the kind we so vividly saw put to work during the Gulf War. Still, some insurmountable obstacle always seemed to get in the way—big dogs, for example, the bane of any audience engineer.

Until lately Nielsen could afford to pursue this quest at a leisurely pace. Now, however, Nielsen's three largest customers, ABC, CBS, and NBC, openly charge that the company's existing "people meter" technology is unreliable, perhaps obsolete. After an exhaustive investigation they concluded in 1989 that their $10 billion industry had become a helpless captive of some rather flimsy statistics. Soon Nielsen reported steep, inexplicable declines in key segments of TV viewing which seemed to confirm the network's worst fears and deeply shook their faith in the company's ratings.

"The thing we've always had has been this set of numbers," says Alan Wurtzel, ABC's senior research executive. "It's the foundation upon which program decisions are made, deals are made, advertising dollars are spent. When those numbers became unreliable, inconsistent, inaccurate, unexplainable, they just threw into chaos almost everything we did, because they were the basis on which the business was built."

To make matters worse, last April the networks invited all comers to present ideas for alternative ways of measuring the U.S. audience, the television equivalent of having your spouse suddenly begin advertising for a new lover. The competition has begun to stir. The Arbitron Company, which competes fiercely with Nielsen to rate local TV markets, continues to threaten to go national; it has funded an effort at the Massachusetts Institute of Technology's Media Lab to develop a passive meter and last November began tracking public response to the full network schedule. A French company has already deployed a kind of passive meter; Arbitron has begun testing the system for use here. Britain's AGB International, which was deeply gored in a past encounter with Nielsen, hints that the U.S. market is simply too lucrative to resist.

Nielsen, therefore, finds itself virtually forced to deploy its newest secret weapon—a device that may be the ultimate passive meter. I met the machine in New York. It can identify viewers and even gives a rough indication of whether their heads are turned toward the TV. The system could fix a lot of the problems cited by the networks, but its deployment would have a significance far beyond its capacity to produce accurate numbers. By tracking the TV audience on a second-by-second basis, Nielsen's passive meter may yield the first accurate ratings of commercials—not shows, commercials—and thus at last solve that great nagging mystery about the "reach" of advertising. If it does, however, it will sharply alter the way consumer products are marketed in America, even the way television shows are written and produced. "The implications," says John Dimling, Nielsen Media's executive vice-president, "could be quite staggering."

But does anyone really want to know the truths that Nielsen's black box (and for now it really is a black box) may bring? What's wrong with Nielsen's numbers? Why did everyone accept them until now? And how did television, arguably the most powerful influence on American culture, become so dependent on such a fragile collection of digits in the first place?

Sonar in the Living Room

This may be hard to imagine, but at the dawn of broadcasting, advertisers doubted that radio and TV would ever be useful for wooing consumers. They needed proof. They hired market researchers, themselves newly arrived on the commercial landscape, to conduct surveys, first simply to find out how many homes in America had a radio and later to determine what programs drew the most listeners. Somewhere along the way, however, ratings took on a power they were never meant to have, much to the chagrin even of Robert Elder, a co-inventor of Nielsen's first meter. In a 1978 letter he wrote that television "suffers greatly from the misuse of the [Nielsen Television Index] and for that reason I am not too happy about my part in getting it started."

. . . A word of explanation here: Nielsen reports two numbers, the rating and the share. The rating is a measure of average audience and is expressed as a percentage of America's total potential audience of 93.1 million TV-equipped households. During prime time only about 60 percent of these households actually watch their TVs. Nielsen's share figures show how this active nightly audience divides itself among the various programs and stations. Suppose, for example, that this Thursday night 50 million households watch TV. Suppose that 25 million of these active households watch *Cheers*. The episode's rating would be 26.9 gross rating points, or 26.9 percent of all 93.1 million TV-equipped households. The share would be 50 percent, or half of the 50 million viewers who actually watched TV during that portion of the evening.

Nielsen began documenting the cruel fact of the networks' declining audience in the 1978–1979 season, when the three still drew a robust 91 percent of prime-time television viewers. Their share has shrunk every year since. By 1985 the average household could get 18.8 channels, and the networks' share of audience had shrunk to 77 percent. By last year the average home got thirty channels and the networks' share had fallen to 63 percent.

For a bit of culture-shock, consider this: Seven of the fifty highest-rated programs of all time are 1964 episodes of *The Beverly Hillbillies*. Each had a rating of 41.8 to 44. In the most heavily watched of these, Jed, Jethro, and Granny somehow managed to command a 65 percent share of viewers—more than the combined share of all three networks today.

By the mid-1980s the explosion in TV choices had begun to outpace Nielsen's ability to keep up. By now advertisers cared less about reaching masses of households and more about reaching the demographic segments of the population best suited to their products; for example, women twenty-five to fifty-four, men eighteen to forty-nine, or kids. Nielsen's set meters, sophisticated versions of the original Audimeter, recorded only that a TV was on and that it was receiving a particular station. Nielsen got its demographic data from viewer diaries kept by a second panel of families. Researchers feared that one member of each family, usually the already harried woman of the house, typically kept the diary for everyone. With so many channels, they worried, how could anyone remember exactly what a family watched, let alone the channel on which it appeared? They fretted, too, about the so-called halo effect that occurred when distracted diary-keepers wrote down what they *would* have watched or *should* have watched, rather than what they really did watch.

By 1985 the networks were ready for a change, and AGB, the British ratings giant, offered a tempting one. AGB had previously announced that it wanted to wire America with a new kind of meter, one it had already deployed in Ireland, Thailand, and the Philippines, which captured tuning and demographics simultaneously, continuously. AGB offered all this, moreover, at a lower cost.

. . . AGB's year-and-a-half-long Boston test gave Nielsen time to dust off a meter it had begun testing a decade before, which worked very much like AGB's fearsome new weapon. Both were called people meters, because they sought to provide an electronic measure not just of tuning but of who was watching. Both began producing ratings in September of 1987, and thus gave broadcasters an opportunity to see how competing ratings systems would describe the same objective reality.

The two new systems produced radically conflicting results. The variations, moreover, occurred in a pattern that defied reduction to a mathematical constant. On the first Monday night, for example, Nielsen's people meter rated ABC's football game 15.3. AGB gave it 11.9, a discrepancy of roughly three million households. Nielsen's meter-and-diary system, which the company continued in order to provide stability during the transition, gave the game 14.5.

Nielsen flatly declared that AGB's numbers were "wrong." AGB said Nielsen's were too high. Confusion reigned; advertising negotiations faltered. Ultimately the industry voted to stay with Nielsen, which was at least a known entity. AGB fled the country, reportedly trailing $80 million in losses.

The new meter brought more data more quickly, including overnight demographics, but it was no friend to the networks. That first season the networks' share of audience dropped from 75 percent to 70 percent. The networks, acting together as the Committee on Nationwide Television Audience Measurement (CONTAM), a body that had been founded in 1963 in response to the congressional hearings, hired a respected media-research firm, Statistical Research, Inc., of Westfield, New Jersey, to investigate the new system.

The resulting report was completed in late 1989 and weighed six pounds. It was 550 pages long, in seven volumes, and arrived in a slick, heavy-gauge gray box meant to last a century. I read the report—every killing, if soporific, detail. This may be my imagination, but I thought I detected a kind of deep and weary sorrow in its text, a disappointed sigh: so this is what went on behind the curtains of Oz all these years! The report "documented an erosion in the quality of the Nielsen service," in its authors' words. "The vision, the actions, and the commitment of the past have been diminished."

Jonn Dimling, of Nielsen Media, read the final, most critical volume in his room in a Northbrook, Illinois, Holiday Inn. "I was about as depressed as I've ever been," he told me. "Even though I was prepared for everything they were going to say, seeing it all, just one thing after another—you think, 'My God, what have we done?'"

To make matters worse, a few months later Nielsen reported the sharp declines in some audience segments which so troubled the networks.

Viewers disappeared. In particular, kids failed to show up for Saturday-morning cartoons. Droves of viewers in key segments deserted the prime-time hours. The declines were so steep, so unexpected, that they caused an immediate combined loss to the networks of about $200 million, the value of commercial time the networks had to cough up to make good on previously arranged audience guarantees.

Where Statistical Sampling Goes Wrong

At its very best, statistical sampling is fraught with problems. The initial response rate for the 1990 census was the lowest in history, even though all we had to do was fill out a single questionnaire, and are required by law to do it. Nielsen runs a huge, continuous, partly automated survey of America twenty-four hours a day, 365 days a year, and intrudes on the daily life of each recruit for two years at a stretch.

In the real world, as Nielsen has found, sampling is hell.

The process begins with the creation every ten years of a "sample frame," the population of households in America from which all Nielsen families are selected. First, using Census Bureau data, Edward Schillmoeller's department divides the country into successively smaller hunks of territory until at last it has a collection of some 5,000 "block groups," or units of census geography comprising on average about 425 housing units each. Next, Nielsen sends squads of field agents into each of these block groups to count every housing unit, both to account for any changes in the number of homes since the Census Bureau made its report and to note the addresses of potential Nielsen candidates. The crews merely count, until they reach a number selected at random by Schillmoeller's department. Assume there are indeed 425 homes in a block group. Nielsen picks a random number from 1 to 425. If the number is 125, the enumerator counts the first 124 homes without jotting down a single address. The next housing unit, be it a cave, tree, or converted beer truck, is the primary target household, a "Basic" in Nielsen-speak. This is the home Nielsen most dearly wants to recruit, and the one that sampling theory dictates Nielsen indeed *must* recruit. If the house is vacant, or even a vacant slab in a trailer park, Nielsen will keep coming back for five years in hopes that someone will have moved in.

In theory, every household has an equal shot at becoming a Nielsen family; in practice, however, the odds for some of us are zero. Nielsen would never allow me to be a member of its sample, because I am "occupationally disqualified," as are all my fellow journalists, every editor, producer, and advertising executive, and of course every single employee of CBS, NBC, ABC, CNN, MTV, local television stations, and Arbitron. The presumption is that we could not be trusted to behave ourselves and at the first opportunity would rush out and write about the experience or tune our TVs to the stations we work for. (Nielsen has good reason to worry: station employees included by chance in diary panels have been known to "load up" the diaries with their own stations' programs.) Nielsen also builds in demographic safety valves to avoid the unlikely but statistically possible selection of an aberrant sample—say, 4,000 black households.

. . . Today's people meter demands a lot from its hosts. Arthur Nielsen, Sr., wrote in 1955 that one of the beauties of the Audimeter system was that it operated "entirely automatically and outside the collaborating family's day-to-day awareness." Today's meter is a nagging shrew, consisting of three components; a computer the size of a compact-disc player, known as the home unit; a smaller box with a numerical keypad and a faceplate of red and green lights, which sits atop the TV set; and a remote control, typically with eight numbered buttons and an "OK" button. Nielsen assigns a button to everyone in a household, even children as young as two. And everyone, even the two-year-old, is expected to behave in appropriate Nielsen fashion—that is, to press his button whenever he starts to watch TV and whenever he stops. Visitors pick an unoccupied button, enter their sex and age on the numerical keypad, and then also report their arrivals and departures. When a viewer punches in, the lights associated with his number change from red to green. Periodically the meter demands a little reassurance that someone is indeed watching, and will blink a single red bulb at the far right of the set-top box. One press of the "OK" button calms the machine. The longer the prompt goes unanswered, however, the more adamant the meter becomes, blinking its bulbs in an increasingly frenzied manner until it is ablaze with flashing lights, like the scene of a midnight car wreck. Some meters finally cry out in frustration, emitting a pained and disappointed beep.

. . . Today's typical Nielsen home, says Larry Patterson, the company's director of field operations, has two TVs, one VCR, and one cable converter, requiring an array of equipment that takes five or six hours to install. The most complex house he has come across had six TVs, five VCRs, and cable access; installing the meters took two full days.

In return for all this equipping and pestering, each family can pick gifts from a Nielsen catalogue and gets cash payments of two dollars a month for each TV or VCR in the house. A household with one TV would get just $24 a year; the family with the complex system mentioned above would get $264.

The networks worry that the burden is too great, that Nielsen families experience "button fatigue" and begin engaging in such inappropriate behaviors as failing to log in, or letting a visitor *just sit there* without first registering his age and presence. CONTAM conducted exit interviews with families leaving the Nielsen stable and found that one out of three reported getting tired of the meter; half of these said that as a result accuracy had suffered. More than one in ten said they "hardly ever" logged out when they finished watching a show.

The networks fear that button fatigue is especially pronounced among children. Almost half the kids (or their parental spokespeople) interviewed by CONTAM said that they did indeed get tired of pushing buttons. Nielsen takes great pains to win their cooperation. It gives them a Nielsen coloring book and shows them a video called "The Nielsen People Meter Show." Nielsen wants kids to bond to their buttons, and practices some subtle human engineering. It gives them a choice of animal stickers to place next to their buttons—but not commercial figures like Donald Duck or the Ninja Turtles, of course, because these might bias their viewing behavior.

. . . Nielsen's cooperation rate is actually far worse than 48 percent. In its routine disclosures the company reports only the percentage of Basics who refuse to participate, and doesn't mention the number of "Alternates" it had to approach before achieving its 4,000-household sample. In fact, Nielsen must approach three Alternates, on average, before it finds a willing participant. In some cases, according to Schillmoeller, recruiters have had to approach up to thirty additional homes.

Moreover, on any given day about 10 percent of Nielsen's people-meter households produce faulty data that cannot be included in the daily ratings calculations. The families most likely to be excluded, CONTAM discovered, were the heaviest viewers, reflecting a Catch-22 phenomenon literally engineered into the people-meter system; the more TVs and VCRs and Nielsen equipment you have, the greater the chance something will happen to bump your data from the day's tabulations.

Fatigue causes some families to drop out of the sample altogether. Other households leave for quirkier reasons: one family bought a slick new TV and didn't want Nielsen's installers tinkering with it. Larry Patterson lost another Nielsen household to one of the cold realities of ghetto life in New York City. He and a partner had recruited an elderly woman living in a tough housing project in the borough of Queens. Early the following week he got a call from a city homicide detective who told him that the woman had been found strangled in her bed the previous Sunday morning. He requested all the woman's viewing records for Saturday night, in case they held some clue to the timing of her murder.

She had turned off the set at 11:23 P.M. on Saturday, Patterson found. But he also discovered a curious thing: someone had watched a lot of television in the woman's apartment the Sunday afternoon after she'd been killed.

The detective was silent a moment. "Oh, yeah," he said. "That was us. We were watching the football game."

"For him, at least," Patterson told me, "it certainly confirmed our credibility."

Readings from America's 4,000 people-metered households are automatically transmitted every night from 3:00 A.M. to about 7:00 A.M. Florida time, the machines dutifully calling home to Nielsen's Dunedin

Center. Most people assume that the people meter alone produces all the information Nielsen needs for its ratings. In fact this nightly torrent of data is by itself utterly useless.

The meter tells only who is watching the TV set and how the set is tuned. Nielsen must merge this data with a second torrent of information, the detailed records of exactly what programs appeared on thousands upon thousands of TV stations and cable "headends" around the country—not what the stations planned to broadcast but what they actually did broadcast, and the exact times at which they did so.

On any day the task is monumental: The networks supply Nielsen with their daily lineups, but typically these succumb to special reports, late-running baseball games, natural disasters, and so forth—regional events that might cause an affiliate to interrupt the network "feed." Nielsen keeps track of all this by stationing robotic TV watchers in the TV markets where Nielsen families reside to watch television twenty-four hours a day, *forever*. They watch for a basic network signal, hidden from human viewers, that indicates when the network feed is being broadcast by an affiliate. If the signal arrives at its scheduled time, Nielsen assumes that all is well. Any discrepancy is called a conflict. In a typical week Nielsen's program-records department in Dunedin will resolve 12,000 to 15,000 such conflicts, often by calling stations to find out just exactly what did air. During the first week of the Gulf War, Nielsen confronted 50,000 conflicts and in the process exposed a bit of affiliate treachery. A few stations had dumped their network feeds to broadcast CNN instead.

CONTAM factored together all the forces tending to reduce cooperation and the supply of usable data, and determined that Nielsen's people-meter sample had a final net response rate of only 37 percent, meaning that only 37 percent of Nielsen's originally targeted Basics produced usable household data on any given day—a rate "below all industry or government standards for high quality operations," CONTAM reported. "The rate has declined steadily over recent years and indications are that, unless a different effort is introduced, it will continue to do so. At some point . . . a totally different measurement approach will have to be considered."

The New Passive People Meter

"As you can see, this is your typical living room," said Christopher Lubniewski, a Nielsen client-service representative, in a recent interview. The room was a barren, windowless office in Nielsen Media's executive headquarters in New York. Nielsen's new passive people meter, a squat black box the size of a videocassette recorder, was perched before me on the shelf of an incongruous breakfront, the only thing even remotely living-room-like.

The machine and I had already been introduced—that is, it had scanned me and then stored four images of my face: three head-on portraits and one quarter-profile. It was now ready to try matching the real me to these digital mug shots.

If it succeeded, it would display on a nearby video screen my name and a number indicating how confident it was about the identification. A number and no name would mean that it had failed. I did not want a zero. A zero would be a pretty good indicator that I had died or at least stopped breathing. A number from 60 to 83 would mean that I was a person, although not someone the meter knew. Anything higher would mean that it knew me well enough to display my name.

The meter scans the room every two seconds, looking for signs of life. It compares each fresh image in a given location with its predecessor to produce a digital representation of movement, the hallmark of humanness. A life-size photograph brought into the room might fool the system for a moment, Lubniewski told me, but over the next few scans its lack of movement would cause the meter to ignore it.

The system next locates the melange of digits most resembling those for a human head, a search program that may at last help Nielsen separate the men from the dogs. "If a cat or a big dog jumped up here," Lubniewski said, "the system would scan it and try to find the head, and during the match-off would give it a score of zero to sixty." A nonhuman moving object.

The machine notices every departure and return. Its reliance on head-on or nearly head-on views, moreover, means that it will not count people who are present but involved in other activities, such as reading the newspaper or making love on the floor.

The machine gets good but deeply qualified reviews.

"It's very accurate," Robert A. Warrens, a senior vice-president and the director of media resources and research for J. Walter Thompson USA, told me not long ago. "I sat in a room in different positions and overall it was able to pick me up a hundred percent." But many who have seen the meter worry that it could worsen Nielsen's already poor cooperation rate, especially given today's heightened concern for privacy. "We know that one out of every two households has a TV in one or more bedrooms," says Nicholas P. Schiavone, NBC's vice-president of media and marketing research, and the current chairman of CONTAM. "Now, I come to your home and tell you I'm going to set up a recognition meter in every room of your household where there's a TV. Will people allow a device that can recognize—that can *see*—into those rooms?"

. . . If the meter works, it will solve Nielsen's problem of button fatigue. One school of thought holds that the passive meter could even improve initial cooperation rates by eliminating the workload associated with the current people meter. It would do nothing, however, to help Nielsen keep up with the proliferation of miniature portable TVs and track the ranks of so-called "out-of-home" viewers, the great uncounted masses who watch television while on vacation, in hotels, away at college, or on the job. To help meet these challenges, Nielsen's Dunedin researchers are experimenting with a pocket-sized electronic "diary" that people would, in theory, whip out to record the shows they watch in bars and elsewhere. They are also testing ways by which various pieces of Nielsen equipment could communicate with one another through the ordinary plugs and circuits of a house, thereby eliminating the need to run so many wires through homes. Moreover, Nielsen recently hired its first chief research officer, a kind of research cop, to study Nielsen's existing rating methods and look for simple ways to improve them.

The passive meter, however, is the thing Nielsen most likes to show off. "Try moving your chair backward and forward," Chris Lubniewski suggested. The meter registered my identity with scores of about 90.

Lubniewski took a seat in an adjacent wheeled chair and together we kicked our way throughout the meter's field of vision. It named us both. I tried covering the top half of my head with a legal pad, something I often do when I watch TV. The machine hesitated. I was a person, all right, but it couldn't say who.

Changes in hairstyle won't throw the meter, Lubniewski said— although he did mention a recent exception. "One woman came in here wearing her hair very tight," he said. "She let it go and it fell in front of her face, and the system *did* get confused."

. . . I asked Nielsen's public-relations man, sitting nearby, if I could borrow his glasses. The machine named me with its highest score yet.

It was time to get serious. Man to machine. I stuck out my tongue, yanked back the corners of my mouth, and closed one eye, a maneuver I picked up from my three-year-old daughter.

Lubniewski smiled, but the smile looked thin to me; it masked, I was certain, the kind of ennui that can come only from watching armies of otherwise sober people suddenly let down their hair or flourish surprise pairs of glasses.

"A lot of people try to fool the system," Lubniewski said. "You have to remember, it scans the room every one or two seconds. You could fool it, but chances are if it misses you—if you sneeze or make a face—we'll still know you're there."

I smiled past my fingers but held the pose a bit longer, just to make sure the system got it. It identified me as human, but otherwise didn't recognize me.

Satisfied, I tucked in my tongue.

An instant later, the monitor displayed my name with a cautious score of 85.

What Lies Ahead

A true passive meter is almost certain to appear over the next few years. Barring the unexpected arrival of a new challenger, that meter will function like the one I saw demonstrated in Nielsen's offices. In the past, fundamental advances in ratings technology have brought far-reaching change to the business and culture of television. What changes will this meter bring? What revelations about the audience-holding power of commercials? Of TV itself?

. . . If Nielsen now stands on a threshold, so does television itself. Ratings began simply as a way for advertisers to prove to themselves that radio and television could help them reach masses of consumers. The numbers soon took on a life all their own and an authority they were never meant to have. They became the soul of television. But when is enough enough? How much information is too much information? Does TV now risk snuffing the last ember of creativity under a yet huger cascade of deceptively precise numbers? Before Nielsen takes that next great technological leap, I'd like to invoke the old FTC warning: Even at their best, Nielsen's ratings will always be estimates. They will always be "inherently imperfect."

Questions for Discussion

1. The author states, "Most viewers know Nielsen as the maker of the bullets that killed *Star Trek* and *Twin Peaks,* but to think of its ratings exclusively in terms of their show-stopping power is to underestimate the depth of Nielsen's influence over the culture, content, and business of television, and thus over the evolution of our consumer culture itself. Nielsen *is* television." In what way is Nielsen television? How would television programming be different without Nielsen?

2. Many problems with the Nielsen system are cited throughout this article. Cite these errors that make the system as it is "inherently imperfect." (It may be useful to first review the impressive process by which Nielsen produces its ratings.) Note especially the problems associated with surveys that are mentioned in the article.

3. Despite the problems with Nielsen, the inability of their ratings to match those of the British ratings agency, and the major networks' unhappiness with them, the American television industry is contin-

uing to rely on Nielsen. Why do you think the networks have chosen to stay with Nielsen?

4. In discussing the new "passive people meter," NBC's vice president says, "Now, I come into your home and tell you I'm going to set up a recognition meter in every room of your household where there's a TV. Will people allow a device that can recognize—that can *see*—into those rooms?" Would you allow such a device into your home in the interest of influencing television ratings? Why or why not?

5. What changes in television ratings and in our culture could the new "passive people meter" bring? What are other possible implications of this technology?

6. Look up a Nielsen rating in the television section of your local paper and then check yourself and your family and friends against it. Are your viewing habits reflected or not? What does this say about how you view television?

Ideas for Writing or Speaking

Using the following format, create a persuasive speech or essay on an issue of your choice. Use statistical research to support your conclusion.

1. Find an issue that interests you. The more interest you have in the issue, the more conviction you will have in your writing or speaking.

2. Write out your conclusion about the issue. Your position on the issue should be clearly articulated and will form your thesis statement.

3. Begin your essay or speech with an introduction that provides a context for your issue and your position. You may also use important statistics to gain the attention of your readers or listeners. Put your thesis statement at the end of your introduction.

4. Identify and expand upon the reasons that support your conclusion. Present these reasons in the body of the essay or speech. Concentrate on statistical evidence. You may also include examples and expert testimony to complete your support.

5. Use the conclusion of your speech or essay to restate your major points and to reemphasize the importance of your conclusion. Remind your readers or listeners of the points you brought out in your introduction, bringing these points full circle in your closing thoughts.

Longer-Term Writing Assignment

The purpose of this assignment is to give you an in-depth understanding of a social, national, or international problem and the many factors that enter into changes in policy. This may be done as a long-term project for an individual or a group.

Begin by asking yourself "What is a continuing community, campus, national, or international problem that concerns me?" Or, take the advice of English professor Bruce Reeves of Diablo Valley College, California, and fill in the blank on the following question: "If we can send a man to the moon, why can't we_____?" For example, you might think, "If we can send a man to the moon, why can't we solve world hunger?" Or, "Why can't we stop the drug cartels?" "Why can't we provide jobs for everyone?" "Why can't we have peace in the Middle East [or somewhere else]?" "Why can't we rid our town of pollution from the local factory?" "Why can't we balance the national budget?"

Then, begin researching the problem. You will learn more about research in the next chapter, but begin with the knowledge you have gained in this chapter. Look up statistics that relate to your problem, being careful to note how the research has been carried out.

After you read Chapter 5, begin the rest of your research, using a minimum of six sources of information, including studies done about this problem and the opinions of experts who have written or spoken about the problem. If the problem you are studying is local, try to interview officials who are in a position to address the problem or who have worked on the problem.

Take notes on the background of the problem, noting the history of the problem, the scope of the problem, and the impact or effect of the problem.

As you research this problem, consider past efforts to solve it. To what extent were those efforts successful? Where there have been failed policies, explain why they have failed.

Note also any current or recent proposals about this problem. For example, if you are writing on the difficulty of balancing the federal budget, consider why recent proposals made by congresspersons have not been approved. Also, consider the chances of success for any current proposals.

When you have finished studying this problem, make a proposal for a solution to this problem. Support your proposal, showing how it will resolve the difficulties that previous proposals have come up against. Also, explain how it will not create more problems than it solves.

If you find that you can't come up with a solution to the problem, then explain what variables make it too difficult to solve. State what would have to change for a resolution to be possible.

In short, your paper or speech should include a complete explanation of the background of the problem, the scope, the harm it creates, the policies that have not worked against this problem, and your proposed solution to the problem or analysis of why it can't currently be solved. Also, include a bibliography of all sources you used in researching this problem.

CHAPTER FIVE

Evidence

Who Said So?
Who Are *They* Anyway?

A critical thinker understands the proper use of controlled studies in supporting arguments.

In the previous chapter, we considered the use of statistical studies as evidence (reasons) to support conclusions. In this chapter, we will examine *controlled studies*. Researchers use controlled studies to make observations and draw conclusions about many subjects, including animal and human behavior; scientific discoveries and solutions to medical problems are obtained through these studies. They are called *controlled* because they use specific methods for comparing groups of subjects that can be duplicated by other researchers. In this way, the findings can be proven to be true in most cases.

The conclusions drawn in carefully controlled scientific studies are inductive; a good study shows us what will *probably* and *usually* occur in a given circumstance.

Some of the elements of controlled studies are the same as those used by polling organizations. A researcher still works with three questions:

1. What do I want to find out? (the characteristic of interest)
2. Who do I want to know about? (the target population)
3. Who can I study to get accurate answers about my entire target population? (the sample)

As with polling, researchers usually can't study everyone in a given target population, so they have to observe *some* members of the population. The number of subjects depends on how precise an answer is needed by the researcher. Preliminary results leading to *additional* studies can be gathered by using a very small sample. For example, if a researcher discovers that 20 women with kidney problems have a negative reaction to Ibuprofen, his findings can be used to justify the funds for a larger study.

In medical research, the design of a study is called the **protocol**. Two groups of subjects (people or animals) who are alike in all important (relevant) aspects need to be studied in order for the research to have the element of **control**. Control involves weeding out extraneous factors that could affect the outcome of a study.

Research Design

A good research design includes:

1. A question to answer. This is the characteristic of interest concerning a targeted population. A researcher begins with a question,

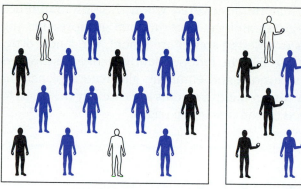

Control Group   Experimental Group

Figure 5.1

such as "What is the effect of the new drug Z on migraine headaches?"

2. A **hypothesis**, which is a speculation about what will be discovered from the research. For example, "The drug Z will shorten migraine headaches caused by restricted blood vessels."

3. A sample of individuals to study. The sample should be randomly selected and representative of the target population. The sample is divided into two groups (see Figure 5.1):

   a. A **control group**: a group of subjects from the sample who get no treatment or a placebo treatment.

   b. An **experimental group**: a group of subjects from the sample who are exposed to a variable created by the researcher; for example, this group might be given a new drug to assess its effects in comparison with similar people who are not given the drug or who are given a placebo (sugar pill).

4. **Data**: The observations made and information collected by the researcher as he or she completes the study.

After the study is carried out, the researcher compiles the data and draws conclusions; the researcher interprets the meaning and significance of the data. In addition, the researcher will carefully consider the *implications* of the findings, which means that he or she will speculate about further research that can be done to answer questions related to the study.

Significant results may be discovered when the only difference between the control group and the experimental group is that the experimental group is exposed to special treatment, like a new drug; this special treatment is called the independent variable. Researchers can draw accurate conclusions and eliminate alternate explanations for the results of their research if the studies are carefully designed to fit the criteria described on the preceding pages.

SKILL

Understand the basic components of a controlled study.

Criteria for Evaluating Research Findings

"Science is always simple and always profound. It is only the half-truths that are dangerous."

George Bernard Shaw, *The Doctor's Dilemma* (1913)

Interesting findings from research studies are often reported in newspapers and magazines or on television programs. Most of these reports don't give complete information about the research design. Before accepting the results of research as reliable, the following questions should be asked.

1.   **How large was the sample?** A small sample can suggest areas for further research, but should not be accepted as establishing factual information.

Sometimes, studies with an inadequate sample are reported in the news media because of the interesting results claimed by the researchers. If you read about a controversial report, be especially careful to listen for information about the sample used by the researcher. Consider the following:

In 1988, the New York Times and the Los Angeles Times ran front-page stories about research by the Canadian neuroscientist Doreen Kimura, who claimed her experiments showed that women's ability to perform different tasks varied according to their estrogen levels. Kimura later denounced the media for overplaying the social significance of her work. In addition, her study has been criticized on a number of grounds, including the

small number of women studied and the method used to measure "verbal skills" (repeating the phrase "a box of mixed biscuits in a biscuit mixer" five times).1

Remember that newspapers, magazines, and television programs
want to present interesting information to readers and viewers. Most
reporters are not trained in research design any more than their audience members, so they are not usually skilled at examining methodology; their primary job is to create a good story.

2.   **Is the study biased?** As we discussed in Chapter 4, if a sample
is not representative of the target group, then the study is biased.
Remember that being representative means having the same characteristics in the same proportion as the target population.

3.   **Have all of the important factors of the data been collected?**
There might be explanations for results in research other than the ones
given by the researchers. For example, if part of the sample knows they
are receiving the treatment, they may report positive changes based
solely on their expectations (i.e., if Joanne knows she received the new
drug that cures headaches, she may *expect* to feel better and then actually feel better). To control for this kind of error, researchers generally
try to conduct *blind* studies in which the participants are not told
whether they belong to the experimental or control group.

Also, researchers may unconsciously exaggerate the improvement
they see in the experimental group, especially if the study results are
very important to them. For this reason, *double-blind* studies are often
conducted. In these studies, neither the experimenter nor the participants know which is the control and which is the experimental group.

4.   **Are the results statistically significant?** When a finding is
labeled *statistically significant*, it is probable that the reported effect
will occur again in similar circumstances. For example, let's say there
are 100 persons in an experimental group and 100 persons in a control group, and 13 more in the experimental group react to the treatment (the variable). With that proportion of difference in reaction,
researchers can conclude that there is a 95 percent probability that
the variable (and not a chance occurrence) caused the effect, and
they can call their study *statistically significant*.

5.   **Have other researchers been able to duplicate the results?**
There is always a first discovery of a link between a variable and an

---

1   Keay Davidson, "Nature vs. Nurture," *Image*, January 20, 1991, p. 15.

effect on people. However, if a study reveals an important finding, then other researchers may try similar experiments to verify the results of the research and look for applications of the discovery. When others have tried to do the same experiment and failed, the results are considered unreliable, as exemplified by the following.

> In 1986, scientists reported that extremely gifted 12- and 13-year-olds were especially likely to be left-handed and to suffer from allergies. They proposed that the kids, while in the womb, had been overexposed to testosterone, which might have triggered both the allergies and the intellectual excellence. But this exotic idea vaporized in the summer of 1990 when different researchers —Jennifer Wiley and David Goldstein of Duke University—did a follow-up study; they found no evidence of a link between gifted-ness and left-handedness and allergies in children.[2]

6.   **Does the researcher claim that the study proves more than it was designed to prove?** Some researchers may be too hopeful or excited about the implications of a study they conducted; if a small sample of cancer patients may have been helped by an experimental drug, the researcher needs to limit the report of results to the findings of this particular study.

When a study is promising, the researcher can suggest further studies which would be needed to make broader discoveries about the effectiveness of treatment.

7.   **Has the research been done by a respected institution?** Research from a well-established institution such as the National Institute of Health or Stanford University is generally considered credible. Be careful in your judgments, however, if research from one reliable source contradicts research from another reliable source; it is best to withhold judgment or to accept conclusions tentatively in these cases.

EXERCISE

Purpose: To understand and utilize criteria for evaluating research.

Analyze the following examples in light of the criteria given for evaluating research findings. Then, answer the following questions:

---

2   Ibid.

1. To what extent did each study meet the criteria for evaluating research? What are the strengths and weaknesses of each design?
2. Are there factors the researchers overlooked in designing their studies? If so, what is needed to improve the design?
3. Does one study have a better design than the other? If so, how?

A researcher is interested in a new treatment for controlling the effects of the HIV virus. He designs a study, called the *protocol*, which involves two groups of patients who have recently (within the past six months) tested positively for the virus. One group receives the new drug, and the other group receives a placebo. There are no special dietary changes, and no other treatments are given to the two groups. The only difference between the groups is that one is taking the drug and the other is not. The subjects in the experiment don't know whether they have the real drug or the placebo; that way the alternate explanation that they felt better because they expected to feel better (the placebo effect) is eliminated. As progress with the two groups is monitored, the researchers should be able to determine if the new drug has had any positive effect.

A researcher wants to find out if test performance in college is improved when students eat a breakfast that is high in carbohydrates. She chooses two randomly selected groups of students and asks them to follow a breakfast plan for a semester. Because she does not want them to know that she is trying to discover the effect of diet on test scores, she tells them the test is for cholesterol ratings.

The control group is given a skimpy breakfast of a low-carbohydrate drink. The experimental group is given a breakfast loaded with carbohydrates like toast and cereal. Each subject keeps a diary of what they had for breakfast. Teachers are asked to report on the morning test scores of the groups of students. At the conclusion of the semester, the test scores are compared to see if the experimental group did better than their peers in the control group.

EXERCISE

Purpose: To give you a hands-on sense of how research is done (i.e., to give you experience in designing a study).

Design a study of your own. Pretend you have unlimited money and people and decide what you want to find out. Then create a study (with a control group and an experimental group). You can be serious or humorous—the research topic is not important. The only important thing is your understanding of the scientific method.

This is a good exercise to do with a partner, because you can get more ideas on how to control against alternative explanations for your results.

You might also try to carry out your study with a small sample and to report your results to the class, telling them your design, your results, and your conclusions.

Examples of Questions to Study:
- Does garlic cure the common cold?
- At what time of day are people more likely to answer the phone and talk to a salesperson?
- Would more people buy a green or a maroon camera case?
- Do people get more or less work done when they are sitting in an attractive room versus an unattractive room?
- Do young children learn math better if they work with real items (coins, beads) or with dittos?
- Do people who have no seasickness when sailing also have no seasickness when on a motorboat?
- Do people who have not eaten for a few hours buy more food at a supermarket than those who have just eaten?
- Do athletes perform better after watching comedians?
- Do people who have a list buy less food at a supermarket than people without a list?

As you can see, the possibilities of what inquiring minds would like to know are endless. Once you decide on your question and determine your hypothesis, state how you would find a control group and an experimental group, how you would guard for error, and how you would analyze your results.

If at all possible, try to do your experiment on a small group of people and report your results, keeping in mind that a small sample can only point to an interesting study to be carried out with a larger, more representative group.

Controversy in Research Findings

If you have studied the previous section and completed the exercises, you should have an appreciation of how difficult it is to do an accurate study. Good studies require time and money to complete. Even studies that use the scientific method and produce clear results are sometimes criticized by scientists or others who find flaws in the researcher's methods or conclusions. You may be familiar with studies of the effects of a substance (like saccharin) on rats, which showed that the substance causes cancer. These studies were criticized because researchers were comparing human and rodent metabolisms; the findings were also criticized because the doses given to the rats were much higher than most humans would ingest.

Read the following excerpt from an article about another controversial research study that has been criticized by some groups and praised by others:

Two recent studies that conclude that abortions have little negative psychological impact on women have renewed debate over a politically charged issue that, many researchers concede, appears unlikely to be resolved soon.

Representatives of anti-abortion groups contend that the studies are methodologically flawed and biased because the researchers favor abortion.

In particular, the critics say the studies did not follow women for a sufficiently long time after their abortions to assess accurately the occurrence of delayed effects; that they used a sample of women unrepresentative of the general population; or that they employed inappropriate measures of psychological distress.[3]

The problem of divided opinion about the validity of a study is a difficult one (see the next section on the use of expert testimony), but as consumers of information, we can either withhold judgment until more conclusive evidence is presented or give credence to a study with evidence we believe is strong enough to influence our current decisions. For example, if we read that one study showed that a low-fat diet contributed to reduced cholesterol rates and another study

---

[3]   Chris Raymond, *The Chronicle of Higher Education*, February 7, 1990, p. A6.

showed no significant relationship, we may still choose to believe that there might be a chance of reducing cholesterol with the low-fat diet. The critical thinker realizes that researchers are not in agreement about the ultimate prevention and cure of elevated cholesterol levels, but he chooses to make some dietary changes based on limited research because "It can't hurt and it might actually help my heart."

A more difficult problem with research is avoiding errors that could affect the results of a study. Consider the following commentary on the subject of research studies conducted by young scientists.

> Errors may occur through improper laboratory practices, faulty equipment, accidental mix-ups, poorly designed experiments, inadequate replication of research results, or any number of other reasons, some involving negligence and others occurring through no fault of the scientist.
>
> . . . Error is, in fact, inherent in any endeavor carried out by fallible human beings. The great possibility of error is one of the reasons why judgment is so important in science and why a scientist who has avoided error, designed good experiments, exercised good judgment, and discovered something new about the nature of things in the universe can experience such a thrill of achievement.[4]

Given the possibility of error in experimentation, the question arises: "Whom should I believe?"

As critical thinkers, we must live between two extremes. One extreme is an attitude of cynicism and anti-intellectualism that says, "Scientific research studies can never be trusted because there are too many possibilities for error." The other extreme is an attitude of passive reverence for the scientific method that says, "Scientists are the geniuses who are trained to carry out the studies that have brought us so many great advances, so I am not intelligent and/or educated enough to question any research I read." Both of these attitudes are dangerous for the critically thinking individual. Research can be trusted if it is carried out in the correct manner, and you are very capable of understanding the basic elements of research and evaluating specific studies you read or hear about.

In deciding what to believe, we also need to consider the credibility of the publication or news station reporting the study. Do the

4 Francisco J. Ayala, "Point of View: For Young Scientists, Questions of Protocol and Propriety Can Be Bewildering," *The Chronicle of Higher Education*, November 22, 1989, A36.

reporters have a reputation for being thorough and careful before they report on a study? Is there a science editor for the newspaper or magazine who knows which studies deserve to be reported? We also need to consider the credibility of the institution that did the study: Was it carried out by a questionable sex researcher who spends much time on the talk-show circuit? Was there possible bias in the research, as in a tobacco company finding that cigarettes improve lung capacity? Or was it done by a reputable research institution with no known biases?

Consider the following article, reported by the Associated Press news service.

Nicotine Gets A Good Grade: Aid for Alzheimer's

Contra Costa Times, December 20, 1989

LONDON (AP)—Nicotine, the drug inhaled by cigarette smokers, can help reduce the symptoms of Alzheimer's disease, psychologists reported Tuesday.

"Giving nicotine resulted in the patients becoming more alert, responding more vigorously, and doing better on a variety of mental tests," Reading University psychologist David Warburton told the London conference of the British Psychological Society.

Compared with the effects of a placebo, nicotine helped the patients suffering from premature senile dementia symptoms associated with Alzheimer's to be more alert, the psychologists said. Yet, they said nicotine did not improve their memories.

Alzheimer's is a progressive disease characterized by degeneration of the brain cells.

Reprinted by permission of the Associated Press.

The careless thinker might read this article and conclude that smoking cigarettes has a significant effect on improving Alzheimer's disease, and go no further in analyzing the article.

The cynical reader might dismiss the research and focus only on the vague wording of this report—"What kind of 'mental tests' were done?" he asks, or "What does *alert* really mean anyway? What's alert to you might not be alert to me."

Neither of these positions features an open mind; to be fair, we can question what the term *alert* refers to specifically but acknowledge that the patients who were given the nicotine were more responsive than those who were given a placebo.

We can note that the study was done by a psychologist whose paper was accepted for presentation at a national conference and tentatively conclude that there is a connection between nicotine and temporary alertness. We might wonder what the effects of caffeine and other related drugs would be. We can even quote the study at parties when someone says there is absolutely no redeeming value to nicotine.

But what if you have to do a report on developments in Alzheimer's disease research, or perhaps your parents or grandparents have the disease and are losing not only memory but also responsiveness?

SKILL

Read and discuss original studies before making decisions on controversial research findings.

Let's say you have to do a report. Making an argument in a public context is not the same as having a casual conversation. If you are going to state that significant research is being done on the effects of nicotine on Alzheimer's patients, you should get the original study from the journal in which it was published so you know exactly what was done and what was discovered. How long were these patients given the nicotine? What kinds of tests were given to them? How many patients were involved? You can ask a professor, doctor, nurse, librarian, or group concerned with the issue to help you understand the importance of a particular study.

In your research, you may find that health care professionals don't give much credence to the study, or you may find that it was an exciting breakthrough that would greatly enhance your report. The general rule of thumb is that, if you are going to report information to others, you need to verify your sources, just as a good journalist would.

If you have a personal interest in research that is reported in an abridged manner in a magazine, newspaper, or televised segment, you can, as we have discussed, get more complete information by going to the source of the research. You might find the study detailed in full by a scientific journal, or you may be able to contact the researcher through the institution that sponsored the research. In addition, you can ask physicians who are treating your friends or relatives for their opinions concerning your specific situation.

In short, we can't possibly keep up with all advances in any given field of research. As critical thinkers, we can look at the credibility of the reports we hear or read, and we can choose to do more intensive study of those reports that are relevant to our situations.

EXERCISE

Purpose: To explore the effect of reported research on decision-making.

For a few days, consider how decisions you have made are based on information you've read about or heard about. Do you use seat belts or air bags because of research? Have you invested in a particular stock or mutual fund based on reports of a successful track record? Are any of your decisions about the food you eat (fat content, cholesterol content, sugar or salt content, balance of food groups) based on research? If so, do you remember what the research said and where you read or heard about it? If you take vitamins, ask yourself why you take them and what research led you to make vitamin supplementation a daily habit.

What about exercise options? Do you regularly exercise, and if so, have your decisions about what kind to do and what equipment or clothing to wear been based on research studies? Do you read consumer magazines before making purchases, or listen to friends or salespeople, or do you just buy impulsively?

To complete this exercise, answer the following:

1. What is the habit you have acquired, the action you have taken, or the item you have purchased?

2. What factors led you to make the decision to acquire the habit or buy the item?

3. What have been the effects (if any) of your decision? To what extent has your life been enhanced by your decision? How might your life be different if you had not made the decision?

Read the following humorous article as a review of some basic elements of controlled studies.

Sickening Experiment on Human Subjects

by Steve Rubenstein
San Francisco Chronicle, May 25, 1990

Scientists were paying people $200 to throw up in San Francisco this week. It was too good a deal to miss.

They do these sorts of things at the University of California at San Francisco. Researchers are always looking for guinea pigs willing to try experimental drugs. In this case, the drug was a new anti-seasickness pill. The ad said you could make $200 for popping the pill and taking an eight-hour boat ride.

There was only one condition. You had to be the nauseous type. Somehow I qualified.

Dozens of people, many with holes in their pants, signed up for the voyage. It was encouraging to see so many selfless people pitching in for science.

"People will do anything for $200," explained one researcher. "Even this."

Before sailing away, we had to take a physical. It was a snap. The main thing the doc seemed interested in was whether I was the throw-up type. It's no good testing seasickness pills on people who don't get seasick.

"How do you feel on boats?" the doc asked, in that concerned demeanor of his calling.

"Terrible," I said. "Lousy. I head straight for the rail."

It was the right answer. The doc's face lit up like the penlight in his breast pocket. He put my chart in the active file. I was in.

On the appointed day, we men and women of science assembled at the hospital to take our pills. Since it was a scientific study, only half of us would be getting capsules containing the actual drug. The other half would receive capsules containing sugar, a placebo. A researcher handed out the pills randomly.

We weren't supposed to know which capsule was which, of course. That wouldn't be scientific. But the capsules, made of clear plastic, were easy to tell apart. The drug looked like tiny time pills, and the placebo looked like sugar. Someone sure screwed up, the doc said, especially because many people believe seasickness is a state of mind.

"What did you get?" we guinea pigs asked each other.

"Placebo," said one sad-eyed soul. "Darn. I'm a goner."

We were to swallow the pill precisely at 8 A.M. The researcher took out her digital watch.

"Place the pill in your right hand," she said. "Prepare to swallow."

We three dozen strangers stood abreast, pills in hand, united in time and place.

"Five, four, three, two, one. Swallow."

Gulp.

Into the buses we marched, and off to Fisherman's Wharf. We had a job to do.

The seas looked calm, which did not sit well with one of the passengers on the boat. His name was Kirt, and he turned out to be the president of the company that was trying to market the new drug. He had paid $80,000 to UCSF to conduct the impartial study—which he cheerily denied would be any less impartial because of his busybody presence on the boat—said the last thing he wanted to see was calm seas. Sick people is what he wanted.

"I don't want everyone to throw up," he said. "I just want the right people to throw up. The placebo people."

And then we shoved off on our mission. Eight nauseating hours on the high seas.

"Don't worry," the skipper told Kirt. "I'm going to get these people sick for you."

Questions for Discussion

1. What controls did the researchers use for this study?
2. Since this article was humorous, and probably exaggerated, we can't claim it as factual evidence of faulty research. Given that disclaimer, what areas of potential error in results did the author point out?
3. If you were to set up a study to test a new anti-seasickness pill, how would you design your research?

EXERCISE

Purpose: To gather data from personal research.

Choose one of the following options for a personal experiment.

1. Chart your study habits for a week or two. Note if you have a regular time and place for studying. Is the equipment you need readily available (pens, paper)? Do you review notes shortly after class?

Do you study alone or with others? What distractions intrude upon your study time (television, radio, phone, snack breaks, visitors)? After you have charted your habits, look at your record and draw conclusions about where time is well used, where it is wasted, and how it could be put to better use.

2. Chart your eating and exercise habits for a week or two. Then look at your record and draw some conclusions about your life-style. Does your record reflect healthy nutritional choices, a rushed, erratic schedule, or a combination of both? Do you exercise regularly? Try to predict what will happen to your health if you continue to eat and exercise in this way.

3. Try a life-style experiment on yourself. Change an aspect of your daily life: set and stick to consistent study habits, do a certain aerobic or bodybuilding exercise, reduce your intake of fat or sugar, or eliminate caffeine, tobacco, or a food you crave (some nutritionists believe that people are allergic to foods that they crave). Keep a record of how you feel after adhering to your new program for two weeks or a month, and report the results to your instructor. (It might also be interesting for several people to work together on this, forming an experimental group.)

Use of Authority: Expert Testimony

In addition to citing controlled studies, writers and speakers frequently support their conclusions with the testimony of experts. An **expert** is an individual who has education, significant experience, or both in a given area. We turn to experts in many areas of our daily lives: We consult doctors, dentists, lawyers, mechanics, counselors, and salespersons who are supposed to have more knowledge and experience in their fields than we do.

We also rely on friends and acquaintances who have become knowledgeable about various subjects because they spend time on and keep up with these subjects; for example, we might consult a friend we respect who has read all about the local candidates for an upcoming election. We listen to what she says because she has credibility as an informed voter. When we buy a car or a stereo, we might consult a friend who works a lot on his car or who has had several stereos because we see him as more of an expert than we are. Even for small purchases, like clothing, we may ask a friend to help us if we believe this person has more knowledge of fashion trends than we do.

The phenomenon of consulting acquaintances before we make decisions has been called the *two-step flow* of information (Figure 5.2). Our expert friends, who are called **opinion leaders**, first (step 1) get their information from the media (television, magazines, newspapers, circulars), and then (step 2) they pass this information on to us. In our information-saturated age, this method makes sense; we can't be informed about everything, so we become experts in the areas we spend our time on and others become experts in other areas, and we share information. We learn from one another's experiences, mistakes, and successes and save time (and sometimes money) in the process.

Advertisers and campaign managers are well aware of this two-step phenomenon as they carefully choose the magazines and television shows to best reach their target audiences. If they can get the opinion leaders to vote for them or to use their products, the rest of us will follow. News of the person or product will travel by word of mouth to the secondary audiences.

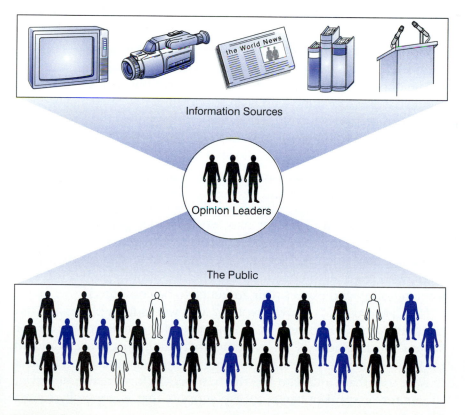

Figure 5.2

EXERCISE

Purpose: To find examples of how the two-step flow influences decision-making.

Consider some voting or buying decisions you've made lately or some decisions about medical treatment. Did you consult an expert or a knowledgeable friend before making your choices? If not, on what basis did you make your decisions?

Try to list your three most recent decisions and trace any outside influences on those decisions.

Examples:

"I used to read a popular weekly newsmagazine to be informed. A friend of mine who is a professor told me about another magazine he likes better because it gives more in-depth coverage on issues. I switched to this other magazine and I really like it. I enjoy getting a broader report on current events." (from a retired student)

"I developed a breast infection—very common for nursing mothers—and didn't want to make a trip to the doctor for antibiotics. The doctor wouldn't prescribe the drugs without seeing me, so I called a friend of mine who is an expert in herbs. She suggested home remedies, which I took for several days; they did keep me from getting worse. But I wanted to get better faster, so I gave in and made the appointment." (from a mother of an infant)

Use of a network of friends may work well for personal decision-making, but it won't work to quote these friends in papers or speeches. You can't say, "Vote for Candidate X for senator; my friend Mark, who reads all the major newsmagazines, thinks he has the best foreign policy" and expect your audience to be convinced.

Nor can you say, "I know a woman who works for a pharmacy and she thinks that 80 percent of the people who get prescriptions for Valium are drug addicts" as evidence that Valium users are addicted to drugs. It may be true that this drug is carelessly prescribed and it may be true that Candidate X is the best person for senator; however, the writer or speaker needs to use support that is generally recognized as valid.

A real expert has relevant academic credentials and/or significant experience in the area in question. People who are seen as experts in a field have been recognized by their colleagues and/or by the general public. This recognition often comes as a result of publishing articles or books, earning advanced degrees, or attaining success or acclaim.

People who fit these categories have credibility, and their opinions are generally considered reliable sources of evidence for a particular argument.

An Opinion with Substance

The following is an excerpt from *The Search* by Tom Brown, Jr., a tracker. He founded a survival school and teaches from coast to coast.

I took the class into the woods and stopped by a drainage ditch. The bottom was covered with soft sandy soil. It was also covered with animal prints. I asked the class to notice all the prints that were visible. They named two animals and guessed at two more. There were eleven, not counting the dog.

When I ask for prints, I'm not just looking for clear sharp markings of large well-known animals. I'm searching for an explanation of every mark on the ground. . . . As I study the markings a picture begins to form in my mind of what passed the spot I am checking before I arrived. My mind begins to place animals in space and time.

Something began to take shape as I noticed the age of the different tracks. . . .

"Wow!" I yelled. "Look at that." It had all come together, and I began to explain the scene to the class as I pointed to the markings that were the tracks of a dog and a rabbit, which had been on this spot at the same time.

"Dog came down, saw the rabbit before it smelled him. Maybe a cross wind. He jumped after the rabbit. Here is his first set of four running prints." I pointed. "Here, here, here, and here. Here is the rabbit moving up the side of the ditch to that sweet new grass." Again I pointed to markings that looked almost as if someone had scraped the dirt with a branch. "The rabbit sees the dog, does a boogie here, and races down the hill. He made two gigantic leaps. See where he jumped? See where the dog leaped for him and missed? Skidded here, regained his balance, and followed up the other side, there." . . .

"How did you do that?" Kay asked.

"I sat for days on the edge of a field and watched rabbits feed, breed, bear young, and avoid danger. After each happening, I would study the marks that had been left in the earth. I can tell when a rabbit is sitting or standing, agitated or calm. Whenever a dog came through the field and happened on a chase, I would follow its every marking, remembering what my eyes had seen just moments before. After a great amount of time, I began to recognize those signs as I happened onto them."

Tom Brown, Jr., with William Owen, *The Search: The Continuing Story of the Tracker* (Englewood Cliffs, NJ: Prentice-Hall, 1980), pp. 215–216.

SKILL

Recognize legitimate and illegitimate uses of expert testimony.

Problems with Expert Testimony

There are some common problems associated with expert testimony that a critical thinker should consider when listening to an argument. These problems are:

1. Use of experts in the wrong field of expertise.
2. Use of experts who are not recognized as experts.
3. Use of experts who are paid for their opinions.
4. Use of experts who are clearly biased.
5. Expert testimony that is contradicted by equally expert testimony.

1.   Use of experts in the wrong field of expertise: The most visible form of this problem occurs in advertisements in which a person who is respected in one field is used to endorse a product out of his or her area of expertise. It is a legitimate use of authority for an athlete to promote sports equipment, but some ads capitalize on handsome or popular athletes by using them to promote cars, shampoos, or cereals.

When the medical program "Marcus Welby M.D." was popular, Robert Young, who played Dr. Welby, was used to promote Sanka coffee; the advertisers hoped we would think of him as a doctor dispensing medical advice (or that older viewers would remember Robert Young as the wise father in "Father Knows Best"). It seems advertisers have recognized our increasing sophistication as thinkers by having a new T.V. doctor announce, "I'm not a doctor, but I play one on T.V." The way the actor states this fact implies that "playing one on T.V." makes him *sort* of a doctor, maybe even *more* than a doctor, especially since he looks so impressive in the white coat he wears on the commercial. And why else would he be dispensing medical advice on prime-time television?

Be careful of slick expert advertisements by non-experts, which are generally accompanied by impressive costumes and backgrounds. If real credentials aren't mentioned in an endorsement, don't assume there are credentials lurking somewhere in the person's background.

2. **Use of experts who are not recognized as experts**: Most areas of expertise today are in the midst of increasingly new discoveries. If someone is used as an expert based on experience or education completed years ago and if the person has not kept up with his field, then he is questionable as an expert. When someone quotes a finding by an expert, a date should accompany the quotation so we know when the discovery was made.

The importance of current information accounts for your instructors' advice to look up recent journal articles when you want to support a position. Books are good sources of support; still, in some fields, a book even a few years old becomes obsolete due to new information. The fact that some of your textbooks are in the sixth (and more expensive) edition reflects the need for updating information in all areas. For example, history books that end with George Bush as president are missing vital information. Although foundational theories are essential, current ideas and events in any field are just as important.

Sometimes a person's credentials are distorted. Having *Doctor* in front of one's name can mean that one is a physician, a dentist, a recipient of a doctoral degree in an academic field, a chiropractor, or a psychologist. As a critical thinker, you need to understand what a title means, the institution that conferred the title, and, if possible, the reputation the titled person has with his colleagues. The claims made by this person are then considered in the light of his or her position as an expert.

3. **Use of experts who are paid for their testimony**: One fairly obvious consideration in listening to evidence based on expertise is to find out whether the authority is paid for the testimony or

endorsement. Some people are paid to promote products, particularly salespeople. A salesperson may genuinely believe that a brand new truck will meet your needs, but he is not the only person to ask about it because of the conflict of interest built into his role. Similarly, an expert witness, such as a psychologist, who is called to testify on behalf of a defendant in a trial may lose credibility if she is paid for her testimony.

4. **Use of experts who are clearly biased**: Many people feel so strongly about an issue that they join with others who have similar beliefs, forming clubs, unions, and associations. They often are or become experts in their interest areas, but their expertise is sometimes accompanied by a strong bias.

For example, those who lobby together for gun control may become highly knowledgeable about laws and regulations across the various states; similarly, members of the National Rifle Association gain expertise on the various statutes. Neither of these groups can be considered impartial and unbiased in a discussion of gun control. This does not mean a critical thinker should not listen to them; in fact, most editorials and televised debates on this issue and other controversial issues involve individuals with strong biases, and many of these individuals try to present a balanced viewpoint. However, critical thinkers keep in mind that they are hearing the facts from particular points of view, and they listen for possible exaggeration of the benefits of or problems with proposed policies.

EXERCISE

Purposes: To discover examples of bias in books, magazines, or televised programs; to consider biased viewpoints.

1. Try to isolate an incident of possible bias in your reading or viewing. You might go through your textbooks and note that examples given seem to support a particular viewpoint or political stand. When you watch a television interview show, note whether the host gives equal time and courtesy to all points of view, or whether he or she seems to favor one side over the other. Many newsmagazines are considered to have a bias, conservative or liberal, or radically left or right; find an issue that is covered by two magazines with different biases and contrast the presentation of the issue.

Example:

This passage is from an English composition textbook. In a chapter about being fair to many points of view, the author begins with these statements:

> Yvonne is a first-year college student of eighteen. . . . Among other lessons, her parents taught her that no man likes a woman with brains, that tears make a woman appealing, and that motherhood is a woman's sacred duty.
>
> When Yvonne left home for college, her worried parents warned her to watch out for radical young college instructors who would try to put wrong ideas in her head. Yvonne really didn't pay much attention, though she dutifully promised to watch out. But then, the very first day she walked into her English composition class, there was the young instructor she had been warned about. And sure enough, after the instructor checked the roll, she assigned an essay on, of all things, the subject "runaway mothers"! [5]

The chapter continues with a dialogue in which Yvonne's unreasonable words are contrasted with the instructor's wisdom. Yvonne is described as being impulsive, crying, waving her fist in her instructor's face, not understanding the instructor's simple explanations, and calling people who need social workers "icky." Later in the text, Yvonne's father is portrayed as a boob from another century who feels that women are only good enough to make coffee on the job.

This text is biased in its presentation of parents as stupid and behind the times. They are portrayed as backward, while the instructor is seen as progressive; they are old and the instructor is young; they are worried and controlling and the instructor is calm and reasonable. It doesn't make sense that such controlling parents as those described here would even allow their daughter to go to college.

Throughout the book, the instructor is seen as the person with all truth, and the parents are seen as bigoted and judgmental with no sense of reality or fairness. The first paragraph quoted lists three lessons taught by Yvonne's parents. Since the first two lessons are ridiculous, the third rule—seeing motherhood as

---

[5] Ray Kytle, *Clear Thinking for Composition* (New York: McGraw-Hill, 1987), p. 7.

sacred, if not a duty—becomes crazy by association with the first two reasons. Criticism of motherhood would be intimidating to a student who considered it an important profession.

What is really unfair is that all of these comments and many more like them are put in a book claiming to teach fairness and empathy and to warn against hasty moral judgments and stereotypes. I wonder if this author is aware of his own bias.

2. Take an issue and create viewpoints for several characters. For example, you could imagine the responses of a police officer, an addict, a pusher, a parent, and a politician to the notion of legalizing drugs. What natural biases might influence their responses? Write out each of their possible responses (alone or in groups) and see where the similarities and differences are.

5.   Expert testimony that is contradicted by equally expert testimony: One characteristic of the "age of information" is the proliferation of research that is carried out by individuals, corporations, universities, and think tanks. The outcome of one study may be diametrically or partially opposed to the findings of another study done by an equally prestigious person or group. In addition, we are seeing that today's discovery can sometimes be tomorrow's mistake; that is, current research often makes research of a few years ago obsolete, and even dangerous. Such was the case for the pregnant women of the 1950s who were given the drug DES, which was later found to have done significant damage to their daughters and grandchildren.

When we consider these problems, we can understand why some people have become cynical about all medical pronouncements; they may fear catching AIDS from drinking fountains because "next year, they'll find out that AIDS is transmitted through water." This attitude is not reasonable, but there is wisdom in choosing a *healthy* skepticism.

A healthy skepticism looks at pronouncements from authorities and considers their credentials, whether they have support from their colleagues (which is not necessarily important as a factor by itself—consider Copernicus) and whether their ideas make sense.

When two respectable experts or institutions disagree, critical thinkers have two options: they can remain neutral until more confirming studies are completed or they can do more personal research. Personal research includes going to libraries for relevant journal articles, interviewing people in the field, and calling the institutions who have done the studies and asking for copies of their findings (because, as previously discussed, they are usually summarized only briefly by the standard media sources).

Consider this passage from *American Health Magazine.*

Circumcision's Comeback?

Now Pediatricians Say the Surgery May Be More than Cosmetic

by Vicki Brower
American Health Magazine, September 1989

Circumcision has been controversial more than once during its 3500-year history. Recently, an American Academy of Pediatrics' (AAP) task force reversed its earlier position that there is no valid medical rationale for routine circumcision of newborns. The AAP now says the procedure "has potential medical benefits and advantages."

The AAP's more positive stand is largely based on studies by Army pediatrician Thomas Wiswell, which show that uncircumcised male infants suffer 11 times more urinary tract infections (UTI's). Researchers suspect bacteria get trapped under the foreskin and move up the urethra to the kidneys. UTI's can be serious and may even have lifetime consequences.

The AAP also notes that circumcision virtually eliminates cancer of the penis, and may reduce sexually transmitted diseases and cervical cancer in women.

Not all pediatricians and urologists agree with the AAP's new position. Dr. Howard Snyder, associate director of urology at Children's Hospital of Philadelphia, calls circumcision "unnecessary surgery and unnatural," pointing out that post-circumcision rates of infection and other complications run about 1 percent to 3 percent.

Reprinted by permission of the publisher.

If you have a son or if you someday have a son, you will decide one way or the other about circumcision. How would you know what to believe from an article like this? All you know from reading this article is that there is disagreement among pediatricians about the medical value of this procedure.

You might, in your frustration, forget the medical aspect of the operation and focus on other factors, such as choosing to circumcise so the child will look like his father or friends. Another option might be to first consider personal religious beliefs, then medical benefits; a critically thinking parent would have to look up the studies cited and/or discuss the findings with one or more pediatricians.

Being thoughtful takes time and effort, and that's why we can't be thorough about every decision. Each of us needs to choose our priorities according to individual values. Once we have decided something is really important, we can do the homework necessary to make sound judgments and to avoid actions we will later regret.

The preceding article included the story of one mother who had made a hasty decision to circumcise, given her approval to the doctor, and is now suing him for performing the surgery—because, she claims, it was done against her son's will! If only she had poured her energy into the initial decision, she wouldn't be wasting time and energy and experiencing personal agony over her choice. Clear thinking has emotional benefits!

EXERCISE

Purpose: To recognize controversial expert testimony.

Find an example of expert testimony contradicted by equally expert testimony; editorial pages sometimes contain pro-con arguments of this nature, or you can find them in *U.S.A. Today* on the debate page, or on programs such as "The MacNeil-Lehrer Report" or ABC's "Nightline." State the basic areas of disagreement and the reasons given for each side's conclusion. Then decide which of the arguments you would support and explain why.

Chapter Highlights

1. Scientific discoveries are often made through controlled studies; a good study can be repeated by other researchers and thus can lead us closer to the truth about an issue.

2. A good research design includes a characteristic of interest, a hypothesis, and a sample, which is divided randomly into a control group and an experimental group.

3. The only difference between a control group and an experimental group is the treatment received by the experimental group.

4. The data gathered from a study is used to draw conclusions and to suggest areas for further study.

5. A critical thinker will review a study according to specific criteria to determine the extent to which the study is valid or biased.

6. The findings of many studies are considered controversial by experts in the field. When studies are controversial, critical thinkers withhold judgment or accept findings provisionally.

7. When using authoritative testimony as a support for conclusions, critical thinkers should consider whether the expert is educated or experienced in a field that is relevant to the issue under discussion.

8. Problems with using expert testimony include the use of experts in the wrong field of expertise, the use of experts who are not recognized as experts, the use of experts who are paid or biased, and the use of expert testimony that is contradicted by equally expert testimony.

Article for Discussion

Food News Blues

by Anthony Schmitz
In Health, November 1991

Not long ago I set a coffee cup on the table and opened the newspaper to a piece of good news. "New Study Finds Coffee Unlikely to Cause Heart Ills," read the headline. One thing less to worry about, I thought, until I remembered a story from a few weeks before. That morning the headline warned, "Study: Heart Risk Rises on 4, More Cups Coffee Daily." My paper does this all the time. Concerning the latest dietary findings, it flips and flops like a fish thrown to shore.

"Medical research," it declared one Wednesday, "repeatedly has linked the soluble fiber in oats with reductions in serum cholesterol." By Thursday of the next week all that had changed. "Studies Cast Doubt on Benefits From Oat Bran," the headline cried. Once again the paper offered its readers a familiar choice. Which story to believe? This week's, or last week's, or none at all?

The paper in question is the *St. Paul Pioneer Press*. It's a respectable provincial daily, not unlike the papers in Houston, Detroit and dozens of other cities. One day, recently, the news editor, Mike Peluso, said he'd take a crack at explaining his paper's flip-flops.

Peluso is compact, graying, more grave than jocular. He met me at the newsroom door. "You want a cup of coffee?" he asked, pointing at a vending machine. No, I said, trying to recall whether this week coffee was good or bad. Peluso shrugged and headed for his cluttered cubicle. Beyond its flimsy walls reporters jabbered into phones.

I arranged the coffee and oat bran clippings on a paper-strewn table. Peluso examined them one by one. He grimaced. He sighed. He swallowed black coffee from a paper cup.

"How do you reconcile the conflicting claims?" he asked himself. "One month coffee can't hurt you, the next month quit coffee and your heart will tick forever."

Exactly.

Peluso shook his head. "I don't know, I don't have any answers for that. You've got to talk about the real world here."

For Peluso, the real world looks something like this: News of a hot nutrition study gets beamed into the newsroom from wire services such as Associated Press, the *New York Times* or the *Baltimore Sun*. Peluso and his staff poke at the story, trying to find flaws that argue against putting it in the paper. By and large it's a hamstrung effort. Never mind that the reporter who wrote the piece is thousands of miles away. She'd defend the story anyway. The paper's own health reporter is scant help; he's been on the beat two months.

Meanwhile, Peluso knows that his competitors—another daily paper, plus radio and television news—won't spend a week analyzing the study. They'll run it today. Which is to say Peluso will, too. But the story the reader sees won't be as detailed as the piece that came over the wire. Compared with the *New York Times* or the *Washington Post*, the *Pioneer Press* is something of a dwarf. Stories get trimmed to fit. Subtleties and equivocations—the messy business of research—don't always make the cut.

"Look," said Peluso, "we're not medical authorities. We're just your normal skeptics. And it's not like we're inventing the research. We're simply reporting on it. We present what's there and let people draw their own conclusions."

"So what should readers make of all the contradictory advice you offer them?"

Peluso sighed again. "I don't know," he said. "You've got to take everything with a grain of salt until the last word comes in. I hate to tell people I don't believe everything I read, but the fact is anybody who believes everything they read is nuts."

Researchers whose work makes news soon learn that the match between science and journalism wasn't made in heaven. Richard

Greenberg, a microbiologist who directs the office of scientific and public affairs at the Institute of Food Technologists, has watched what happens when the scientific method collides with journalistic technique.

"The first thing you've got to remember," says Greenberg, "is that science is not fact. It is not truth. It is not holy scripture. It's a compendium of information. You try to put all the research together and come to a consensus. Just because somebody runs a study that comes to a particular conclusion doesn't change everything that's gone before."

Scientists don't generally reach consensus in time for the next deadline. After 30 years of study, coffee's link to heart disease remains an open question. Four plus cups a day may slightly increase the risk, though some research suggests only decaf is linked to heart problems. Similarly, a decade's worth of oat bran experiments have served only to get a good argument going. Some studies suggest oat bran isn't any better at lowering cholesterol than white bread. If you eat enough of either, the message goes, you won't have room for fatty food. Others say oat bran has innate—though so far inexplicable—cholesterol-lowering properties.

While on their way to answering the big questions about fat or cholesterol or fiber, researchers often pause and dicker merrily about the design flaws in one study or the dicey statistical analysis in another. "Among ourselves," says one epidemiologist, "we're more interested in the detail of how things are done than in saying right now whether oat bran's good for you."

For journalists it's exactly the opposite. The arcana of statistical analysis and research design are boring at best, baffling at worst. The big question is whether oat bran will keep your heart ticking.

"The reporter and headline writer are trying to distill the meaning of the latest piece of research," says Greenberg. "They're trying to grab the eye of the reader. They're searching for absolutes where there are no absolutes. And this is what happens. One day you read caffeine is bad. Then you read that if you take the caffeine out, coffee is OK. Then you hear that the solvent that takes out the caffeine is dangerous. Then you find out the caffeine isn't dangerous after all. It so confuses the public they don't know whom to believe. And the truth is, there wasn't really any news in any of these studies. Each of them was just another micromillimeter step toward scientific consensus."

For Greenberg, news exists in those rare moments when scientists weigh the evidence and agree to agree—when the American Heart Association, the National Cancer Institute or the National Academy of Sciences pronounces that you ought to eat less fat, or more vegetables.

But by the terms of journalism, scientific consensus is a dead-letter file. If everybody agrees, there's no conflict, there's no news. In comparison, debates such as those about coffee or oat bran are a newsroom gold mine. Contradictions and conflict abound. Better still, almost everyone has oatmeal or coffee in the cupboard.

"You can't convince an editor not to run this stuff," says Howard Lewis, editor of the newsletter *Science Writers*. "My advice is that they do it for the same reason they run the comic strips and the astrological columns. But I feel it's all a hoax. Usually they're not accomplishing anything except sowing panic or crying wolf."

A Purdue communications professor raised a stir few years back when he suggested that research news might be more harmful than helpful. Writing in the journal *Science, Technology and Human Values*, Leon Trachtman observed that 90 percent of the new drugs touted in newspaper reports never reached the market or were driven from it because they were ineffective, too toxic or both. Readers relying on this information would have made wrong choices nine times out of 10.

So who's served, Trachtman asked, by publicizing these drugs before there's a scientific consensus on them? "When there's no consensus, why broadcast contradictory reports?" Ultimately, he said, readers are paralyzed by the pros and cons. He asked whether the result will be contempt for research, followed by demands to stop wasting money on it.

Not surprisingly, Leon Trachtman got blasted for implying that a scholastic elite ought to be making decisions for us. Among the critics was David Perlman, a science editor who writes regularly about health and nutrition. Often, Perlman says, research leads to public debates. Will avoiding fatty foods really lengthen your life? Should government experts try persuading people to change their eating habits? It's debatable. But citizens can hardly take part if they're capable of nothing more than numbly accepting expert advice. "To abdicate an interest in science," says Perlman, citing mathematician Jacob Bronowsky, "is to walk with open eyes toward slavery." Perlman trusts people's ability to sort through well-written news.

"It's not just the masses who are confused," says Trachtman. "It's the same for well-trained scientists once they're out of their field. I think people ought to establish a sensible, moderate course of action, and then not be deflected from it every morning by what they read in the paper."

But let's face facts. Do you have the resolve to ignore a headline that declares, "Sugar, Alzheimer's Linked"? If you can't help but play the game, you can at least try to defend yourself from nonsense by following these rules:

Count the Legs. First, ask if the group studied bears any relation to you. Don't let research done only on four-legged subjects worry you. Pregnant rats, for instance, are more likely to bear offspring with missing toes after getting extremely high jolts of caffeine. What's this mean for humans? Probably nothing. There's no evidence that drinking moderate amounts of caffeine causes human birth defects.

If research subjects have two legs, read closely to see if they're anything like you. Early research that helped launch the oat bran fad involved only men, most of whom were middle-aged. All had danger-ously high blood cholesterol, which reportedly fell after they ate a daily cup-plus of oat bran—enough for a half-dozen muffins. Fine, unless you're female, have low cholesterol already, or can't stand the thought of eating half a dozen bran muffins every day.

Check for Perspective. Even if you're a match for the group being studied, don't assume the results are significant. "Check if the journalist gets the perspective of other people in the field," says Harvard epidemi-ologist Walter Willett. "People who have watched the overall flow of information are in a good position to say, 'Well, this really nails it down,' or 'That's interesting, but it needs confirmation.'"

Ask How Many Guinea Pigs. Quaker Oats research manager Steven Ink, who's written a guide to nutrition studies, says the best research uses at least 50 subjects. By this standard, we should look askance at the recent study showing that eating 17 tiny meals a day lowers cholesterol. Only seven people took part. But rules of thumb don't always work. A small number can be meaningful if the effect observed is large and consistent. You don't need to feed 50 people cyanide to figure out that it's going to be bad for everyone.

What's more, Ink advises, subjects shouldn't be fed quantities of food that no one in his right mind would eat. One example is the recent study showing that trans fatty acids such as those in margarine may be bad for your heart. Subjects ate three times more trans fatty acids than the aver-age American.

Finally, any group tested should be compared to a similar group. Early studies that linked coffee to heart disease were skewed because coffee drinkers differed greatly from the control group. The coffee drinkers were more likely to smoke and eat a high-fat, high-cholesterol diet. Both habits carry bigger heart risks than does drinking coffee.

Wait for Confirmation. "Don't let one study change your life," says Jane Brody, the *New York Times* health writer. She waits for three types of food research to agree before changing her eating habits.

First, she looks for studies of large groups that show a link between a food and good or bad health—Italy's big appetite for olive oil and its low rate of heart disease for instance. Then she watches for lab evidence in test animals that suggests how the food causes its effect in people. Finally, she considers human experiments in which two groups are com-pared—one eating the food, the other not eating it, with neither group knowing which is which.

Applying this rule to her own meals, Brody skimps on butter and favors olive oil. She eats plenty of fruits and vegetables, lots of pota-toes, rice, beans and pasta, and modest amounts of lean meat. "This plan won't make you sick, has a good chance of keeping you well, and is immune to these fads that are here today and gone tomorrow," Brody says.

Hunt for Holes. No matter how carefully you read, you'll have to rely on the information your newspaper chooses to supply. If the big mattress ad on an inside page gets dropped at the last minute, the editors may suddenly have room for an exhaustive treatment of the latest coffee study. But if a candidate for national office gets caught with his pants down, the space required for a thorough expose may mean the coffee piece gets gutted.

When editors at the *St. Paul Pioneer Press* got hold of a wire service report debunking oat bran, they found room for the first two-thirds. The third that didn't fit held a stern critique by other experts. They charged that the study contained too few people (20 female dietitians), didn't control the rest of what they ate, and started with subjects who had unusually low cholesterol.

"The reader really has to be skeptical," says Frank Sacks, the Harvard researcher whose oat bran study was under attack. "Take my case, for instance. The reporter really ought to say that this is a new finding, that it needs to be replicated. This is a warning sign that you have to wait a while. Reporters hate that when you say it. They call it waffling. But the truth is your hot new finding might not be confirmed down the line. You hate it when that happens, but it happens time and again.

"The real conservative advice is not to take any of this stuff in the newspaper with a whole lot of credence," says Sacks. "You could just wait for the conservative health organizations like the American Heart Association to make their recommendations and then follow their advice."

I called the American Heart Association to get its line on oat bran and coffee. "We don't have an opinion," said John Weeks somewhat plaintively.

"We get calls every day from the media," said Weeks. "They want to know what we think about every new study that comes out. And we don't have an opinion. We don't try to assimilate every new study. Our dietary guidelines would be bouncing all over the place if we did. Once the evidence is there, we move on it. Until then, we don't."

The Heart Association is sticking with the same dietary advice it's dispensed since 1988, when it last revised its model diet. Eat less fat. Eat more grains, vegetables and fruit. The evidence that oat bran lowers cholesterol is so limited that the association makes no specific recommendations about it. Concerning coffee, the group has nothing to say.

Weeks' advice for whipsawed newspaper readers has a familiar ring. "What people need to keep in mind," he said, "is that one study does not a finding make."

"You mean," I asked, quoting Mike Peluso's newsroom wisdom, "I'm nuts to believe everything I read?"

Said Weeks, "That's exactly correct."

Questions for Discussion

1. Comment on the following paragraph from the article: "But by the terms of journalism, scientific consensus is a dead-letter file. If everybody agrees, there's no conflict, there's no news. In comparison, debates such as those about coffee or oat bran are a newsroom gold mine. Contradictions and conflict abound. Better still, almost everyone has oatmeal or coffee in the cupboard." Should newspapers and magazines report controversial studies or wait until there is scientific consensus for the findings of the studies? What are your reasons for your answer?

2. What habits, if any, have you changed because of research that was reported by the popular media? (Consider dietary and exercise habits as well as advice on car safety, crib safety, durability of consumer goods, and so on.) To what extent has the advice been helpful?

3. What is the best approach to the reading of research in the popular press? Should you believe nothing, everything, or some things? Do you agree with the guidelines for reading research that are given in this article?

4. Do you believe that scientific journals such as the *New England Journal of Medicine* should be more readily available to the public by being sold in bookstores and supermarkets? Would people buy these publications, and if so, would they be capable of understanding them? Give reasons for your answers.

Ideas for Writing or Speaking

Research Paper or Speech

1. The purpose of this assignment is to help you become familiar with using research to support your conclusions. Many highly intelligent people will give strong reasons for their conclusions; however, they may not take the time to study current research findings to support their reasons.

    Your objective for this paper or speech is to find out how well you can substantiate the reasons for your conclusion.

    Since the issue you choose will be controversial, there will be opinions on both sides. You need to show, with your research, that your reasons are stronger than the reasons given by the opposition.

The steps to take to prepare this essay or speech are as follows:

a. Choose a controversial issue that you can research. Ideally, the issue will have been studied by researchers and discussed by experts.

b. Take a stand on the issue, or formulate a tentative **hypothesis**. A hypothesis states what you believe your conclusion will be after you conduct your research.

c. Find at least four sources of research to support your conclusion. These sources include reports of studies done on the issue, and articles and comments by experts that can be culled from professional journals, newsmagazines, or broadcast interviews. If you know an expert, you can arrange for an interview and record the comments as authoritative testimony.

   Also, find some arguments for the opposing side of the issue, so that you can address their reasoning in your essay or speech.

d. Complete a rough draft of your essay or speech, which should include your issue, conclusion, reasons, and evidence to prove your reasons. Also, in the body of the essay or speech, address the strongest reasons given by those who draw the opposite conclusion, and say why these reasons are not strong enough to justify that conclusion.

e. Write the final form of your speech or essay, adding an introduction and conclusion. The introduction should highlight the importance of your issue; you can use quotes, statistics, analogies, or anecdotes to gain the attention of your audience. The conclusion should summarize your reasons and reemphasize the importance of your issue and the validity of your conclusion.

Pro-Con Paper or Speech

2. The purpose of this assignment is to have you understand, first-hand, that issues are controversial because there is usually valid reasoning on both sides. In addition, when you complete this assignment, you will be a more experienced researcher and a more discerning thinker about the quality of reasoning given to support conclusions.

To complete this assignment, do the following:

a. Choose a controversial issue. For this assignment, it is best if you do not feel strongly about the issue because you need to be objective about the good reasons on both sides. However, do choose an issue that is interesting to you, so you are motivated to read about it.

b. Write your issue in question form, so you can clearly see the pro and con side of the issue by answering "yes" or "no" to the question. For example, you might write: "High-school principals should be able to censor articles from student newspapers." Those who answer yes are on the pro side of this issue; those who say no are on the con side.

3. Find eight sources of research on your issue. Four should be pro and four should be con. The sources may be journal articles, newspaper or magazine articles, books, transcripts of radio or television broadcasts in which experts testify, or personal interviews you conduct with an expert on the issue. (Some experts will give you their time, so don't hesitate to call for an interview.) A bibliography of these sources should be handed in with your finished product; use standard bibliographical form.

4. Study the research that you compile and choose three reasons for supporting the pro side of the issue and three reasons for supporting the con side. These reasons should be the best you can find for each side. Write out the reasons for each side, using evidence to support each reason.

5. Finally, take a position on the issue, and state why you found the reasons for that position to be the most sound. (You can see now why you should start off being as neutral as possible on this issue.) Acknowledge the strengths of the other side while explaining why you found your chosen side's position to be stronger. Conclude your essay or speech by commenting on what you learned in the process of studying both sides of an issue.

CHAPTER SIX

Reasoning Errors

I Know What I Think.
Don't Confuse Me with Facts.

A critical thinker recognizes errors in reasoning.

Understanding an argument is a complex process, as we have seen. We need to know what someone is concluding (claiming) about a particular issue or problem and the reasons for his or her beliefs. The strength of an argument depends on the quality of evidence used to support a conclusion.

When we look at an individual's support for his beliefs, we may perceive that something doesn't make sense, but we may not have words for whatever seems faulty in the reasoning. This chapter will teach you some terms that are used to characterize typical errors in reasoning. These errors occur so often that they have acquired a name of their own: **fallacies**.

Keep in mind, as you read this chapter, that the fallacies discussed are simply labels we give to faulty reasoning. Don't be concerned about labeling every faulty reason perfectly. Instead, use this discussion of fallacies as a general tool to help you analyze the quality of reasons given for a conclusion.

Fallacies can be seen as (1) reasons that seem logical but don't necessarily support the conclusion, or (2) statements that distract listeners from the real issue. This second type of fallacy is a form of verbal defense mechanism.

Adequate and Inadequate Reasons as Fallacies

Reasons that sound good and logical but are not adequate support for the conclusion are the first ones to consider. These are tricky because they use the form of good reasoning, but they don't have the real substance.

The major categories for insufficient reasons are: **faulty analogies, false cause (post hoc), ad hominem,** and **slippery slope**. In this section, we will first consider the legitimate and then the illegitimate uses of these types of evidence.

In considering legitimate support for conclusions, we will look at two patterns of reasoning that are commonly used: **reasoning by analogy** and **cause-effect reasoning**. These two patterns of reasoning are powerful in their ability to persuade, but subject to error and thus frequently misused.

Reasoning by Analogy

Have you ever taken a test with questions like these?

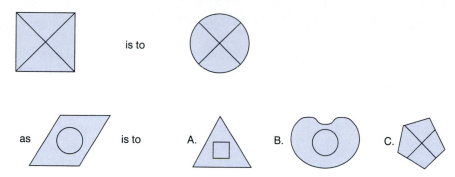

This test measures the ability to reason by analogy. If you answered "B" you correctly identified the analogous drawing: Both drawings contain two figures (X and 0) that have the same relationship to the figures that enclose them.

When speakers or writers use analogies, they describe something (an object, event, idea, or process) and compare it to something else. The *claim* is that the two things are alike in important ways. Reasoning by analogy can be coded as follows:

A is to B as C is to D.

Reasoning by analogy, comparing one idea or plan to another, is one of the major forms of evidence used by speakers and writers. For example, school teachers, police officers, firefighters, city planners, and other professionals often share ideas with others who hold similar jobs, because they know that what worked in one community might work in another. Conferences and conventions for people in the same profession are all about sharing what is useful in one context, under the assumption that it will also be useful in another.

Let's consider effective reasoning by analogy and then look at faulty analogies.

The human mind's ability to reason by analogy begins at an early age and continues throughout life. A child may reason, "Camp is just like school—I have to get up early and do what the counselors tell me." A friend may help parents understand a child's jealousy of a new baby by comparing the arrival of a new baby to a spouse bringing home a new mate. An elderly person may complain "This nursing home is like prison—the food is lousy, I have to follow strict rules, and no one comes to visit me."

Reasoning by analogy is useful in two ways:

1. We are able to explain a new or difficult idea, situation, phenomenon, or process by comparing it to a similar idea or process that is more familiar.
2. We are able to give reasons for a conclusion by showing that our idea or program has worked at another time or in another place. We are also able to show that an idea we disapprove of has not worked well in another context.

When we reason by analogy, we assume that since an idea, process, or event is similar in one way to another idea, process, or event that it is also similar in another *significant* way.

Reasoning by analogy is commonly used in argumentation. When we report studies of experiments on animals and draw conclusions on predictions for humans, we are reasoning by analogy.

Example: A researcher may report that when rats are confined to an overcrowded cage, they exhibit antisocial behavior; a conclusion is then drawn about humans, comparing crowded rats to city dwellers. The researcher may imply that crime is a result of overcrowded conditions.

When we look at a specific past event for a clue about what is likely to happen in a similar present situation, we are reasoning by analogy.

Example: Someone may argue, "Prohibition didn't work in the 1920s—people still found a way to make alcohol, and an underground criminal network was supported. In the same way, making drugs illegal today only forces people to get them from pushers at a high price."

When we compare a system in one nation to a system in another, we are reasoning by analogy.

Example: Employees may cite the generous maternity leave policies of European countries to argue for better leave packages in the United States and Canada.

When we compare one condition to another to justify attention to the condition, we are reasoning by analogy.

Example: A lobbyist for a recovery group may claim, "Addiction to shopping is like addiction to drugs; the shopaholic can no more change his behavior than can the drug addict. Therefore, we should spend federal funds on the prevention and cure of shopaholism."

When advertisers compare a product to an experience, they are using an analogy.

Example: "Springsoft fabric softener smells great. It's like hanging your clothes out in the fresh air."

EXERCISE

Purpose: To understand the usefulness of analogies as learning tools.

Although we are considering analogies as they relate to persuasion, analogies are also useful in understanding information. Ask a teacher you respect how he or she has used analogies to explain a difficult process to students. Find two or three examples of these kinds of analogies and share them with the class.

Because analogies are used commonly, we must be careful not to accept them uncritically. The key to an accurate analogy is that *the two things being compared are alike in all significant aspects.* If there are significant differences between the items being compared, then we have a faulty analogy. Sometimes the comparison is easy for a critical thinker to make. Let's consider our Springsoft example.

Similarities:

Both are used in getting clothes dry, and both presumably smell good.

Differences:

Springsoft	*Fresh air*
smell induced by chemicals	smell from fresh air
clothes feel soft	clothes feel rough
recurrent cost involved	one-time clothesline cost
quick when used with dryer	time-consuming

You can see that comparing Springsoft with fresh air is not accurate in all of the dimensions that are significant to a consumer. It would be more accurate to ask consumers to buy Springsoft because it has a nice fragrance and makes clothes feel softer. So why don't advertisers just state the facts?

Advertisers, politicians, teachers, and other advocates usually realize that a powerful picture is worth more than a detailed argument. A swim instructor may know that asking children to put their arms out straight is more effective when she adds "like Superman does." Campaign managers realize that a powerful negative image leveled against an opposing candidate may have greater impact than a reasoned case against him. Likewise, parents who want to feel they are doing the best for their children may respond to the idea of infusing fresh air and sunshine into their clothes, especially since the fresh air and sunshine come in an easy-to-use product.

Faulty analogies occur when we compare one situation or idea to another and disregard significant differences that make this comparison invalid. For example, to compare plans for overcoming racism in the United States to plans that work for the Finnish people would be fallacious: There are very few races in Finland compared to the United States. Or someone might suggest that we look at the low rate of theft in some Middle Eastern countries and adopt a similar prevention plan. The problem is that in those countries, the punishment for stealing is the removal of a hand—that method is not likely to be adopted by American voters and legislators.

Faulty analogies are used frequently when social issues are discussed. You might hear someone claim there is no problem with violence on television or in movies. The person taking this position might say, "I watched cowboy shows all of my life and I turned out just fine." Besides the ambiguity in the term *just fine*, the problem with this reasoning is that Hopalong Cassidy and the Lone Ranger are quite different from the Terminator and Predator. The speaker may or may not be right about the effect of televised violence, but the analogous reasoning does nothing to prove his or her point.

You might note that faulty analogies are often accompanied by a poor understanding of history—i.e., how our current world is different in significant ways from the world of previous generations.

You can often see faulty analogies when one person gives advice to another. For example, if a grandparent tells you that he or she used to walk five miles in the snow to get to school, implying that you or your children should do the same, you would have to consider the difficulty of implementing this plan in a culture where parents are afraid to let their children play in the front yard alone.

Or let's say a friend of yours is advising you about how to prepare for a speech you have to give in a class. He or she might say, "Just relax and don't prepare too many notes. That's what I did and I got an A." That method may work for your friend but may be totally inappropriate for you; you may be the kind of person (like most of us) who needs to have good notes and to practice a speech before giving it to a class.

The biggest problem with people who give advice is their assumption that what worked for them will work for you—a classic case of faulty analogy.

When you see someone supporting a position by comparing one idea, situation, or plan to another, stop and evaluate whether the comparison is valid. If it is, you have a good analogy and a good reason to listen to the speaker. If it is not a valid comparison in some important way, then you have a faulty analogy.

EXERCISE

Purpose: To utilize criteria for evaluating reasoning by analogy.

Consider the following analogies and evaluate their validity. Note similarities that make the analogy useful and persuasive and/or significant differences between what is being compared that make the analogy misleading.

1. This excerpt is from an introduction given by Ted Koppel of ABC's "Nightline" when he did a program on 1992 presidential candidate Ross Perot.

   Koppel: How do you figure the phenomenon of Ross Perot? Why do so many people who know next to nothing about the man seem so enchanted by him? A few years ago, I mulled over the same question with regard to the enormous popularity of Vanna

White. She of "Wheel of Fortune," you ask? The very one. She is, after all, a lovely woman with an engaging manner and a charming smile, and no one, but no one, lights up letters on a board better than she. But that still doesn't explain the depth and breadth of Vanna's popularity. The world is full, after all, of thousands of equally lovely, engaging, and charming women. What is it, then, about Vanna?

And then it struck me. Of all the people on television whose names we know who are not playing somebody else, we probably know less about Vanna, that is, what she thinks and believes, than almost anyone else, and so we can project onto her what we would like her to believe.

So, too, with Ross Perot. He is enjoying the support of conservatives, liberals and moderates precisely because, like Vanna, Ross doesn't go into much detail.[1]

2. Homosexual men and women have traditionally been excluded from the armed forces. In 1992, 29 members of Congress introduced legislation to end this exclusion, and in 1993 President Clinton also proposed lifting this ban. One argument given for changing this exclusionary policy is that gay men and women are a minority group like African-Americans and that no other minority is banned from the military. An argument given for keeping the policy is that separate living quarters would have to be provided to keep straight and gay personnel apart, just as similar policies provide separate quarters for heterosexual men and women.

3. A couple sued a landlord for refusing to rent to them because of their sloppy appearance; they claimed discrimination in the form of "lookism" (prejudice against someone because of how they look). In defending himself, the landlord stated, "You wouldn't hire someone who was out of shape as an employee in a health spa, and you wouldn't want a receptionist for an investment firm who had purple hair. So why should you have to rent an apartment to people who look sloppy?"

Cause-Effect Reasoning and False Cause

When we want to understand why something happens the way it does, we look for causes. We tend to look for causal connections for

---

1   Ted Koppel, "The Unknown Ross Perot," "Nightline," April 23, 1992.

several reasons: First, we seek to eliminate and prevent specific problems that arise for individuals; secondly, we want to resolve general problems that affect large groups of people; and finally, much investigation often is motivated by sheer human curiosity.

On an individual level, we look for causes of problems that arise in daily life. We might seek to understand why our car is making a certain sound, why our checkbook doesn't balance, why our dog seems lethargic, or why we lost a job. If we find a cause, then we hope we will find a cure for our present difficulties.

We also seek causes in order to eliminate *potential* problems: Seat belts and air bags were created as a result of understanding the causes of the kinds of human injury that can occur after the impact of a collision; baby furniture and toys are created or modified based on our understanding of their harmfulness to children; government officials may look at inflationary trends caused by the infusion of more money into the country before they take action to stimulate a failing economy; and premarital counselors can advise engaged couples about the major causes of divorce and help them address important issues before they get married.

Philosophers and scientists have worked to develop theories of cause and effect. The next section will review these theories and then consider common errors in causal reasoning.

HUME'S CONDITIONS FOR CAUSE AND EFFECT

One definition of cause and effect was put forth by the British philosopher David Hume (1711–1776). He reasoned that we are justified in saying that one thing is the cause (x) of an effect (y) if the following three conditions are met:

1. X, the cause, preceded y, the effect, in time.
2. X and y are contiguous (in contact with one another) in time and place.
3. There is a history of (1) and (2); i.e., there is a history of x preceding y and of x and y being related in time and place.

The first condition is clear; if one thing causes another, the cause must come before the effect. But we should also note that sometimes the cause and effect appear to occur at the same time; for example, as soon as I pull the plug on my lamp, the light goes out.

The second condition specifies the need for a relationship in time and space between a cause and an effect. In outbreaks of diseases caused by "sick buildings," a connection is made between workers (often on particular floors) and the onset of the same illness. The reminder that causes and effects must be connected wards against superstition and against unlikely causes.

The third condition helps us to justify a causal effect by pointing to a regular tendency. A florist can reason that every year, on certain holidays, the demand for flowers goes up. A school teacher can chart a tendency for a consistent reduction in math skills over summer vacation. A driver can note which roads are regularly jammed during the week because of rush hour. Conversely, if there is no history of regularity between a particular cause and a particular effect, then a critical thinker should wait for such a trend to surface before accepting an alleged causal connection.

TECHNICAL CAUSATION

Another format for determining causation specifies two different types of conditions between causes and effects.

A **necessary condition** is a condition (state of affairs, thing, process, etc.) that must be present if the effect is present. Equivalently, if the necessary condition is absent, then the effect cannot occur.

One of the necessary conditions of life as we know it is oxygen. Some of the necessary conditions of a fire are oxygen, a flammable material, and a form of ignition. If we know the necessary conditions of an event, then we can *prevent* it from happening. Remove any of the necessary conditions and the effect does not take place. Thus we can speak of a necessary condition as a cause, or one of the causes, of an event.[2]

A **sufficient condition** is a condition (state of affairs, thing, process, etc.) that automatically leads to the production of another event. If the condition is present, the effect will definitely occur. The sufficient condition creates the effect.

Swallowing cyanide is a sufficient condition for death. The difference between a necessary and a sufficient condition is that although a necessary condition must be present, by itself it will not produce the effect. The sufficient condition is "sufficient" by itself to produce the effect. Usually the sufficient condition is really a set of necessary conditions, all of which must be present at the same time and place. For instance, a combustible material, oxygen, and the combustion point are all necessary conditions for a fire. Together all three constitute the sufficient condition for a fire. If we know the sufficient condi-

2   Nicholas Capaldi, *The Art of Deception* (Buffalo: Prometheus Books, 1987), p. 158.

tion of an event, then we can produce it at will. Thus we can speak of a sufficient condition as a cause of an event.[3]

Finding the exact cause of an event or an effect can be very difficult, even in technical matters. We often must look at *multiple causes*, a combination of causes leading to a specific effect. A particular business might be successful because of a *combination* of the needs of the community, the location of the store, and the advertising campaign. A person may die because of a combination of a weak heart and an overexertion in exercise. The weak heart could be further traced back to a family history of heart disease. Taken in combination, these factors may have been sufficient to cause death.

The phenomenon of multiple causes makes it difficult to provide evidence beyond a reasonable doubt in many cases. For example, for years people have tried to sue tobacco companies because, they claim, the tobacco caused them to develop lung cancer. However, despite convincing evidence on the harmfulness of tobacco, people have difficulty proving that tobacco is the *only* cause, sufficient by itself, for the development of lung cancer. Lawyers for the tobacco companies can argue that there are, in any given case, other possible causes for a person's susceptibility to lung cancer and that other people who smoke a similar amount of tobacco have not contracted the disease.

The new practice of allowing juries to assign a portion of blame for an injury to the plaintiff and a portion to the defendant is a recognition of the difficulty of determining the precise cause of a problem. In one recent case, a male psychologist was accused of causing pain, suffering, and suicidal tendencies in a female patient with whom he had had sexual relations. The psychologist admitted to having had sex with his patient, but he produced explicit love letters she had sent to him. In addition, his attorneys presented information about the patient's previous sexual history; the psychologist, as defendant, was not required to reveal details of his own sexual history. As a result of the evidence presented by the defense, the jury softened the verdict by assigning 18 percent of the blame to the patient and 82 percent of the blame to the psychologist. They reasoned that, although he had broken his professional ethics, she had contributed to that breakdown.

In searching for causes, we should also consider the notion of an *immediate* or situational cause of a problem. We can ask, "What is the factor that makes the difference between an event happening or not happening?" (In folk wisdom, this might be expressed as "the straw that broke the camel's back.")

---

3   Ibid.

The immediate cause is preceded by other factors that led up to the effect. If someone causes an accident because of driving drunk after a party, we have the immediate cause of the collision. However, if no liquor had been served at the party, the accident probably would not have happened, or if the driver's father or mother had not been an alcoholic, the driver might not have been predisposed to drink. The driver's predisposition to drink would be termed a *remote* cause of the accident. In many cases, critical thinkers have to ask the question, "Where do we draw the line in our search for causes?"

EXERCISE

Purpose: To distinguish immediate from remote causes of an event or effect.

1. Do some research on a social or national event and try to isolate the causes, both immediate and remote, of this event. For example, if you researched the United States' entry into World War II, you would go beyond the attack on Pearl Harbor, as far back as World War I to see all the influences that both compelled and restrained U.S. involvement. Another example would be the rioting in Los Angeles in 1992 (which is discussed in an article at the end of this chapter). You might find the immediate cause of the rioting to be the verdict acquitting the police officers of beating Rodney King; however, in your research you would also discover deeper, although less immediate, causes for these events.

2. Study the arguments used by prosecution or defense attorneys in a trial that attempts to prove a cause-effect relationship between events. Examples would be trials against manufacturers of faulty products, such as breast implants or dangerous toys, or trials in which one person claims damage done to them by another person or by a company, such as complaints about the effects of second-hand cigarette smoke or video display terminals. Investigative news programs, such as "Frontline," "60 Minutes," "48 Hours" and "20/20" often feature stories about such trials, and they make transcripts of their programs available to the public.

In looking at the statements made by the attorneys for both the prosecution and the defense, find examples of arguments claiming or denying a cause-effect relationship. Summarize these arguments and comment on their persuasiveness both to the jury and to you as a critical thinker.

MILL'S ANALYSIS OF CAUSE AND EFFECT

Another British philosopher, John Stuart Mill (1806–1873) formulated several specific methods (which he called *canons*) to help us systematically discover causes. Let's look at two of these methods, the method of difference and the method of agreement (or similarity).

Method of Difference

Using this method, the cause is found by noting that the only difference between the event or effect (called y) happening or not happening is whether one element—x—is present.

Let's say a family of four goes to Chicken King for lunch. Dad orders the fried chicken, while Mom and the kids have nuggets. All of them order root beer to drink. That night, Dad wakes up with painful cramps and stays up most of the night dealing with an upset stomach. At this point, Dad concludes that he probably got sick from the fried chicken, since it was the only thing he had that the rest of the family did not have. The fried chicken is the element (x) that caused the upset stomach (y).

If a patient reports to a psychologist that he is depressed, he might be asked to keep a journal, detailing the times of most and least depression. If the psychologist discovers the most and highest depression (y) occurring on Sunday night and Monday morning, then he or she might conclude that the depression is related to a return to work (x) after the weekend. Although the return to work may not turn out to be the cause, it provides a useful avenue of inquiry.

A famous example of looking for a difference occurred when Edward Jenner, a 19th-century British physician, tried to find a cure for small pox. He discovered that there was a group of people who rarely got the disease—dairy maids. What was the difference between the dairy maids and the larger population?

On further investigation, Jenner discovered that most of the dairy maids had had cow pox, which is similar to small pox but not usually deadly to human beings. Because they had had cow pox, they were immune to the small pox; the cow pox had "vaccinated" them against small pox. So cow pox (x) caused the positive effect (y) of immunization from the illness. From this discovery, Jenner came upon the notion of vaccinating people against small pox.

Method of Agreement

Using this method, the cause is found by noting that x is the only factor always present when y (the problem or the good effect) occurs; therefore, x causes y.

Let's look at our family example again. This time, the family gets up and has plain bagels and cream cheese for breakfast. They then go to a carnival and all share a pizza for lunch. Then, after a few hours, the children have some cotton candy. Later that night, both of the children develop upset stomachs. Using the method of agreement, the parents conclude that since both children had cotton candy, cotton candy is the cause of the problem.

USING DIFFERENCE AND SIMILARITY TOGETHER TO DETERMINE CAUSE

Often, we are able to use both the method of agreement (similarity) and the method of difference together. In our previous example about the Chicken King incident, let's imagine that the next day, while Dad sleeps in, Mom goes outside to do some yard work. She chats with a passing neighbor and tells how her husband got an upset stomach, which she suspects came from his meal at Chicken King. The neighbor relates how, several days ago, she also got sick from eating the same meal, whereas her children, who had nuggets, were OK. In this case, x is the only difference between what Dad ate and what Mom and the kids ate. X is also the only similarity among the people in the neighborhood who got sick.

If a patient is having allergic reactions, a doctor may begin a systematic search for the causes of the ailment. The patient might be told to stop eating food typically involved in allergies (for example, wheat, sugar, and dairy products). Then, after a period of time, the suspected allergens are introduced one at a time; if the allergic reactions reoccur, the patient is advised to eliminate the food that triggered the reactions. If the patient continues to eliminate this food and finds that the allergic reactions are gone, then the process of reasoning from evidence to a cause has been successful in this case. X is the only food that caused the reaction (y); and in every case in which x is eaten, the reaction occurs.

False Cause

Most of us use a form of the methods we have discussed when we encounter a difficulty; many professionals also use these methods to solve problems. However, it is easy to make errors if we use these methods uncritically, especially when the human element is involved: It is much easier to zero in on a cause of a blown fuse or an upset stomach than it is to determine what causes a person to go "over the edge." Because people are very complicated, we can't easily find the causes of human difficulties or resolve some of them beyond a reasonable doubt. Consider the phenomenon of copycat crimes, where a criminal copies someone else's modus operandi in order to shift the blame to the other criminal. How do we really know the same criminal committed two crimes unless we have more information with which to make a judgment?

In assigning causation, some common errors are made in the following ways:

1. The sample size is too small. Whenever we have a small sample, we run the risk of making hasty generalizations. In the example involving Dad, the neighbor, and the fried chicken, we don't really have enough sick people to draw a firm conclusion (one that would stand up in court). Maybe Dad got sick from the chicken, but the neighbor got sick from a new medication she was taking.

2. There may be other probable causes to consider. In the case of Dad's sickness, we would also need to consider whether both Dad and the neighbor ate too much or whether both Dad and the neighbor caught a virus that was going around the neighborhood. The virus alone, or the virus in combination with the chicken, could have caused the illness.

3. Correlation is taken to be causation. Because two events are contiguous (linked in time and place, so that the first and second of Hume's conditions are met), we may jump to the conclusion that the first event caused the second event. Dad's and the neighbor's illnesses are correlated with eating the chicken. However, if we find that other people ate the fried chicken and remained healthy, then the fried chicken cannot be the only—the *sufficient*—factor causing the stomach upset; the correlation cannot be considered causation.

Closely related to the error of assuming causation with correlation is the fallacy known as **false cause** or *post hoc ergo procter hoc*. The

Latin translates to "after this, therefore because of this," and refers to the practice of stating that because one event followed another, the first event caused the second event. As we have seen, cause-effect reasoning is sometimes relevant and valid; it is used extensively in psychology (a person may have a fear of abandonment because he or she was abandoned as a child), history (Jewish people became a merchant class in parts of Europe because they were not allowed to purchase land), business (sales have increased since we've been using the new advertising campaign), medicine (you are tired and run down because of low blood sugar), politics (she had 70 percent of the votes and lost 50 percent after the last-minute smear campaign of her opponent), and economics (the economy began to recover when interest rates were lowered).

In all the cases listed above, research and reasoning could prove that one event came after another and that, in all probability, the first event caused the second event. The fallacy of post hoc occurs when there is no real proof that one event *caused* another event; there is only evidence that one event came *after* another event.

The clearest example of post hoc occurs in superstition. Superstitious thinking is non-critical thinking. A superstitious person may reason fallaciously, "I got fired because I walked under that ladder yesterday," or "The reason I failed the test is because a black cat crossed my path right before I got to class." What's especially dangerous about superstitious thinking is that if someone really believes they are somehow "cursed," they may act as if they are cursed and make the curse come true because of their expectations.

However, the post hoc fallacy is more subtle than mere superstition; it consists of reasons unsupported by evidence. For example, politicians are fond of blaming budget deficits and unemployment rates on their predecessors ("I didn't get us into this mess—the previous administration did"). The problem with this reasoning is that it ignores the more complicated factors needing to be understood to change the current situation for the better. The blaming process is often at the root of a post hoc fallacy and it stops constructive action that could alleviate a problem.

Here are some examples of post hoc fallacies based on shifting the blame and therefore not taking responsibility:

> "The reason our team lost is because we weren't playing at home."
>
> "I failed the class because the teacher hated me."

"I saw how you put your television set in your car. The reason it doesn't work is that it was poorly placed in your car after you left our repair shop."

"I ate three pieces of pie at Joanne's house because I didn't want to hurt her mother's feelings."

"I can't find my soccer ball because a large green and brown monster came and ate it while I was sleeping." (Who says small children can't use the reasoning process?)

Although many post hocs are based on blame and use rationalization (why is it so hard for us to admit error?), some are based on a lack of information to substantiate a valid reason—i.e., we don't know the cause of a particular problem.

In our frustration to find reasons and therefore solutions or explanations for situations, we may rush to assign blame without fair and careful analysis. Then we are in trouble, because we are addressing surface and not deeper causes for problems.

For example, if we say that homelessness is usually the result of a lack of desire to work (false cause in most cases), then we look for a solution to fit the false cause. So homeless people are given jobs, training, and motivational lectures. A year later, we still have the basic problem of the homeless, although some individuals have been helped. We would do better to get at the root causes and the diverse causes of social problems, rather than to try to find quick fixes to what may not be the complete problem.

For example, some of the homeless may be mentally unfit for employment or seminars; some may be displaced homemakers who would rather be in the parks with their children than shuffled off to training; some may be perfectly happy in a homeless condition, and then cities need to decide what to do about them; and some may welcome job training but find it difficult to get hired. Problems are complex and a single cause usually doesn't address them accurately.

EXERCISE

Purpose: To discover multiple causes for a given phenomenon.

1. Look at the problem of drug abuse in our culture and answer the following questions: What are some of the simplistic (post hoc) reasons given for the problem? What might be some of the deeper

causes of this problem, and what solutions are implied by these causes?

2. If you completed the research suggested at the end of Chapter 4 concerning a social, national, or international problem, do a short paper or speech on the causes of this problem. Take a position on which causes were immediate, which remote, which sufficient, and which necessary for the problem to develop. If some analysts of your problem commit the fallacy of assigning a false cause, say how. Support your position with evidence.

Attacking the Person

Ad hominem is a Latin term meaning "to the man" or attacking the person. Ad hominem occurs when a person is attacked on a personal quality that is irrelevant to the issue. For example, someone might say that a woman is not qualified for a position on a city council because she's a homemaker, or that an actor has no right to take a position about environmental issues.

In these cases, the people should not be judged because of their professional affiliations: A homemaker could do as well as anyone else in city government, and an actor is also a citizen who has the right to speak out (even if he or she does have the advantage of a larger audience than the average person).

Many logicians believe that ad hominem is always a diversionary tactic. However, there are times when attacking the person is valid, because the area of attack is very important to the position the person is taking. For example, it is relevant to say that you won't vote for someone for class treasurer (or Congress) because you know he can't balance his checkbook and has overspent his credit cards.

It is relevant to refuse to vote for a certain person to be a deacon in your church if he is continually gossiping about other church members. It is relevant to refuse to vote for a candidate who promises to care about the homeless but who lacks a record of supporting legislation aimed at helping homeless citizens. In these cases, personal character *is* relevant to the position being sought.

It is hard to determine the relevance of some aspects of personal character. For example, is it valid to refuse to vote for a man or woman because he or she is known to have had extramarital affairs? Interestingly, in one famous case, that of Gary Hart running for the

Democratic presidential candidacy in 1988, many claimed they wouldn't support him, not because he was sexually immoral, but because he was so indiscreet as to be caught with another woman while in the midst of campaigning. The reader can decipher what this says about our culture and about ad hominem reasoning!

If someone attacks the character of another person, ask yourself, "Is the character of the person an important part of the issue?" If not, you have an ad hominem fallacy.

Attacking a person is valid when that person is claiming to be an authority in an area where he has no real expertise. For example, someone may make claims about archeological finds when he does not have the proper background to evaluate any discoveries in the field of archeology. For further examples of fallacious appeals to authority, see the section on expert testimony in Chapter 5.

EXERCISE

Purpose: To determine if there are cases in which personal qualities are relevant reasons for rejecting political candidates.

List the elements of personal character that are important for a President or congressional representative. What in a candidate's background, if anything, would prevent you from voting for him or her? Are there things about a person that would bother you if they had occurred recently, but you would overlook if they occurred in his or her past? How far back into someone's background would you look when making your voting decision?

The Slippery Slope

Slippery slope refers to the domino effect: If you push one domino in a pattern, then all the others will fall. A slippery slope argument states that if one event occurs, then others will follow, usually in an uncontrollable way. If you think about it, any domino effect argument is based on a prediction about the future and is therefore based on inferences and interpretations. Still, this form of reasoning can be valid, even when opponents call it a slippery slope, if the interpretations are soundly based on existing facts and reasonable probabilities.

For example, in the 1970s people used to discredit the possibility of a domino effect in Southeast Asia; they believed if the United States left Vietnam, then not only Vietnam but also Cambodia would fall to the Communists. This concern proved to be valid.

When school-based health clinics were introduced, some parents complained that this was the first step in birth control devices being distributed by schools. This argument, which was dismissed as a slippery slope argument, did prove to be valid. Many school-based health clinics now offer birth control and reproductive counseling.

There are also cases in which an individual is refused a reasonable privilege because it would probably call for the privilege to be extended to too many others. For example, let's say you are a day late for paying your auto registration. The clerk would probably still have to charge you a penalty because "If I make an exception for you, I would need to make an exception for everyone."

The slippery slope fallacy occurs when the consequences of a single act are predicted and not substantiated by evidence. For example, many people fight the idea of making tobacco advertisements illegal despite overwhelming evidence concerning the harmfulness of this substance. The slippery slope argument given is that if tobacco advertising is made illegal because tobacco hurts people, then pretty soon advertising for eggs and milk would be curtailed because of their cholesterol content.

The problem with this argument is that eggs and milk are not analogous to tobacco; although there is a high cholesterol content in these products, they are also extremely nutritious in other ways, whereas no nutritional or health value has been found for tobacco. Therefore, it's not likely that advertisements for eggs or other healthy products would be disallowed just because tobacco ads would be.

Another example of the use of the slippery slope fallacy concerned Gregory K., a severely abused child in Florida who successfully sued to "divorce" his parents so that he could live with his foster family who wanted to adopt him. The boy's parents were divorced, the father was an abusive alcoholic, and the mother was so neglectful of the child that he had been placed in foster homes for several years. Lawyers for the boy feared for his life should he return to this environment. Lawyers for the state social workers, however, claimed that allowing a boy in this circumstance to sue his parents could lead to other children suing to leave their parents because they were denied the latest style of shoes or video games. As one writer stated in revealing the fallacious nature of this argument:

If the lawyers really believe that, it doesn't say much for their own profession. Are there attorneys who would handle some brat's Ninja Turtle-deprivation case? Not likely, especially if the kid didn't have a fat retainer fee in his piggy bank. And are the lawyers saying there are judges who would take a frivolous suit seriously, and not toss it out as nonsense?

No, if the Florida boy wins his case what we'll probably see are other suits filed by kids who will be saying that they have had it with parents who are dope heads, drunks, sadists; parents who don't know how to take care of children and are unwilling or incapable of learning. And that they've had it with social service agencies that don't provide real social services.[4]

There are also examples in personal communication in which the slippery slope fallacy occurs. If you ask for a day off work to take your sick dog to the vet and your employer says, "I can't give you the day off because then everyone would want the day off," you have probably encountered this fallacy. Not everyone is going to want the day off, and most people would not take advantage of your situation to ask for similar time off. Your need for time off is not based on negligence (as is the case with people who pay bills late and are penalized); your need is based on an emergency.

SKILL

Recognize when reasons given to justify a conclusion are not sufficient.

Fallacies that Mislead

To this point, we have examined errors that occur when the reasons given for a particular conclusion do not clearly support the conclusion. The second type of fallacies are those characterized by reasons that lead the listener away from the real issue. Common examples of this type of fallacy are **red herrings, ad populum, appeal to tradition, false dilemma,** and **begging the question.**

---

4   Mike Royko, "When Mother and Father Don't Know Best," *This World*, May 3, 1992, p. 4.

The Red Herring

The **red herring** fallacy gets its name from the old practice of drawing a herring—a smoked fish—across a trail to distract hunting dogs from following the trail. In this manner, the hounds were led away from finding their prey; this technique has been used by criminals who didn't want to be found and had access to smoked fish. Similarly, when someone can distract your attention by getting you on the defense about an issue other than the one under discussion, that person has taken you off track of the real, or original, issue.

Children are particularly skillful at using red herrings; it's one of their best defense mechanisms against parental demands.

Example

Mother:	Get that sharp stick out of here!
Child:	That's not a stick. It's a laser beam. I need it to perform surgery on some space aliens.

Or,

Father:	Joey, it's time to brush your teeth and get in bed.
Joey:	You didn't tell that to Suzy.
Father:	(getting off track) Suzy's older than you.
Joey:	But I'm taller than she is.

If this child is successful, he will have gained extra time, and he might even be able to stall long enough for his parent to forget what time it is!

What a child does purely in the pursuit of having his way, he may learn to do as an adult in defense of a larger cause.

Example

When 1992 presidential candidate H. Ross Perot was first in the race, he was questioned at a conference of newspaper editors. *Philadelphia Inquirer* columnist Acel Moore wanted specific answers about Perot's proposals concerning the drug problem in the United States.

Acel Moore:	Let this audience know. I haven't heard it.
Mr. Perot:	Do we have to be rude and adversarial? Can't we just talk?

> *Mr. Moore:*   If you're going to be a candidate for the President of the United States, I think you should have to go through that process. And part of the process is being asked questions of a very specific nature, and coming forth with some responses.[5]

Or, consider this fictional example:

> *Reporter:*   Mr. Secretary, why won't the President admit that he wrote those memos with his signature on them?
>
> *Secretary:*   Why are you reporters always attacking this president and defending his opponents?

If the secretary can get the reporters to defend themselves, they will have been led away from the issue of whether the President wrote the memos. Red herrings serve to move the dialogue away from an uncomfortable topic to a topic that can be more easily discussed.

Ad Populum: Jumping on the Bandwagon

The **ad populum fallacy** is another one we seem to learn from early childhood. This fallacy consists of a false appeal to the authority of "everyone." A course of action should be taken or an idea should be supported because "everyone" is doing it or believes it.

American society has been said to produce individuals who are *other-directed*, which means the opinions and approval of others are important motivating factors for Americans. (The other-directed person is contrasted with the individual who is inner-directed and derives his motivation and approval mostly from internalized sources.)[6] Some of our societal cliches reveal this tendency, such as "keeping up with the Joneses," "the in-crowd," or "the in thing to do," or simply "everybody's doing it."

Advertisers capitalize on our tendency to jump on the bandwagon and follow the crowd with such slogans as "Coke is it," "The Pepsi generation," and "He's a pepper, she's a pepper, be a pepper." Sometimes advertisers don't even use words; they just show large numbers of people who are happily using their products. If you stop and think

---

5   Ted Koppel, "The Unknown Ross Perot," "Nightline," April 23, 1992.

6   David Riesman, *The Lonely Crowd* (New Haven: Yale University Press, 1950), pp. 19–26.

4-5   © 1985 Universal Press Syndicate   Larson

The Far Side by Gary Larson

about these "reasons" for buying products, they seem silly. So why do advertisers continue to use them? Because they work; many people want to identify with the "right" products, to be cool and be accepted.

Examples

> "Join the millions of satisfied customers who have purchased a Crocodile pick-up. What are you waiting for?"

> "That's not fair. All the other kids get to go to the Dismembered Junkies concert!"

> "Hey, America: Introducing your new turkey stuffing mix!"

Appeal to Tradition: "We've Always Done It This Way"

Closely related in its logic to the ad populum fallacy is the **appeal to tradition**, which occurs when a belief or action is supported simply because it conforms to traditional ideas or practices. In both ad populum and appeal to tradition, the conclusions of the speakers or writers may be fine, but the reasons are not relevant to the conclusions. You should drink Pepsi or Coke because you like the taste but not because "everyone is drinking it." Similarly, you may not want to change the way you are doing something because it works well for you, not because it has always been done that way; the folk wisdom on that is "if it ain't broke, don't fix it."

Yet, there are times for a reasonable discussion about whether something should be done a different way or with a different person. In such cases, it is not useful to say, "We need to do it this way because we've always done it this way." That statement is an appeal to tradition that short-circuits useful dialogue or needed change.

Examples

"Vote for Smith. We've always had a member of the Smith family in our state legislature."

"All the men in our family are lawyers; you will be too."

"Our workers have always been happy working 9 to 5; there's no need to change that schedule."

Traditions that are held by families, organizations, and nations are wonderful in their ability to bind us together and give us a sense of belonging. These traditions are not what we are suggesting when we discuss "appeal to tradition" as a fallacy. In fact, in our new and improved society, we might note the fallacy of "appeal to change" or "appeal to the novel."

Sometimes a newly elected candidate or manager in a corporation may make changes without considering the reasons why a particular system is in place. Often, non-incumbents campaign on the idea that we need change, but they don't tell us what that change will involve, or how the change will be an improvement over the current situation. Neither tradition nor novelty is an adequate reason to vote for a candidate, to support legislation, or to buy a product.

As noted by the above examples, the fallacious appeal to tradition gives an irrelevant and distracting reason for an opinion. It may very well be that the company mentioned in the last example should not change their working hours or create flex-time for their employees; they may find they need all the workers available at the same time. However, to offer "we've always done it this way" as a reason does nothing to engender a meaningful discussion of the possibilities of useful change, and in fact, obscures the issue.

The False Dilemma

Another error in reasoning, common in both personal and political communication, is the **false dilemma** or the **either-or fallacy**. When someone makes this error, he or she polarizes a situation by presenting only two alternatives, at two extremes of the spectrum of possibilities. Any other reasonable possibilities besides these two extremes are left out of the statement, and the careless listener may believe that the issue is limited to the two choices given.

Examples

"Do you want four more years of overspending and poor priorities, or do you want four years of prosperity and sensible spending?"

(Note: You may be able to prove that the incumbent candidate can be fairly criticized on his spending priorities, but does that mean the only alternative is the new candidate or that the new candidate will be as flawless as is implied?)

"Do you want to give your family the same, boring potatoes for dinner tonight, or do you want to give them the exciting taste of Instant Stuffing?"

"Sure, you can go ahead and date Terry and end up with a broken heart and bad memories; but wouldn't it be better to go out with me since I know how to treat you right and show you a good time?"

"If you don't go to college and make something of yourself, you'll end up as an unhappy street person."

The false dilemma leads a listener away from a reasonable consideration of the complex problems involved in most decision-making

Hagar the Horrible by Chris Browne
Reprinted with special permission of King Features Syndicate.

situations and presents one conclusion as perfect while the other is seen as disastrous.

This is a dangerous fallacy because it leads us to simplistic solutions, and it encourages us to put our allegiance to a person or idea above a fair consideration of a solution that would address all concerns.

The error of false dilemma is appealing to us for two reasons:

- We like to think solutions are clear-cut and simple; a simple solution saves us time and effort in understanding all the complexities of a situation.
- Our language encourages polarized thinking by including few words to describe a middle ground between extremes. Look at this list:

Beautiful	Ugly
Strong	Weak
Extroverted	Introverted
Brave	Cowardly
Happy	Sad

Although we have words that describe the extremes (poles) of a state of being, we have no words describing a middle ground. To put yourself in the middle of these adjectives, you have to say "sort of happy," "somewhat happy," "average," or "medium."

Since our language is polarized, our thinking tends to be polarized if we don't make the effort to be more accurate. In our statistically oriented culture, we tend to use numbers to let us know where things stand on a polarized continuum. We might say "On a scale of 1 to 10, how happy are you with our relationship?" or "On a scale of 1 to 10, how close are we to closing this deal?" We use numbers to fill in where words are lacking.

As a critical thinker, you can tell someone using a false dilemma that you see the situation as more complex than it is being described. You can then draw attention back to the issues, by asking questions such as "What specific changes does your candidate propose to make if she is elected?" or "What is so good about Instant Stuffing?"

Begging the Question

The fallacy of **begging the question** is one of the more subtle ways a speaker or writer distracts attention from an issue. Begging the question takes place in two ways:

1.   The speaker asks you to prove that his or his belief is not correct. Instead of giving reasons for his conclusion, he places the burden of proof on the listener or on the person he is debating. For example:

> "How do you know I can't do psychic surgery?"
>
> "Show me that space aliens don't exist!"
>
> "Why do you think they call it Close-up?"
>
> "Why wouldn't you call 1-800-DENTIST?"

Don't be trapped into proving someone else's conclusion. It's hard enough to prove your own!

2.   The second way a person can beg the question is by building on an unproven assumption in his or her argument as if it is a given fact. The classic example is: "Have you stopped beating your wife?" This question *assumes* the husband has beaten his wife. Notice how there is no way to answer this question with a "yes" or "no" without admitting that the speaker's assumption is correct.

Other examples are:

> "Why are you always so defensive?"
>
> "How can you vote for a dump site that is going to destroy the environment?"
>
> "Why are you supporting a team that is going to lose the Super Bowl?"

Begging the question does not always mean that a question is asked. A person can beg the question as he gives reasons to support his conclusions. For example, a speaker might say:

> Since legalizing drugs would reduce the crime rate, we have to consider where our legislative priorities are.

Can you see that the speaker here has made the assumption (interpretation, inference, guess) that the crime rate would be reduced if drugs are legalized and then has moved on to his next point? It could be that the legalization of drugs *would* reduce crime, but that possibility has to be proven before it can be used as a reason. (Many of the examples of basic assumptions given in Chapter 3 are also examples of begging the question.)

Begging the question is also called *circular reasoning*:

If it's on television, it has to be a good show, because only good shows get on television.

The speaker in this example is using the assumption that only good shows get on television as proof that a particular show is good. The assumption that only good shows get on television has not been proven.

SKILL

Recognize reasons that are irrelevant and distract from the conclusion.

STOP AND THINK

You may find it hard to categorize errors in reasoning under one label or another; some speakers manage to use a whole group of fallacies at once!

Example

Everyone knows the governor is unreliable; if we keep trusting him not to raise taxes, we could all be in debt by next year.

This statement could be an example of begging the question, since the speaker reasons from an unproven assumption that the governor is unreliable. It could also be ad populum, because the speaker uses the phrase "everyone knows" to support his claim. It also could be seen as ad hominem, an attack on the character of a person that is unconnected to an issue. Finally, it could be called a slippery slope argument, because the speaker predicts catastrophic results from the action of trusting the governor.

The bad news is that speakers and writers who are not careful in their reasoning may lump several errors together and leave you to wade through the mess! The good news is that you don't need to be obsessed with finding the exact title of a fallacy and attacking your opponent with it. You only need to see that there are reasons people give to justify their conclusions that are insufficient or irrelevant. The labels we give to the reasoning errors are useful only in helping us define and avoid inadequate and faulty support for our conclusions. These labels also provide guideposts for evaluating and refuting the reasons others give.

EXERCISE

Purpose: To practice isolating errors in reasoning; to notice overlap in categories of fallacies.

1. Find errors in reasoning in magazine, newspaper, or television advertisements, or in letters to the editor. You may discover that a particular inadequate reason may fit the description of several fallacies. Share the errors you find with your class.

2. There are other common fallacies in reasoning. Find examples of other types of fallacies that are not listed in this chapter (from other instructors or textbooks). Explain these to your class.

3. In a class group, offer two examples of each of the fallacies. Then, as a class, play the game explained below called "What's My Fallacy?"

What's My Fallacy?
FALLACIES INVOLVED

Faulty Analogy   Red Herring
Post Hoc (False Cause)   Appeal to Tradition
Begging the Question   Slippery Slope
Either-Or (False Dilemma)   Ad Populum
Ad Hominem (Attacking the Person)

GAME RULES

Object of the game: To accumulate points by correctly guessing the fallacies of the other teams.

   Form class teams of 3–6 persons each.

   Each team should put 18 fallacies (2 for each category) in random order on paper or cards; this step may be done in groups during class, or the team can assign several fallacies to each member to do at home. These fallacies should be no more than a few sentences. For example, a team might say, "How can you vote for him for student body president—he's a vegetarian!" This would obviously be an instance of attacking the person rather than his policies.

Each team needs: 1 reader, 1 scorekeeper, 1–2 referees.

SCORING

Each team must have 18 errors in reasoning to read to the other teams.

The lead team (each team is the lead team when they stand in front of the class to read their list of fallacies) earns 1 point for each appropriate example and loses 1 point for each inappropriate example.

Guessing teams win 2 points for each correct answer and lose 1 point for each wrong answer.

In order to get 2 full points for a right answer, the guessing team must be recognized by the referee of the lead team and say why the fallacy was chosen. The answer must satisfy the lead team and the instructor. Instructor may award 1 point for a close answer.

Your instructor may decide to award points toward a grade for this exercise, or just to use the game to help you practice recognizing fallacies.

In most classes, an interesting discussion of what distinguishes one fallacy from another will occur. This discussion will help you to recognize fallacious reasoning more easily.

Articles for Discussion

"We Mustn't Open Drug-Use Floodgate"

by Dan Boatwright
Contra Costa Times, December 10, 1989

Hometown: Concord, California

Occupation/credentials: State senator, chairman of Senate Committee on Bonded Indebtedness, member of Joint Committee on Prison Construction: former assemblyman and member of Legislature since 1972; former mayor of Concord; former deputy district attorney in Contra Costa County.

Education: Bachelor's degree in political science and law degree from UC–Berkeley, attended Vallejo Junior College.

Can you imagine walking into the local market with your children and seeing packages of cocaine marketed alongside cereal? How about grocery stores offering coupons—"Save $1 on your next quarter gram of nose candy!" Or picture drug manufacturers and distributors offering promotional prizes—"Enter our sweepstakes and win two weeks in Bogota!"

How about the corner crack cocaine peddler telling his customer, "That's $10, plus 73 cents tax. The county road tax and special earthquake tax have knocked the price up a little."

Is this the kind of society we might have if drugs were legalized? I don't know. But I do know I'm not anxious to increase drug usage, and legalizing drugs will do just that.

Frankly, it continues to amaze me that some people argue that we ought to legalize drugs at least for people who would "register" as drug users, and use the taxes to finance treatment programs. It makes me wonder what they have been smoking.

When methadone (a heroin substitute) was legalized in Great Britain, the heroin problem was not curtailed. Instead, they now have methadone addicts in addition to their heroin junkies.

Does anyone really believe that the legalization of drugs will take the profits out of the hands of drug traffickers, funneling them instead into drug prevention and treatment?

Are we to assume that people who wish to use drugs would "register" as drug users? (I'm sure an employer would love to know if he or she had a "registered user" on the payroll!) And those who didn't register—can we assume they wouldn't make any attempt to buy drugs? Of course not.

And, once drugs have been legalized, do you think we can count on producers to pay state and federal taxes, warehouses to remit their property taxes and street-corner dealers to forward sales taxes?

Even in a simplistic world, the legalization of drugs doesn't make sense. It will cause consumption to go way up. In 1980, West Virginia allowed table wine to be sold in grocery stores rather than state liquor stores. During the first year, wine sales increased by 700 percent.

In fact, every state that has changed policies to make liquor more accessible has experienced a huge increase in consumption. What makes any rational person think the same increase wouldn't hold true for drugs?

The National Institute on Drug Abuse estimates that 14.5 million, or 7 percent of the over-12 population, uses illicit drugs. Even if we make a conservative estimate of a 300 percent increase in consumption under legalization, it would mean that more than 20 percent of our population would be drug users. What would this mean for society? It could mean more car wrecks because of stoned drivers, more spousal abuse and child neglect by addicted parents, more accidents on the job, more babies born addicted to drugs, more deaths from drug overdoses, and more cases of AIDS from heroin users sharing needles.

It would also mean that more of society's resources would go into rehabilitation for addicts, new health programs and lost job productivity.

The Research Triangle Institute of North Carolina estimated in 1988 that the national cost of drug abuse is $100 billion. Approximately 30 percent of this amount, $30 billion, is spent on law enforcement.

Even if enforcement costs were saved by legalization, it is estimated that the doubling or tripling of the other social costs would still bring the price up to $140 billion to $210 billion.

Drug legalization won't lessen our crime problems. Organized crime and black markets will not disappear, nor will other problems such as prostitution or theft as a means to get drug money. In fact, crimes like reckless driving and abuse would surely increase,

Now is not the time to back down, especially since drug trafficking has been shifting toward the West.

Passage of the Crime Victim's Justice Reform Initiative on the June ballot will result in a more efficient, speedier criminal process, and will enable us to get convicted drug dealers into prison sooner. Longer prison terms will keep them off our streets. Confiscation of their personal property will deny them some of the tools of their trade.

We need to use all of our energies right now to fight drugs. We shouldn't be diverting our energies into conjuring up methods of legalization.

Progress has been made. Drug-awareness programs in the 1980s have helped to bring about a decrease in the number of people using drugs. After spending years trying to convince our youngsters to "say no" to drugs, it would be devastating to suddenly tell them "it's OK after all."

I've personally seen too many victims of drugs. I don't care to hear another innocent infant, born to a drug-addicted mother, cry helplessly in the midst of a heroin withdrawal.

I don't want my children's children to grow up in a society where harmful drugs are marketed like candy. I don't think you do either.

Reprinted by permission of the author.

"Prohibition Only Worsens Drug Woes"

by Dr. Tod Mikuriya
Contra Costa Times, December 10, 1989

Hometown: Berkeley, California

Occupation/credentials: Psychiatrist with 22 years of East Bay practice; advisory board member, National Organization for the Reform of Marijuana Laws; member, California Society for the Treatment of

Alcoholism and Other Drug Dependencies; author of numerous papers on drug policy.

Education: Bachelor's degree from Reed College, Portland, Ore; medical degree from Temple University, Philadelphia.

In the heat of the first "drug war"—Prohibition against alcohol in the early 1920s—the New York district Prohibition commissioner and the district director of the Treasury Department extended this prohibition to physicians. They then declared drug addiction to be a moral defect, not a disease.

This enforcement initiative, which started out as an informal directive, was then codified into laws through the efforts of prohibitionists.

Federal and state laws now preclude the prescription of narcotics or cocaine to addicts in the "good-faith practice of medicine."

Since the early 1920s, hundreds of physicians have been sent to jail for following their belief in the Aesculapian duty to relieve their patients' pain.

The pre-emption of control over narcotic addiction by police and prosecutors has created the current crisis in dealing with illegal drugs. These efforts have clearly failed.

Defining drug abuse as a moral transgression and equating illegal drug use with drug abuse have set in motion coercive policies and a giant underground economy. Enforcement-corrections expenditures are escalating with dubious results. Treatment and prevention remain largely unavailable.

The definition of drug abuse as a matter of right and wrong precludes the prioritization of drug-control policy. Low-danger marijuana is treated the same as crack cocaine or heroin by the law.

Drug Enforcement Administration agents are now tracking down purchasers of halide lamps, used for growing marijuana, and busting nursery-supply stores that allegedly cater to growers.

Drug prohibitionists, while voluble on punishment and demonology, become tongue-tied when the discussion turns to ways to pay for jails, prisons, probation and police. On treatment funding for the nine out of 10 drug abusers asking for help, they are positively mute.

The toxic side-effects of invasive, statist activities are embodied in lawyer-drug czar William Bennett, who recently told the American Medical Association and the American Bar Association to demonstrate their leadership by submitting their members to random drug testing.

His other proposals, including shock prison camps, informers and the publication of arrestees' names, are perverse products of the moral model of drug abuse.

Already, guidelines are being implemented to subject all employees in any institutions receiving $25,000 or more from the federal government to random drug testing in hopes of guaranteeing drug-free work places.

Unfortunately, no provision is made for mandating or funding treatment, causing a source of further harm from these policies.

The prohibitionists have not figured out what to do about the homelessness and dependence on public assistance resulting from these punitive policies.

It is time for the AMA and the ABA to convene a joint study committee for the revision of laws to permit medicalization of drug-abuse problems, and to make a serious commitment to treatment and prevention.

Legalizing drugs in order to fund drug-abuse treatment and prevention through earmarked taxes would institutionally connect use with control of abuse. The legal drugs, alcohol and tobacco, lack this connection and continue to visit significant harm on society.

Voluntary drug users' cooperatives, using pharmacies to dispense drugs to problem-free users through transaction fees, would support help for abusers by contracting with physicians and treatment programs.

Experience with such a system would permit the refinement of marketing strategies to minimize drug-caused dysfunction through safer products and a harmfulness-based pricing structure. Less harm would equal a cheaper price.

An arrangement of user-industry accountability to society would be more legitimate than the current, perverted use of the word "accountability"—meaning "we're going to catch you"—being pushed by Bennett.

President Bush, Bennett, Congress, other politicians, sports-team owners, the National Collegiate Athletic Association, other academic officials and the heads of corporate America are not falling over themselves to urinate in the bottle.

Legalizing drugs would, most importantly, eradicate the illicit market that supports most of the secondary problems—including the reactive "war on drugs."

Removal of the "forbidden fruit" allure from illicit drugs would make President Bush's wish come true.

It would transform a bag of social poison into a vice utilized by a sad few individuals who have the need to substitute chemistry for positive experience.

The extraordinary popular delusions and madness of crowds—facilitated by a sensation-mongering media—will, unfortunately, make matters worse before they get better.

Now that the Red menace is subsiding, the prohibitionists can concentrate their efforts on showing the rest of the world how right-wing America can suppress freedom and look stupid.

Questions for Discussion

1. What are the two writers' assumptions about drug usage?
2. What reasons are given for each writer's opinion? Which reasons are supported by strong, cited evidence and which reasons are unsupported?
3. What does each writer seem to value the most for American society?
4. Do you detect any fallacies in reasoning on the part of either writer? Look especially for examples of begging the question, the slippery slope, and false dilemma.
5. Both writers use analogies to make their points. Isolate these analogies and discuss their accuracy and effectiveness.
6. Does either writer resort to name-calling or the use of loaded words to make their points? What effect does this have on their arguments? What images do they both use to paint a picture in the readers' minds that make the opponents' positions seem ridiculous?
7. Does the citing of each writer's credentials at the beginning of their editorials have any positive or negative effect on you as a reader?

Decades of Rage Created Crucible of Violence

by Don Terry
New York Times, May 3, 1992

LOS ANGELES, MAY 2—Large flakes of ash drifted to the ground as the basement of a church in the city's South-Central section began filling up Thursday evening with refugees from the fear and the fire sweeping the streets.

Michael Ming, a 23-year-old college student, stood outside in the falling dusk and watched a building burn to the ground a block and a half away. It had been burning for 12 hours. Gunshots echoed through the dimness, and a little girl asked her mother if they could go home. Their home, her mother said, was in flames.

Mr. Ming had gone to the church that desperate and dangerous night to answer its call for aid, a call written on a banner draped across the face of its modern building: "Brothers, Come Help Us Stop the Madness."

Ambivalence About Rioters

"Yeah, it's madness," Mr. Ming said of the riots, touched off by the acquittal of four white Los Angeles police officers in the beating of a black motorist. "But it's also understandable. And if the social conditions don't change, it will happen again and again and not just in L.A."

Like most people here, Mr. Ming condemned the violence and mourned the dead and the newly homeless. But he and a broad range of others, from solidly middle-class blacks like Al Myles to the young, Hispanic residents like James Garcia, also expressed ambivalence and guarded admiration for the rioter's rage at "the system."

The explosive violence here had been smoldering for 27 years, said scholars, ministers, advocates and residents of the city's arson scarred and riot-torn neighborhoods in more than two dozen interviews.

Many said the acquittal of the four police officers charged with using excessive force in the beating of the black motorist, Rodney G. King, was only a spark put to a tinderbox of anger built up over years of deep poverty, governmental neglect, racism, charges of police abuse and high unemployment.

Warren M. Christopher, a former Deputy Attorney General under President Lyndon B. Johnson who headed a commission that investigated the beating, said the acquittal "uncorked" the same resentment and frustration that burned through Watts in 1965 and this time spread its flames and death across a much larger swath of the city.

In an interview Friday, he said the city had made a crucial mistake after Watts, a mistake that has returned to haunt Los Angeles and other cities: when the fires were put out and the troops were gone, the problems and people of Watts received only half-hearted assistance in rebuilding their neighborhood and lives.

"This is a second opportunity to get at some of the underlying causes," Mr. Christopher said. "You don't get very many second chances."

Rainbow of Rage

But unlike the Watts riot, which was largely contained in the predominantly black neighborhood, this week's violence and arson fires were spread out, and the rioters included blacks, Hispanics and whites, displaying a growing sense of despair.

The riot was a rainbow of anger.

"The police treat us very bad, too," said Mr. Garcia, a 17-year-old Hispanic high school student. "People want justice. They hit Rodney King; we hit them. It cost them money to do us wrong this time."

Although residents were quick to assail Chief Daryl F. Gates as part of the problem, they did not volunteer any criticism or praise for the longtime black Mayor of this city, Tom Bradley, a former police officer.

On the surface, the history of tension and trouble between the police and black and Hispanic residents was at the heart of what happened here. For many, the riot was a simple message to the authorities and the larger society: Treat us right. We've been pushed too close to the edge.

"Almost everybody I know has been harassed and much worse by the police," said Ervin Mitchell Jr., 31, a design engineer from South-Central who was standing with Mr. Ming. "Young blacks and Hispanics have been persecuted, beaten and pulled out of our cars because of stereotypes. We're tired of being treated like garbage. We're tired of living in a society that denies us the right to be considered as a human being."

Disgust All Round

Mr. Ming added: "But it goes way beyond that. The way the whole entire system is structured, the rich get richer, the poor get poorer. It provides almost no hope for most folks, especially black folks."

Not far away, and several hours later, Walter Thompson, 19, stood on a sun-soaked street corner with his friend Cindy Edwards, 16. Ms. Edwards said she was disgusted with the verdict and the looting. Which was worse was a toss up, she said.

"Now I don't have a store to go to," she said. "We had two. They burned one down, the other they looted."

Mr. Thompson cut in and said the looting should have occurred in Simi Valley, the predominantly white suburb where the trial of the four officers was moved.

"That's where the enemy is," he said.

Then, like many others, he bitterly cited the slaying of 15-year-old Latasha Harlins as evidence that blacks are treated unfairly by what he called "the prejudiced criminal justice system."

Bullet in the Rubbish

Miss Harlins, who was black, was shot in the back of the head by a Korean merchant after a dispute in a grocery store. That shooting, like the beating of Mr. King, was captured by a video camera. The merchant was convicted of manslaughter and given five years probation.

"We're mad for a whole lot of reasons," Mr. Thompson said, raising his voice and stepping closer. "First that 15-year-old girl was killed and they got away with it. Then they beat Rodney King like a dog and the jury sets them free. The black people don't get no justice, nowhere, no time."

Telling him to be calm, Ms. Edwards gently pulled Mr. Thompson away. "This has really hurt us," she explained.

Across the street, a growing band of young people led by the actor and community advocate, Edward James Olmos, in cleaning up the riot-ravaged street. They swept up large piles of broken glass, charred beer cans, green olives and even a bullet or two.

Joblessness and Anger

The lack of decent jobs in the inner city, especially for teenagers, was another reason given for the days of rage.

"I don't think it's very difficult to figure out why the riots happened so intensely," said Ramona Ripston, executive director of the American Civil Liberties Union of Southern California. "As far as I can see," she said, "we have a lot of young people, 15, 16 years old, no programs to keep them in school, no jobs, no health care, no stake in society. It's a form of civil war. America had better wake up."

Outrage about the verdict and lack of meaningful opportunity no doubt motivated many rioters, but plain lawlessness seemed to have pushed many more into the bashed-in stores.

"Some people say this is because of Rodney King," said Yolanda Gnat, 33, as she searched for an open store in south central Los Angeles to buy milk for her baby. "Others are doing it just to be doing it. A lot of people probably never even heard of Rodney King. They're doing it because it's like Christmas in the springtime."

Refuge in a Church

Steve D. Valdivia and his staff at the Community Youth Gang Services have been on the violent streets since the rioting began.

"The first night reports from my staff were scary," he said. "They said they had never seen such hatred and despair in people's faces. We've seen this coming. Everything was building up to this. There have been a number of shootings of minority kids. And now everybody is upset about the verdict. Young people always act out the frustrations of a community."

The Rev. Cecil Murray has turned his church, the First African Methodist Episcopal Church, which Mayor Bradley attends, into a shelter from the riots and the fires burning in almost every direction nearby.

Thursday night, 100 men, women, and children, mostly black and Hispanic, crowded into the basement, sleeping and talking on a forest of green cots set up inches apart by the Red Cross.

"Earthquakes is what we're trained for," a Red Cross volunteer said.

Many people watched the riots on two television sets, one tuned to a Spanish-language station.

"That's my house," a woman said, pointing to a building engulfed in flames on the television screen.

One television stayed on throughout the night. So did several babies.

Mr. Murray swept through the room, talking with the children and praying with an 80-year-old woman who had to be carried from her apartment building in a blanket.

Gang Cooperation

That night, David Madise, 30, stood on a dark sidewalk, watching over First A.M.E. and its basement of scared strangers.

"I came out to help," he said. "I'm just making sure everything is cool."

He spent the worst nights of the riot in front of the church and saw two men struggling up the hilly street, pushing a big screen television set in the middle of the night.

They asked him to help but he refused.

"Since this started, I've seen Bloods and Crips working together like crazy, looting and carrying away everything they could get their hands on," he said, referring to the city's infamous and usually rival street gangs. "They don't care about colors. That was a big change."

"Land of Crazy Folks"

The next day, Mr. Murray said sending in the National Guard was "only a Band-Aid" approach to deep-seated problems.

"The War on Poverty became the war on the poor because it was poorly managed," he said. "America is creating a land of crazy folks. Crazy situations create crazy people."

The situation has been extremely crazy for Eddy Zapata and his family. They were burned out of their home on Wednesday and spent two days living with his sister-in-law in a small and overcrowded apartment.

On Friday, the 39-year-old freelance auto mechanic took his wife and two children, 6 years and 1 month old, to Mr. Murray's church. The riot took everything from the struggling family, their house, clothes, tools and maybe their hope.

Holding his baby daughter in his lap, he said he had no idea what the family would do now.

Everyone Lost Something

"We lost everything," he said. "For the last three years I have been trying to make it on my own with my shop. Now it is gone."

The entire city has lost something during these days of violence: businesses, homes, sons and daughters and trust.

Al Myles, a 38-year-old businessman, lost another fragile piece of his faith in "people of color ever really winning our equal rights."

"To me, this feels like a complete duplication of the Watts riot," Mr. Myles said. "The verdict sent a clear message: that there's only one kind of justice and it doesn't apply to people of color in any way.

"I don't condone what's happening but how else are you going to get the idea across that we're tired of this abuse?" he said. "They haven't listened to us in courts or the ballot. But this time it's not just blacks who are upset. I think everybody is upset with injustice, with the lawlessness of the law."

With that, he took a deep breath and looked sad.

Questions for Discussion

1. In the title of this essay, we are told that "decades of rage created a crucible of violence." What, specifically, does the author cite as causes for the violence following the Rodney King verdict in the spring of 1992? Since journalists often make their points through a combination of research and human interest anecdotes, you will have to search through the article to find these reasons. You will also discover that different sources gave the journalist some very different reasons for the reaction. Then, taking into account this chapter's section on cause and effect, discuss which reasons you agree with and which you find unconvincing.
2. Al Myles, a businessman cited in the article, said "To me, this feels like a complete duplication of the Watts riot." Warren Christopher is also quoted as saying the acquittal of the police officers "uncorked" the same resentment and frustration that burned through Watts in 1965. The analogy was made by others who witnessed the aftermath of the King verdict. Comment on the effectiveness of this analogy.

Ideas for Writing or Speaking

1. Research the effects of the original Rodney King verdict for yourself. Then write an essay or speech explaining your views about what happened and why it happened. You might also propose solutions to the problems of inner-city dwellers. What should be done to alleviate these problems and to make positive changes?
2. Research the causes of any political or social problem that interests you. Cite what you believe to be the major factors creating the difficulties. Possible topics for this paper include homelessness, teenage pregnancy, national debt, divorce, the state of the economy, trends in television programming, the state of education in our public schools, the state of the economy, racism, classism, or the relationship between the President and Congress. The problem can be international, national or specific to your own city, county, or campus.

   You may also want to propose solutions to the problems that you cite, but be sure you have clearly and thoroughly supported your conclusions about the underlying causes first.

⬦ More Ideas for Writing or Speaking

1. Write an argumentative essay or speech about a current issue in which you include several examples of fallacious reasoning. At the end of the essay or speech, identify the fallacies you have committed.

   Share your papers or speeches with the class and see if they can isolate your errors in reasoning.

2. Write a critique of an editorial or essay from a newspaper or magazine. Point out the fallacies made by the writer of the editorial.

3. Choose an issue about which you have strong opinions. Read some viewpoints by people who oppose your viewpoint on this issue; errors in their reasoning will usually be obvious! List and explain several errors made by your opponents or one major error that weakens their argument.

   Next, look critically at your own viewpoint. What errors are committed by those who favor your position on this issue? List and explain these errors.

4. Argue for a new program or policy, using one or more analogies. For example, if you wanted to propose a noncompetitive curriculum for middle school or high school students, you could cite the innovative policies at Plainfield Community Middle School in Plainfield, Illinois. No student at Plainfield school is ever cut from a club or a team, no matter how lacking in talent he or she appears to be. The school has noted an increase in self-esteem among the student body and a high quality of performance in music and sports programs.

   In making your argument, show how there are similarities in every significant, relevant way between your idea, policy, or program and the idea, policy, or program to which you are comparing it.

CHAPTER SEVEN

Persuasive Speaking

What's Your Point,
and How Do You Sharpen It?

A critical thinker can organize ideas and
advocate for his or her beliefs.

This chapter will cover:

◆ The three parts of a persuasive message
◆ Methods of organizing persuasive speeches
◆ Techniques for handling speech fear

When you present a formal argument, you are giving a persuasive speech with the goal of convincing your audience to accept certain viewpoints and take certain actions. Many of us have a picture of a person who is convincing as someone with *charisma*, an intangible quality that attracts others to them and to their ideas. Some people seem to have this personal power and we can't explain why.

However, beginning with Aristotle, we have explanations, verified by research, of what makes a clear and convincing argument, and those ideas have formed the recommendations in this book. If you use what you know about the content and organization of a good argument and add some basic tips on public speaking, you can successfully present your ideas to both groups and individuals.

This chapter will explain how to use the principles of argumentation to create formal arguments.

Being an Advocate of Ideas: Communicating Publicly

The primary obstacle to effective public speaking is fear. Research indicates that the fear of public speaking is the most common area of concern to Americans, ranking above the fear of spiders and death. When we stand in front of a group, we expose our ideas, our egos, and our bodies to a group of not necessarily sympathetic people. We may shake, quake, or refuse to show up when we are required to speak.

At one eastern university, every graduate is required to take a basic public speaking class. When the administration discovered many students putting this class off until the last quarter of their senior year, or even not graduating because they refused to take the class, the speech department took action by initiating a special class for those who were terrified of public speaking. The class filled several sections every semester. So if you are experiencing anxiety about speaking and would rather skip this chapter and related assignments, take heart. You aren't alone in these feelings of fear.

It is possible to overcome public speaking fears to a great extent and most students who take a course in public speaking report improvement in their feelings of confidence by the end of a semester. In addition, those who fear the most often prepare the best and therefore have well-researched and convincing arguments.

The Best Ways to Deal with Speech Fear

"All the great speakers were bad speakers at first."

Ralph Waldo Emerson, "Power," *The Conduct of Life* (1860)

What advice would you give to someone who has to give a speech and is feeling terrified? You probably have some techniques you would use, such as breathing deeply to calm yourself or memorizing your opening line to get you started. The basic recommendations of speech professionals are given in this section.

The first way to gain confidence is to choose a topic you believe in. When you really care about your topic (which is most often the case when you take a stand on an issue), you can more easily concentrate on convincing your audience and forget your self-consciousness. Secondly, you need to prepare well; then you can be confident that what you are saying has value to your audience, is solid, and includes relevant information. Preparing involves finding evidence to support your reasons and writing a clear outline of your ideas.

Finally, practice the speech so you know it well. Then, even if your mind goes blank temporarily, your mouth keeps on going. Use brief notes to help you with memory lapses; note cards function as mini security blankets. Number these cards (in case you drop them) and then refer to them only briefly as you speak. Also, get rest before you speak, do whatever relaxation techniques work for you, and concentrate on your audience rather than on yourself. Look for friendly faces as you scan the room, and avoid people who look unhappy (unless everyone looks unhappy—then you might need to think about what you might have said to confuse or offend them).

Aristotle said that rhetoric (argumentation) involves using all the available means of persuasion. He defined the means of persuasion as **ethos** (personal credibility), **logos** (logical organization and reasoning), and **pathos** (emotional appeal).

Ethos: Speaker Credibility

Part of your ethos, your credibility or reputation as a speaker, will come through the same methods that help you to overcome speech fear. When you are well prepared to speak and have conviction about your topic, your audience will give you respect and attention.

Speaker credibility can be achieved through specific effort and planning. Speakers are seen as credible when:

- They can be clearly heard by the audience.
- They show that they have done their homework on a topic by using well-cited research to support their key points.
- They are easy to understand because they are well organized.
- They are easy to understand because they have rehearsed the speech before giving it.
- They show respect for the audience by using language and examples that can be understood (not too complex or too simplified) by the members of that particular audience.
- They reduce nervous, distracting mannerisms to a minimum (this can be done with practice).
- They dress appropriately for the speaking occasion.

Logos: Logical Organization and Credible Content

There are several traditional ways to organize formal speeches. In our time-conscious, media-saturated age, there are also variations to traditional methods of structuring speeches. Regardless of the format you choose, there are some essential ingredients to every organizational pattern that apply whether you have two minutes or twenty minutes to speak. To be a clearly organized speaker, use these principles, illustrated in Figure 7.1:

- Make your conclusion (thesis statement) clear early in the speech, immediately following the introduction.
- Tell us how you plan to support your position; list the key reasons immediately after you state your conclusion. This technique is called the *preview* of your speech.
- Announce/highlight each key point (reason). Figure 7.1 shows that each key point must be supported (with evidence). The evidence must be cited (tell us where it comes from—the publication, author, and date). Each key point should also be strong enough to be a supporting "pillar" for the thesis statement.
- Use transitions between reasons for a smooth flow of ideas.

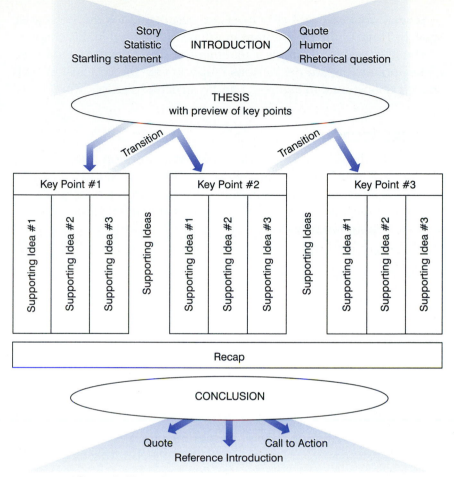

Figure 7.1   Speech Flowchart

- Note that in Figure 7.1, the transitions flow between key points with a brief reference back to the thesis statement.

- Review your key ideas before making a concluding statement. The repetition of your ideas—first previewed in the introduction, then explained in the body, and finally summarized in the conclusion—helps to reinforce them in the mind of your audience.

It is often effective to address and calmly refute the arguments for the opposing side of your speech. Do this early on, in the body of the speech, if your audience is neutral or hostile to your position. On the other hand, if your audience is supportive of your position, concentrate instead on moving them to action.

Several organizational structures are acceptable for the persuasive speech. Three of the most common will be highlighted in this chapter.

The first method is simply a statement of your conclusion followed by key points that are the reasons (support) for the conclusion. This speech is illustrated in Figure 7.1 and is structured as follows.

I.   INTRODUCTION

In the introduction, you get the audience's attention and lead into your topic through the use of examples, quotations, statistics, or relevant anecdotes. In the last sentence of your introduction, you state your conclusion (sometimes called a thesis statement) and then preview (tell about) your key points.

II.   BODY OF THE SPEECH

While the introduction serves to make a strong statement of your conclusion (opinion), the body of the speech answers the question "Why do you have this opinion?" The key points are all distinct reasons for drawing your conclusion. Cover each point, being sure to support each point (reason) with cited evidence.

III.   CONCLUSION

The conclusion of your speech should include a review of the key points that support your opinion. End the speech with a call to belief or action.

The advantage of this method of presentation is that it is clear and simple; you are, in effect, saying "I believe [*conclusion*] because of these reasons, and you should too!"

Sample Speech Outline

Homeschooling for Happy Children

by Patti Preut

Introduction:
Attention Step
I.   Our educational system is in a state of crisis.

A. In 1983, we were confronted with a federal report called *A Nation At Risk* that stated "A rising tide of mediocrity in education is eroding the very foundation of society."
1. Our educational system is a major concern for our society. The children in the schools will someday be in the workforce and in decision-making roles.
2. Educational reform has become an important issue of the 90's, but reform measures are not helping to improve academic performance.
B. Our children are also facing emotional and social problems, according to David Elkind, professor of child development at Tufts University.
1. Suicide and homicide rates for teenagers are triple what they were 20 years ago.
2. Theft and violence in public schools are on the rise.
3. Reform measures are not producing academic progress nor addressing socialization problems in the school.
C. Parents must choose how best to serve their children's social and educational needs.
1. Some choose the public school system, others choose private schools.
2. There is another alternative available: homeschooling.

Thesis Statement/Conclusion
Homeschooling, unlike public schooling, is very effective in producing positive socialization in our children.

Preview
I will first discuss how negative socialization commonly occurs in public schools and then explain how homeschooling effectively produces positive socialization.

Body:
II. Public schools promote negative socialization.
A. A major problem is peer dependency.
1. Dr. Urie Bronfenbrenner, child development researcher, found that children 6th grade and under who spent more time with their peers than their parents became peer dependent.
2. Peer dependent children experience a loss of self-worth, optimism, and respect for parents.
3. Peer dependent children are more subject to pressure in such areas as clothing, language, music, or the use of drugs and alcohol.
B. Closely related to peer dependency is the problem of social competition.

1. Dr. James Dobson, a family psychologist, believes that the epidemic of inferiority and inadequacy in our teens is rooted in the ridicule, rejection, and social competition experienced in young children during the elementary years.
2. Research reported in the July, 1987, *Instructor's Only* Newsletter found that 80% of students entering school feel good about themselves and who they are. By the time these same students become seniors in high school, only 5% have managed to keep a positive self-image.

C. Academic pressure in schools also causes children to experience apathy and to withdraw from others.

D. The threat of violence in some schools creates fear and mistrust among peers.

Transition

I have discussed how negative socialization commonly occurs in schools. To address the fear that home-schooled children are sheltered social misfits, let's examine how homeschooling can effectively nurture positive socialization.

III. Homeschooling promotes positive socialization.

A. Homeschooling gives children the time and attention that is needed to develop positive self-images.

1. Dr. Raymond Moore, researcher, developmental psychologist, and former teacher and principal, states that home is the best place for the first 8 to 12 years, and that staying at home for this time adds to a child's security and self-confidence.

B. Children need to feel wanted and depended upon in order to develop high self-esteem, and parents are best able to fill that need.

1. We have noticed and nurtured our son's good organizational skills and special abilities with young children; as a result, he is beginning to take pride in these qualities and is initiating projects that use these skills both within and without the home.
2. In a study of 4,500 homeschoolers, Dr. Taylor of Andrews University found, based on the best available self-concept scales, that over one-half of home-schooled children scored in the top 10%. That score was 41% higher than the average child in public schools. He also noted that the longer children homeschooled, the higher their self-concept.

C. Children who are homeschooled learn to relate easily to adults and children of all ages.

1. Networks of homeschooling parents hold frequent activities like park days and field trips. At these functions, children interact with other children of various ages.
2. Because of the lack of peer dependency and increased exposure to adults, home-schooled children develop more respect for and rapport with adults.

Conclusion

Today, I have introduced you to homeschooling and talked about the aspect of socialization.

Review

I have shown how negative socialization commonly occurs in schools today through peer dependency, too much academic pressure too soon, and threats of violence. I have also cleared up the misconception that homeschoolers are not well socialized and shown that homeschooling effectively produces positive socialization by providing a secure environment, a feeling of value, and a varied social life that grows with maturity.

Closing Statement

Parents are ultimately responsible for their children's social as well as academic development. They must consider all the options available. We believe that we provide the best place for our children to grow into well-adjusted and educated adults. As counselor and teacher Marita Hayhurt states, "School socialization is not the same as learning to nurture, to give, to receive and to share feelings in the intimacy of a home."

Monroe's Motivated Sequence

A second organizational method is called **Monroe's Motivated Sequence**.[1] This method is very similar to the basic organizational format covered previously. Monroe's steps are especially effective when a speaker wants to motivate the audience to take action. Monroe's sequence involves the following five steps.

1.   *Attention:* Get the audience's interest and attention; you can do this with provocative questions, statistics, or a relevant anecdote. End your attention step with your thesis statement (main idea) and a preview of your key ideas. This step is similar to the introduction step of the first method.

2.   *Need:* The body of your speech begins with this step. Here you show your audience that a serious problem must be addressed. Discuss the extent and scope of the problem and how we are hurt by the problem.

3.   *Satisfaction:* At this point, you present a solution to the problem that was introduced in the need step.

---

[1]   Allan H. Monroe, *Principles and Types of Speech Communication*, 11th ed. (Glenview, IL: Scott, Foresman, 1990), pp. 180–203.

4. *Visualization:* This last part of the body of your speech is used to help listeners form a picture of what it would be like if your solution were in place. If there are aspects of the solution that would be of personal benefit to audience members, visualize those benefits in this step.

5. *Action:* This step is considered the conclusion of the speech and is used to request specific action of the audience members.

Problem-Solution Format

A third method of structuring persuasive speeches has been outlined in the Northern California Forensics Association handbook. This method also follows a problem-solution format.

1. *Introduction:* As in any speech, the introduction to a persuasive speech must put the audience at ease with the topic of the speech, must clearly state the purpose of the speech, and must give some direction about the course of the speech.

2. *Harms:* The harms section of the speech should answer the question, "How are we hurt by this problem?" Financial losses, personal injuries, and deaths caused by the problem are often detailed in the harms portion.

3. *Inherency:* The inherency section should answer the question, "Why does the problem exist?" The reasons for the existence of any problem can be categorized as either attitudinal inherency or structural inherency. Attitudinal inherency occurs when the sentiments of the public create a barrier to the solution of the issue or when those sentiments help to perpetuate the cause of difficulty. Structural inherency is a physical barrier that must be overcome in order to solve the problem. Such a barrier could be a law, the lack of trained personnel, or an inefficient system.

4. *Significance:* The notion of significance addresses the question, "What is the scope of the problem?" Significance is often described by details of the geographic range, quantitative preponderance, or qualitative weight of the problem. More often than not, the significance issue is handled within both the harms and inherency sections.

5. *Solvency:* This final section is arguably the most important part of the persuasive speech. It answers the question, "What can be

done to remedy the problem?" It is important to address two issues within the solvency section. First, be sure to tell your audience how they can help specifically. Second, attempt to give an example of how your solution has worked in the past.

6.   *Conclusion:* The conclusion of the persuasive speech should accomplish two goals. It should initially view how the advocated solution steps will affect the problem and it should also make one last appeal to the audience.[2]

Pathos: Emotional Appeal

Both positive and negative emotions can influence our thoughts and actions. As critical thinkers, we should be aware of a speaker who uses *only* emotional appeals as reasons for a conclusion. As speakers, we should appeal to our listener's emotions only when we believe it is appropriate and relevant to the issue we are discussing.

Most of the big issues we confront as a society, and many smaller ones, involve deep-seated feelings. Consider the reasons why people are for or against capital punishment, abortion, euthanasia, and a host of environmental issues. If a group is protesting the creation and sale of fur coats, the members of this group most likely feel deeply for the animals that are used to make the coats. On the other hand, those who have spent a lifetime learning to make the coats or who have a family depending on the sale of the coats feel equally strongly about their livelihood. Whatever your position on this issue, you can imagine the personal feelings that accompany advocacy on both sides.

Emotional appeal is important in making issues real for audience members. Hearing statistics about thousands of victims of drunk drivers does not move us as much as hearing the personal story of one victim and his family.

Responsible and effective speakers will use emotional appeal to show us the human impact of an attitude or a policy that needs to be changed. Let's say a speaker wants to persuade his or her audience that homeless individuals who are schizophrenic need to be hospitalized and given treatment. The speaker can and should use logos in the form of statistics, giving the estimated number of homeless who

---

[2]   Joe Corcoran, *Northern California Forensics Association Handbook* (Northern California Forensics Association, 1988).

are schizophrenic and the medical needs that they have. However, the factor that will convince the audience to listen, the factor that will highlight the importance of this issue, is likely to come in the form of an emotional appeal. A few case histories of homeless schizophrenics and examples of the problems they face will do much to make an audience receptive to this problem and its possible solution.

Are emotional appeals ethical? Yes, if they are:

1. True and accurate.

2. Used with solid reasoning.

3. Based on healthy emotions.

The third category, healthy emotions, needs to be considered by the speaker. Psychologist Abraham Maslow has suggested that all human beings have the same basic needs, which form the basis of human motivation.[3] When we as speakers or writers want to bring our audience to action, we can appeal to these needs (Figure 7.2).

The needs are listed in a hierarchy. The lower level needs must be satisfied before people become concerned with higher level needs. We can ethically address *these* needs, using examples that stir the emotions of audience members.

1. *Physical needs:* These include the needs that guarantee our survival as people and as a species, such as food, air, water, rest, and the ability to reproduce.

Example of use in a speech: Although you can discuss facts about scarcities of food and water in a speech, you also can use emotional appeals by asking your audience to imagine a world in which their children would not have enough food or water to survive. Since we all have the same needs, you can then ask the audience to empathize with people in other nations who are without adequate supplies of food or water.

2. *Safety needs:* These involve the need to be protected from harm to our persons and to have adequate levels of comfort, such as decent housing, safe products, and avoidance of sickness.

Examples of use in a speech: Speakers can legitimately use emotional appeals, such as graphic examples of accidents that have occurred at a dangerous intersection when they are advocating for a

3   A. H. Maslow, *Toward a Psychology of Being* (New York: Van Nostrand Reinhold, 1968).

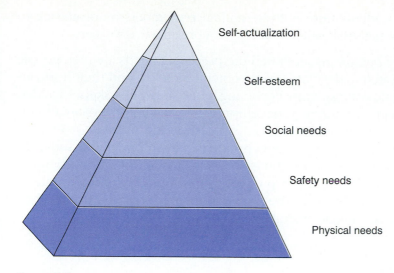

Figure 7.2
Source: A. H. Maslow, *Toward a Psychology of Being* (New York: Van Norstrand Reinhold, 1968).

needed stoplight. They can tell about children who died or were disabled from faulty toys that should be recalled. They can describe the fear of those who live near "crack houses" to emphasize the need for more effective neighborhood law enforcement.

3. *Social needs:* These needs involve our desires to form alliances with others, to be included in group interactions, and to have close friends who love and respect us.

Examples of use in a speech: Speakers can give examples of children with AIDS who have not been included in their peer groups as part of a speech on their need for acceptance in the community. Speakers promoting a social cause sometimes appeal to audience members' social needs by offering some form of group identification to them; for example, the Comic Relief fund-raisers for the homeless offer t-shirts to contributing audience members.

4. *Self-esteem:* These needs concern our desire to feel like worthwhile, contributing members of society, whose lives have meaning and purpose.

Examples of use in a speech: Speakers can appeal to our altruism in helping others in need, which in turn gives us a feeling of making an important contribution. They also can help us to empathize with those whose professions are worthy of more respect than they are generally given, such as homemakers, pre-school teachers, and mechanics.

Seminar leaders often motivate audience members by promising to give them skills that will help them be more effective workers.

5. *Self-actualization:* When the preceding needs are met, people are motivated to develop various potentials, to expand their horizons by trying new things or by becoming better at familiar skills. Included in the need for personal development is gaining a greater understanding of spiritual matters.

Examples of use in a speech: Speakers can appeal to audience members' desires to become more well rounded by using examples of people who have taken on new professions or challenges late in life. They can describe the thrill of an outdoor adventure when encouraging audience members to buy a vacation package.

REMINDER

Use emotional appeals sparingly, as a means of getting your audience's attention and of highlighting important points.

EXERCISE

Purpose: To incorporate the knowledge of pathos into the writing of a speech.

Take each of Maslow's needs and write your own examples of how they could be incorporated into a speech as an emotional appeal.

EXERCISE

Purpose: To recognize the use of pathos in a speech.

Write or tell about a speech you heard that included an effective appeal to emotion. You might use the following format:

1. Explain the issue and the conclusion of the speaker.
2. Discuss the audience's predisposition to the speech and the speaker.
3. Explain how, specifically, the speaker used the appeal to emotion. Was it a story, an example, a personal testimony?

4. Talk about the placement of the appeal to emotion. Did it come in the introduction, body, or conclusion of the speech, or was it referred to throughout the speech?

5. Summarize your reasons for finding this appeal effective. Then comment on whether you felt the appeal was ethical.

Chapter Highlights

1. A critical thinker considers the best ways to organize and present ideas to be a strong advocate for an issue.

2. The best ways to deal with speech fear are to choose an issue of interest to you, prepare thoroughly, and practice.

3. Ethos, the credibility of the speaker, is an important element of persuasion. Ethos is enhanced by the obvious preparation of the speaker and the manner in which he or she presents the speech.

4. Logos, the content and organization of the speech, is crucial to a persuasive message. Several organizational structures can be used to enhance the clarity and persuasiveness of a speech.

5. Pathos, emotional appeal, is powerful in its ability to persuade and should be used ethically.

Articles for Discussion

Speak for Yourself

by Susan Faludi
New York Times Magazine, January 9, 1992

I am at the boiling point! If I do not find some day the use of my tongue . . . I shall die of an intellectual repression, a woman's rights convulsion.

Elizabeth Cady Stanton, in a letter to Susan B. Anthony

"Oh, and then you'll be giving that speech at the Smithsonian Tuesday on the status of American women," my publisher's publicist reminded me as she rattled off the list of "appearances" for the week.

"What?" I choked out. "I thought that was at least another month away."

But the speech was distant only in my wishful consciousness, which pushed all such events into a mythical future when I would no longer lunge for smelling salts at the mention of public speaking.

For the author of what was widely termed an "angry" and "forceful" book, I exhibit a timorous verbal demeanor that belies my barracuda blurbs.

My fingers may belt out my views when I'm stationed before the computer, but stick a microphone in front of me and I'm a Victorian lady with the vapors.

Like many female writers with strong convictions but weak stomachs for direct confrontation, I write so forcefully precisely because I speak so tentatively.

One form of self-expression has overcompensated for the weakness of the other, as a blind person develops a hypersensitive ear.

"Isn't it wonderful that so many people want to hear what you have to say about women's rights?" the publicist prodded. I grimaced. "About as wonderful as walking down the street with no clothes on."

Yes, I wanted people to hear what I had to say. Yes, I wanted to warn women of the backlash to our modest gains. But couldn't they just read what I wrote? Couldn't I just speak softly and carry a big book?

It has taken me a while to realize that my publicist is right. It's not the same—for my audience or me.

Public speech can be a horror for the shy person, but it can also be the ultimate act of liberation. For me, it became the moment where the public and the personal truly met.

For many years, I believed the imbalance between my incensed writing and my atrophied vocal cords suited me just fine.

After a few abysmal auditions for school plays—my one role was Nana the dog in "Peter Pan," not a speaking role—I retired my acting aspirations and retreated to the school newspaper, a forum where I could bluster at injustices large and small without public embarrassment.

My friend Barbara and I co-edited the high school paper (titled, interestingly, The Voice), fearlessly castigating all scoundrels from our closet-size office. But we kept our eyes glued to the floor during class discussion.

Partly this was shyness, a genderless condition. But it was a condition reinforced by daily gendered reminders—we saw what happened to the girls who argued in class. The boys called them "bitches" and they sat home Saturday nights.

Popular girls raised their voices only at pep squad.

Whereas both sexes fear public speaking (pollsters tell us it's the public's greatest fear, rivaling even death), women—particularly women challenging the status quo—seem to be more afraid and with good reason.

We do have more at stake. Men risk loss of face, women a loss of femininity.

Men are chagrined if they blunder at the podium; women face humiliation either way. If we come across as commanding, our womanhood is called into question. If we reveal emotion, we are too hormonally driven to be taken seriously.

I had my own taste of this double standard while making the rounds of radio and television talk shows for a book tour. When I disputed a point with a man, male listeners would often phone in to say they found my behavior "offensive" or even "unattractive."

And then there were my own internalized "feminine" voices: Don't interrupt, be agreeable, keep the volume down.

"We're going to have to record that again," a weary radio producer said, rewinding the tape for the fifth time. "Your words are angry, but it's not coming through in your voice."

In replacing lacerating speech with a literary scalpel, I had adopted a well-worn female strategy, used most famously by Victorian female reformers protesting slavery and women's lowly status.

"I want to be doing something with the pen, since no other means of action in politics are in a woman's power," Harriet Martineau, the British journalist, wrote in 1832.

But although their literature makes compelling reading, the suffrage movement didn't get under way until women took a public stand from the platform of the Seneca Falls Women's Rights Convention.

And while Betty Friedan's 1963 *The Feminine Mystique* raised the consciousness of millions of women, the contemporary women's movement began to affect social policy only when Friedan and other feminists started addressing the public.

Public speech is a more powerful stimulus because it is more dangerous for the speaker. An almost physical act, it demands projecting one's voice, hurling it against the public ear.

Writing, on the other hand, occurs at one remove. The writer asserts herself from behind the veil of the printed page.

The dreaded evening of the Smithsonian speech finally arrived. I stood knock-kneed and green-gilled before 300 people. Was it too late to plead a severe case of laryngitis? I am Woman, hear me whisper.

I cleared my throat and, to my shock, a hush fell over the room. People were listening—with an intensity that strangely emboldened me.

It was as if their attentive silence allowed me to make contact with my own muffled self. I began to speak. A stinging point induced a ripple of agreement. I told a joke and they laughed.

My voice got surer, my delivery rising. A charge passed between me and the audience, uniting and igniting us both.

That internal "boiling point" that Elizabeth Cady Stanton described was no longer under "intellectual repression." And its heat, I discovered, could set many kettles to whistling.

Afterward it struck me that in some essential way I hadn't really proved myself a feminist until now.

Until you translate personal words on a page into public connections with other people, you aren't really part of a political movement.

I hadn't declared my independence until I was willing to declare it out loud. I knew public speaking was important to reform public life—but I hadn't realized the transformative effect it could have on the speaker herself.

Women need to be heard not just to change the world, but to change themselves.

I can't say that this epiphany has made me any less anxious when approaching the lectern. But it has made me more determined to speak in spite of the jitters—and more hopeful that other women will do the same.

Toward that end I'd like to make a modest proposal for the next stage of the women's movement. A new method of consciousness-raising: Feminist Toastmasters.

Reprinted by permission of the author.

Questions for Discussion

1. Comment on the following statement by the author of this article: "Public speech can be a horror for the shy person, but it can also be the ultimate act of liberation." How can public speaking, even when we dread it, be liberating?

2. The author states, "Until you translate personal words on a page into public connections with other people, you aren't really part of a political movement." To what extent do you believe that speaking is essential for those involved with political, social, and religious movements?

Changing a Man's Mind

Anonymous, given as a conference handout at the Seventh Annual and Fifth International Conference on Critical Thinking and Educational Reform

Thomas Aquinas, who knew more about education and persuasion than almost anybody who ever lived, once said that when you want to convert someone to your view, you go over to where he is standing, take him by the hand (mentally speaking), and guide him to where you want him to go.

You don't stand across the room and shout at him. You don't call him a dummy. You don't order him to come over to where you are. You start where he is, and work from that position. That's the only way to get him to budge.

We have lost sight of this elementary psychological fact. The world is full of passionate advocates, screaming their own prejudices, and excoriating their opponents.

This does three things: (a) it makes the people who agree with you feel better, (b) it makes the people who disagree with you stiffen their resistance, and (c) it makes the people on the fence uneasy and skeptical that you are speaking the whole truth.

I have never known a single passionate and partisan argument to win over a person who disagreed with it, or even to persuade a person who was neutral on the subject. The chief reason being that all passionate and partisan arguments overstate their case and understate their opponents' case.

When you think that someone is wrong, and you disagree with him, the first task is to determine in what way he is right. This is not as paradoxical as it sounds: no view can be entirely wrong, and everybody has a little piece of truth by the tail. This is the piece we start with, we work from there, and concede as much as we honestly can.

Lord Acton said that we have no right to oppose a position until we can state that position in a way that fully satisfies those who hold it; until, indeed, we can make out a better case for it than the proponent himself can. (Most of us, of course, distort or lampoon the opposite position, and then proceed to demolish this straw man.)

And all this is much more than an academic exercise. The arts of argument and persuasion are so little known and practiced that disputants have no recourse to anything but violence. If people can't agree on how to disagree, there is no hope of reconciliation or compromise. And the art of argument is learning how to disagree productively.

We begin to fight when words fail us. And words fail us when we use the wrong ones to the wrong people for the wrong reasons.

It is far easier to be passionate in defense of what one believes than to comprehend why somebody believes something different. But, ultimately, only this comprehension (which is not agreement) can replace violence with dialog instead of the deafening monologues that lead to war.

Reprinted by permission of the Center for Critical Thinking.

Questions for Discussion

1. Comment on the following statement from this essay: "I have never known a single passionate and partisan argument to win over a person who disagreed with it, or even to persuade a person who was neutral on the subject. The chief reason being that all

passionate and partisan arguments overstate their case and under-state their opponents' case." Have you found that people who argue passionately overstate their own case and understate their opponent's case? Can you think of examples of this overstatement and understatement?

2. Can someone be persuasive and passionate and still be fair to the other side of the argument? If so, how? If not, why not?

3. Think of an issue that concerns you deeply. Can you see the "piece of truth" held by the other side? How could you use that truth to persuade your opponent to consider the value of your position?

Dr. Martin Luther King, Jr. used ethos and pathos in the following speech, which is considered a classic modern American address.

I Have a Dream

by Dr. Martin Luther King, Jr.
Delivered at the People's March on Washington, 1963

I am happy to join with you today in what will go down in history as the greatest demonstration for freedom in the history of our nation.

Five score years ago, a great American, in whose symbolic shadow we stand today, signed the Emancipation Proclamation. This momentous decree came as a great beacon light of hope to millions of Negro slaves, who had been seared in the flames of withering injustice. It came as a joyous daybreak to end the long night of their captivity.

But one hundred years later, the Negro is still not free. One hundred years later, the life of the Negro is still sadly crippled by the manacles of segregation and the chains of discrimination. One hundred years later, the Negro lives on a lonely island of poverty in the midst of a vast ocean of material prosperity. One hundred years later, the Negro is still languished in the corners of American society and finds himself an exile in his own land. So we have come here today to dramatize a shameful condition.

In a sense we've come to our nation's Capital to cash a check. When the architects of our republic wrote the magnificent words of the Constitution and the Declaration of Independence, they were signing a promissory note to which every American was to fall heir. This note was a promise that all men—yes, black men as well as white men—would be guaranteed the unalienable rights of life, liberty, and the pursuit of happiness.

It is obvious today that America has defaulted on this promissory note insofar as her citizens of color are concerned. Instead of honoring this sacred obligation, America has given the Negro people a bad check; a check which has come back marked "insufficient funds." But we refuse to believe that the bank of justice is bankrupt. We refuse to believe that there are insufficient funds in the great vaults of opportunity of this nation. So we've come to cash this check—a check that will give us upon demand the riches of freedom and the security of justice. We have also come to this hallowed spot to remind America of the fierce urgency of now. This is no time to engage in the luxury of cooling off or to take the tranquilizing drug of gradualism. Now is the time to make real the promises of Democracy. Now is the time to rise from the dark and desolate valley of segregation to the sunlight of racial justice. Now is the time to lift our nation from the quicksands of racial injustice to the solid rock of brotherhood. Now is the time to make justice a reality for all of God's children.

It would be fatal for the nation to overlook the urgency of the moment. This sweltering summer of the Negro's legitimate discontent will not pass until there is an invigorating autumn of freedom and equality. Nineteen sixty-three is not an end, but a beginning. Those who hope that the Negro needed to blow off steam and will now be content will have a rude awakening if the nation returns to business as usual. There will be neither rest nor tranquility in America until the Negro is granted his citizenship rights. The whirlwinds of revolt will continue to shake the foundations of our nation until the bright day of justice emerges.

But there is something that I must say to my people who stand on the warm threshold which leads into the palace of justice. In the process of gaining our rightful place we must not be guilty of wrongful deeds. Let us not seek to satisfy our thirst for freedom by drinking from the cup of bitterness and hatred.

We must forever conduct our struggle on the high plane of dignity and discipline. We must not allow our creative protest to degenerate into physical violence. Again and again we must rise to the majestic heights of meeting physical force with soul force. The marvelous new militancy which has engulfed the Negro community must not lead us to distrust of all white people, for many of our white brothers, as evidenced by their presence here today, have come to realize that their destiny is tied up with our destiny. And they have come to realize that their freedom is inextricably bound to our freedom. We cannot walk alone.

And as we walk, we must make the pledge that we shall always march ahead. We cannot turn back. There are those who ask the devotees of civil rights, "When will you be satisfied?" We can never be satisfied as long as the Negro is the victim of the unspeakable horrors of police brutality. We can never be satisfied as long as our bodies, heavy with the fatigue of travel, cannot gain lodging in the motels of the highways and the hotels of the cities. We cannot be satisfied as long as the Negro's basic mobility is from a smaller ghetto to a larger one. We can never be satisfied as long as our children are stripped of their selfhood and robbed of their dignity by signs stating "For Whites Only." We cannot be satisfied as long as a Negro in Mississippi cannot vote and a Negro in

New York believes he has nothing for which to vote. No, no, we are not satisfied, and we will not be satisfied until justice rolls down like waters and righteousness like a mighty stream.

I am not unmindful that some of you have come here out of great trials and tribulations. Some of you have come fresh from narrow jail cells. Some of you have come from areas where your quest for freedom left you battered by the storms of persecution and staggered by the winds of police brutality. You have been the veterans of creative suffering. Continue to work with the faith that unearned suffering is redemptive.

Go back to Mississippi, go back to Alabama, go back to South Carolina, go back to Georgia, go back to Louisiana, go back to the slums and ghettos of our northern cities knowing that somehow this situation can and will be changed. Let us not wallow in the valley of despair.

I say to you today, my friends, so even though we face the difficulties of today and tomorrow, I still have a dream. It is a dream deeply rooted in the American dream.

I have a dream that one day this nation will rise up and live out the true meaning of its creed: "We hold these truths to be self-evident; that all men are created equal."

I have a dream that one day on the red hills of Georgia the sons of former slaves and the sons of former slaveowners will be able to sit down together at the table of brotherhood.

I have a dream that one day even the state of Mississippi, a state sweltering with the heat of injustice, sweltering with the heat of oppression, will be transformed into an oasis of freedom and justice.

That my four little children will one day live in a nation where they will not be judged by the color of their skin but by the content of their character; I have a dream today.

I have a dream that one day down in Alabama, with its vicious racists, with its governor having his lips dripping with the words of interposition and nullification, one day right there in Alabama little black boys and black girls will be able to join hands with little white boys and white girls as sisters and brothers; I have a dream today.

I have a dream that one day every valley shall be exalted, every hill and mountain shall be made low, and rough places will be made plane and crooked places will be made straight, and the glory of the Lord shall be revealed, and all flesh shall see it together.

This is our hope. This is the faith that I go back to the South with. With this faith we will be able to hew out of the mountain of despair a stone of hope. With this faith we will be able to transform the jangling discords of our nation into a beautiful symphony of brotherhood. With this faith we will be able to work together, to pray together, to struggle together, to go to jail together, to stand up for freedom together, knowing that we will be free one day.

This will be the day—this will be the day when all of God's children will be able to sing with new meaning "My country 'tis of thee, sweet land of liberty, of thee I sing. Land where my fathers died, land of the pilgrim's pride, from every mountainside, let freedom ring." And if America is to be a great nation, this must become true.

So let freedom ring from the prodigious hilltops of New Hampshire. Let freedom ring from the mighty mountains of New York. Let freedom ring from the heightening Alleghenies of Pennsylvania!

Let freedom ring from the snowcapped Rockies of Colorado!

Let freedom ring from the curvaceous slopes of California!

But not only that; let freedom ring from Stone Mountain of Georgia!

Let freedom ring from Lookout Mountain of Tennessee!

Let freedom ring from every hill and mole hill of Mississippi. From every mountainside let freedom ring.

And when this happens, when we allow freedom to ring—when we let it ring from every village and every hamlet, from every state and every city—we will be able to speed up that day when all of God's children, black men and white men, Jews and Gentiles, Protestants and Catholics, will be able to join hands and sing in the words of the old Negro spiritual, "Free at last! Free at last! Thank God almighty, we are free at last!"

Martin Luther King, Jr., "I Have a Dream." Reprinted by permission of Joan Davies. Copyright © 1963 by Martin Luther King, Jr.

Questions for Discussion

1. How did Dr. King use the principles given in the essay "Changing a Man's Mind" to persuade his listeners?
2. What appeals to ethos and pathos were made in this speech?
3. What aesthetic elements were used to create a unified, eloquent speech?

Ideas for Speaking or Writing

Create a persuasive speech using one of the three methods of organization. Consider methods of increasing personal credibility that are covered in the ethos section. Include emotional appeals and solid research. Use the following suggestions to guide your preparation.

1. Choose an issue that concerns you. You can try to persuade your audience about a factual issue (Caffeine is/is not bad for your

heart), an issue of value (It is/is not wrong for couples to live together before marriage), or a policy issue (Ruling by instant replay rather than by the calls of referees and umpires should/should not be mandatory in televised sporting events).

2. Take a stand (conclusion) on your issue and support your stand with at least three reasons.

3. Give evidence to support your reasons; use evidence in the form of statistics, studies, authoritative testimony, and examples. You may also interview an expert about your issue. Be sure to give the source and the date when you cite your evidence in the speech. Strive to keep your evidence current and turn in an outline and a bibliography on the day of your speech.

4. Think about evidence that opponents to your position might offer. Within the body of your speech, discuss the opposing viewpoint and why it is not as sound as your own.

5. Add emotional appeal through anecdotes, examples, or personal testimony.

6. Begin the speech with a story, statistic, or quote that gets the audience's attention and explains the importance of your issue.

7. Close by repeating the issue, your conclusion, and your reasons. End with a strong quote, a reference back to the introductory story, or other reminder to the audience of how they should believe or act now that they have this information.

8. Begin planning your speech as soon as it is assigned to you so that you have time to find evidence, get organized, and practice before the due date. Rehearse the speech so that you feel comfortable looking up at the audience, and make your delivery conversational. Also, practice handling questions with friends or family members before you give the speech.

More Ideas for Writing

1. Find an issue of the journal *Vital Speeches* in your college or community library. Choose a speech that interests you and analyze it, using the following questions as a guide:

   • What were the interests and concerns of the audience the speaker was addressing? Was the audience supportive, neutral, or hostile to the speaker's position? How well did the speaker adapt to his or her audience?

- What were the issue and conclusion of the speaker?
- How did the speaker use ethos, logos, and pathos to be persuasive? In what areas could the speaker have improved the speech?
- Were the reasons given to support the conclusion backed up by solid evidence? Were these the best reasons given?
- Did the speaker address the opposing viewpoints in any way?
- Did the speaker refute the important points of the opposition in a fair and appropriate manner?
- Were there any fallacies in the reasoning of the speaker? Were the studies and experts cited clear and convincing?
- Were there aesthetic elements that helped the speech to be tightly woven and eloquent? Did the speaker use language elements, such as repetition or beautiful prose, to make his or her points? Did the speaker use the conclusion to refer back to attention-getting points made in the introduction?
- What is your overall impression of this speech?

2. Respond to this excerpt from the article "The Lost Art of the Public Speech" by Bob Greene.

> Speeches—eloquent, painstakingly crafted, carefully thought out, and meticulously paced, full-length speeches—are an endangered American species.
>
> The speech has historically been one of the most important means of serious communication. If a person had an essential message to deliver, that message was conveyed in a speech. That's what politicians and great thinkers did when they had something to say: They labored over a speech until it was ready, and then they delivered it out loud to an attentive audience.
>
> No more. The speech is already an anachronism. Twenty or 30 years ago, the serious speech was still a routine part of American life, and now the serious, influential speech is so rare that it's startling when one comes along.
>
> . . .The people you would most expect to want to continue the tradition of the speech—politicians with a national audience—are rushing to help devalue the speech. Next time you watch network TV news, pay close attention to how national politicians talk. They have begun to speak almost exclusively in those cute little bursts expressly writ-

ten to be picked up by television producers—predigested 8 to 12-second nuggets that don't resemble anything an actual person would ever say during a real-world conversation. . . .

This goes on especially on the floor of Congress. . . . Except in the most uncommon of circumstances, reporters and camera crews are only going to pick up the luminescent little word-pellets that have been custom-constructed for them. . . .

If Abraham Lincoln wanted to make a point today, he would deliver the Gettysburg Sound Bite.[4]

Respond to the claims made in this essay. Support your thesis with evidence from newspapers, magazines, journals, radio and television broadcasts, or interviews. Try give specific examples to prove or disprove the points made by Bob Greene.

3. Listen to a persuasive speech or sermon or watch one on television (if you get C-SPAN, you might be able to listen to a speech presented before Congress, the National Press Club, or another organization). Then analyze the speech, using the following suggestions:
   a. What were the speaker's issue, conclusion, and reasons?
   b. Was the audience for this speaker supportive of, neutral, or hostile to his or her ideas?
   c. To what extent did the speaker use ethos to establish credibility, logos to support his or her conclusion, and pathos to appeal to the audience's emotions?
   d. How did the speaker introduce and conclude the speech? Were there clear transitions throughout the speech? Give specific examples of these.
   e. Were you persuaded in any way by this speech? Explain why or why not.
   f. If you were hired as a consultant to this speaker, what advice would you give to improve his or her speaking?

---

4 Bob Greene, "The Lost Art of the Public Speech," *Chicago Tribune*, April 24, 1992. Reprinted by permission of the publisher.

CHAPTER EIGHT

The Power of Language

Talk Is Not Cheap.
So Who Pays for It?

A critical thinker examines the power of language and how it can be used or misused in an argument.

"If language be not in accordance with the truth of things, affairs cannot be carried on to success."

Confucius, *Analects* (6th Century B.C.)

In his definition of man, Kenneth Burke said, "Man is the symbol-using animal."[1] Language is the powerful system of symbols that enables us to communicate in ways no other creatures can. Speechwriters for politicians or businesspersons can be paid thousands of dollars for a short speech. Those who are willing to pay these enormous fees know that the words that are used and the way they are organized can make or break a campaign, a merger, or a crucial proposal.

On a smaller scale, many professionals attend workshops that focus on how to present ideas—how to sell stereos, clothes, or food by using the correct phrasing. Recently, a large supermarket chain trained its checkout clerks to ask, "Is plastic okay?" They assumed that if people are asked if they want paper or plastic, they would opt for the more expensive paper bags. By asking in a way that narrows the customers' responses to a polite yes or a less polite no, they hoped to cut down on the expenses of using paper.

Employees who work in front office positions are often trained to handle the public by speaking to them in ways that reflect courtesy and diffuse anger. You may have noticed that in a well-managed store, you can complain and receive sympathetic words from a clerk (if not your money back)!

In our personal lives, we think about phrasing things to get the desired results. Teenagers and adults may rehearse their opening words carefully before calling a potential date. Children think about and practice how to ask their parents for treats or money. At some time, you probably sat in your room or car rehearsing what you were going to say to someone; we usually engage in that kind of preparatory behavior when we are dealing with an emotional situation—a fight with a loved one, a proposal of marriage, a request for a change in salary or working hours. We believe, consciously or unconsciously, that our choice of words and the way we say those words can influence others.

This chapter explores the influence that words have on people, especially as citizens and consumers. We will look at the way words can help us to clarify issues and, conversely, how words can be used to make issues more obscure and difficult to understand.

---

1   Kenneth Burke, *Language as Symbolic Action: Essays on Life, Literature, and Method* (Berkeley: University of California Press, 1966), p. 3.

Denotation and Connotation

The first principle to understand is that words, as symbols, are extremely powerful. To comprehend this idea, consider two terms, *denotation* and *connotation*.

Denotation is the specific object or act that a word points to or refers to. Concrete words like *dog, van, walk, swim*, and proper nouns like *Marisa* all point to objects, actions, or persons; these objects, actions, or persons are the word's denotations. Abstract words have no definite denotation.

Connotation refers to all the images—positive, negative, or neutral—that are associated with any given denotation. The connotations of words include their emotional meanings. Both concrete and abstract words have connotations that are different for different individuals.

If you think about those definitions, you might conclude that although denotations are the same for everyone, connotations vary from person to person. For example, the name *Terry* simply refers to a given person (denotation); still, I may have a positive connotation for the name while you may dislike the name because of a negative experience you had with someone named Terry in your life. Try this exercise to see if you and another person have a disagreement about connotations of names.

EXERCISE

Purpose: To understand and experience the power of connotations.

1. Meet with a friend, family member, or ideally a "significant other" (boyfriend or girlfriend) and together try to pick out a name for a boy and for a girl that you would both be happy to give to a child. See if in your discussion you can isolate how the connotations of some names are different for both of you because of your memory of different people (denotations).

   When you find a name that you can agree on, state why. What are the positive connotations that you have for the name, either because of past associations or because of the sound or meaning of the name?

2. Ask your parents or someone else's parents what they had in mind when they chose a name for their son or daughter. Specifically, ask

them how they decided upon the name and what connotations they associated with that name.

Since children often live up to parental expectations, try to assess whether the name had any effect on the child as they were growing up. Did the name imply strength, weakness, friendliness, masculinity, or femininity, or did it call forth images of a famous person? Interestingly, teachers in one study favored papers written by children who had typical names (like Mike and Jennifer) and reacted less favorably to papers that were signed by children with less-common names (like Horace).

The Power of Connotation

We may have personal connotations that are based on our unique past experiences; we also tend to have cultural connotations associated with names and words. When the child star Shirley Temple was at the height of her career, there were thousands of parents who named their daughters Shirley after her, but in the succeeding generation, there were very few. In the 1960s, the name *Bruce* was associated with weakness or femininity, but in the 1980s Bruce (perhaps because of the Bruce Lee films) was seen as a strong, macho name.

Semanticists, who study the meaning of words, use a tool that allows them to assess the cultural connotations of a word. This tool is called a **semantic differential**.

fast	…	…	…	…	…	slow
strong	…	…	…	…	…	weak
beautiful	…	…	…	…	…	ugly
active	…	…	…	…	…	passive
brave	…	…	…	…	…	cowardly
good	…	…	…	…	…	bad
powerful	…	…	…	…	…	powerless

Meaning is based upon three dimensions: Is it good or bad? Is it active or passive? Is it powerful or weak? Note that all of the polar dimensions given in the semantic differential fit into one of these three categories.

In several classroom studies of the words *lady* versus *woman*, it was discovered that most students see the term *lady* as good, passive, and weak, while the word *woman* is seen as neither good or bad, but as active and strong. Advertisers commission studies of words to discover if the name they will give to a car, cola, or laundry detergent has positive connotations for their target audiences.

We can say that a name or word is just a label and has no effect on us, but consider the following examples:

- When you go into a gift or novelty store, you are likely to see a section of "over the hill" paraphernalia for persons who are turning 30, 40, 50, or 60. You know that, logically, when you have a birthday you are essentially the same biochemical and emotional being you were the day before. Yet when the label *30* or *40* is attached to you, you may suddenly experience a sense of despair, futility, or mild depression because of the connotations (images) associated with that age. Conversely, ask young children how old they are and they will usually quite conscious of whether they are 5 or 5 1/2 or 5 3/4 and will use these minute distinctions as status symbols among their peers. People who reach the age of 21 in our country (the age of full adult privileges) will sometimes say with surprise, "I don't feel 21" or "I don't feel different." The main difference is in the label.

- If you believe that abortion is wrong, do you want to be described as *anti-abortion, anti-choice,* or *pro-life*? Do you want to use the word(s) *fetus, products of conception, unborn, pre-born,* or *baby*?

     If you believe that abortion is a right, do you want to be described as *pro-abortion, anti-life,* or *pro-choice*? Do you want to use the word(s) *fetus, products of conception, unborn, pre-born,* or *baby*?

- Colorado's governor vetoed a "lettuce libel" law that would have let farmers sue anyone who falsely insulted their agricultural products. Now, the produce police have struck in Louisiana, where a new law prohibits "disparagement of any perishable agricultural or aquacultural food product." Could this lead to a Crawfish Anti-Defamation League?[2]

- Leonore Hauck, a managing editor for the Random House dictionary division, discussed how definitions change to reflect current sensibilities. "One of the definitions of 'girl' in 1947 was 'a young, unmarried woman.' Today we say, 'a young, immature woman, esp. formerly, an unmarried one.' The word 'formerly'

---

[2] Amy Bernstein, "Eye on the '90s," *U.S. News and World Report*, December 23, 1991, p. 17.

shows you how the meaning has changed, and a note warns the reader, 'Many women today resent being called *girls.*'"[3]

Reification: When Words Take on More Power than Reality

Now imagine yourself subject to a classroom experiment. You are sitting in class, about to see a film. To make the session more festive, your instructor gives you crackers and a home-made paté to munch as you view the movie. You enjoy the hearty taste of this snack, and when the film is over and the lights go back on, you ask for the recipe. Your teacher then informs you that you have been eating dog biscuits with canned cat food on top.

If you are like many people, you may experience a sense of nausea and disgust, although some cat food and dog food is perfectly edible for humans and is more nutritionally balanced than most fast food. But the labels put on this food, the words themselves, not the actual products, might make you sick.

In the same way, some people feel special when they are served expensive caviar or sweetbreads (usually at upscale gatherings). The fact that they are eating fish eggs or cow organs has no jarring effect on them because there are such powerful, positive connotations associated with the names of these foods.

When the words themselves become more powerful and real than objective reality, we have a perfect case of non-critical thinking. The formal term for this very widespread but largely unnoticed phenomenon is **reification**. It leads to such human foibles as the following:

- Paying more money for "name brands" that may have the same ingredients as generic brands of products.
- Feeling confident when wearing designer label jeans or unworthy when wearing possibly higher-quality jeans that don't carry the popular label.
- Feeling like you can't succeed in a math or writing course because a teacher in fourth grade called you "poor in math" or because of one previous grade.

---

3 Patricia Holt, "The Woman Who Decides What Goes in Webster's," *San Francisco Chronicle*, October 24, 1991, p. E-5.

- Feeling overweight even when you are at or below your ideal weight because you were called fat years ago. (Karen Carpenter, the singer who died of complications of anorexia nervosa, was reportedly very upset about a reviewer who referred to her as overweight, and that label may have contributed to her obsession with her weight.)

- In "primitive" cultures, being subject to stomach cramps because you know that someone is sticking needles in a doll with your name on it. Or in "sophisticated" cultures, having hotels with elevators that go from floor 12 to floor 14, because no one wants to stay on the (unlucky) 13th floor. (Note that this arrangement is especially true in hotels that house gambling casinos, which are presumably filled with people concerned about maximizing their "luck.")

Sometimes reification can cause life-or-death consequences; our superstitious and confused thinking can get us into deep trouble. Consider the story of a 25-year-old Frenchman, Lucien Schlitz, and his 19-year-old first mate, Catherine Plessz, who set out on a long cruise for the tropics aboard a 26-foot steel cutter. They started in the Mediterranean Sea, which was so rough that it put the boat on its side. The boat righted itself, but later on a freak wave swept over the boat and both Lucien and Catherine found themselves in the water. Through desperate efforts, both managed to get back on board, but they no longer had a rudder (steering mechanism), so they were adrift.

The boat was still whole even though it had been knocked around by the storm. It would seem, to our clear, dry heads, that the logical thing would be to remain on board with the comforts of food, water, and blankets and to wait for help. But Lucien's mind was stressed and fatigued, and he began to think obsessively about the life raft. He was terribly concerned that it wouldn't inflate, so he pulled it open, nearly losing it to the wind in the process. Since it measured six feet across, he couldn't fit it in the cockpit, so he moored it to the back of his steel boat.

> Soon after that, by mental processes that would surely be a feast for any psychologist, the only solution that seemed left to Lucien and Catherine was to take refuge in the *life* raft which represented safety [my italics]—still, as we see it, in a pattern of psychological aberration which explains the inevitability of everything they did. . . . On 14 September, 1972, Lucien and Catherine had now sought safety in their life raft after throwing into it some tinned food, some distress flares, two 20-liter jerricans of water, a compass and the leather sack with their money and their papers. Then the line linking them to the *Njord* parted.[4]

Over the next days, Lucien and Catherine needlessly suffered great thirst, hunger, sleep deprivation, and cold (from being tossed into the water often by the waves that upset the raft). On the twelfth day,

> just as they had decided that survival was too difficult and they would make a quick end to it by drinking all the rest of their water at once for a last sensation of well-being, they were spotted at fifty yards, despite 8 foot troughs, and rescued by a cargo ship.[5]

This extended example reveals that we can give a word or phrase (in this case, *life raft*) power of its own and make faulty decisions based on that word or phrase.

SKILL

Recognize the power we can attach to words. Pause and consider the facts, knowing how labels can be deceiving.

---

4   Bernard Robin, *Survival at Sea* (Camden, Maine: International Marine Publishing Company, 1981), p. 112.
5   Ibid., p. 114.

Meanings Are in People

General semanticists, who study the effects of words on people, have articulated some key principles to guide our responsible use of words.

Their main principle is: *The word is not the thing.* They use the analogy of a map (the words) showing a particular territory (reality). The map can give us information about the territory, but it is not the territory and it can never show all the details of the territory. Our responsibility as thinkers is to realize that words are limited and to check out the territory before we draw hasty conclusions. If Lucien and Catherine, the sailors just discussed, had had the strength and wisdom to think over their options, they would have realized that, though their inflatable raft was *called* a life raft, their lives were more secure if they remained on board their cutter and sent up flares from there, saving the raft for a second vessel. In fact the sailboat *Njord* was found adrift, but sound and dry, many days before Lucien and Catherine were rescued.

The meaning of words lies in people and not, magically, in the words themselves. Dictionary definitions are useful for providing knowledge, but they often fall short in creating understanding among people who use words. *Webster's New International Dictionary* may define *love* as "a deep and tender feeling of affection for, or attachment or devotion to, a person or persons," but we can't rely on that definition when our significant other says "I love you."

We need instead to find out what the word *love* means to an individual (does it mean "I want to marry you," or "I enjoy your company," or "I love every person and you're a person," or "I will always be with you no matter what happens," or something else?). If your friend wants you to meet her at class *early* and gives you no further explanation, there's a good chance that one of you may be there a few minutes before class starts and the other may be there an hour before, waiting impatiently.

SKILL

Realize that meanings are in people. Ask "What do you mean?" whenever a word or phrase is unclear or is a potential source of misunderstanding.

This skill may seem so simple as to be insulting to your intelligence, and yet it is one of the most valuable and underused skills we have. We tend to use a form of what psychologists term **projection** when we hear a phrase, a political speech, or a commercial message; that is, we tend to assume that what the other person means is what we would mean if we had used those words.

Our tendency to project explains why we are so often disappointed with blind dates ("This person is wonderful"), political candidates ("I care about the 'little people' in America"), or products ("Pimples virtually disappear!"). Sometimes we don't take time to question what the people who bring us these messages mean, because we really want to believe there is the perfect date, political solution, or pimple formula for us.

Often, then, the cause of projection may lie in our emotional need to believe something is true; other times, we are just untrained or too busy or lazy to pursue the reality of what is being said to us. And sometimes speakers or writers make things so confusing that it takes a grand effort to understand them. Consider a report that reads: "We have confirmed that the overturning of the presidential veto to create an amendment protecting the flag has been enforced."

In states where voters are given choices through propositions, there is often confusion in the wording of these propositions. For example, years ago, in California, if you voted *yes* on a particular proposition, that meant you were saying *no* to nuclear power plant expansion; if you voted *no* that meant you were saying *yes* to this expansion. Uninformed voters probably often cast votes they didn't really mean.

To help us defend against words that don't clearly represent reality, we will examine four common problems with language: **vagueness**, **ambiguity**, **doublespeak**, and **weasel words**. All are used by advertisers, salespersons, politicians, and others.

The Problem of Vagueness

As we have seen, abstract words are words that can easily mean different things to different people; they have a variety of connotations and no fixed denotation. The problem that arises with the use of abstract words is **vagueness**. A word or phrase is vague when its meaning is unclear.

Vagueness is a common problem in public discourse. Some politicians will use only vague terms that have generally positive connotations and not define what they mean, hoping that each listener will like the sound of the promises being made. When asked for specific details about their plans, they may commit the fallacy of "ignoring the question" (see the following example). Conversely, a good politician will say he has a plan for "increased aid to the needy," and then define what he means by *aid* and what he means by *the needy* and then what, exactly, he has in mind.

Good reporters will notice vague language and press politicians to explain themselves. If the politicians explain using only more vague, abstract terms, be careful about supporting them (because you don't know what you're supporting).

Example

Reporter: Mr. Candidate, you mentioned you have a comprehensive plan to deal with our terrible freeway delays. Can you tell us what is involved in this plan?

Candidate: Gladly. I plan to use all available resources to create a wide-range solution to this problem that has plagued us for years.

Reporter: Can you be more specific? Are you planning expansions, and would these cause greater bridge tolls or taxes for the citizens?

Candidate: As I've said, the program will be really comprehensive, and each citizen will be considered and served. If I'm elected, you're going to see some incredibly positive changes.

This candidate appears bright enough to describe his program in glowing terms, but he is unwilling or unable to detail what he is actually proposing. Perhaps the candidate hasn't formulated a plan, or perhaps he avoids giving details about his plans for fear of alienating special interest groups.

Example

Concerned Family: Can you tell us if this operation on our mother's hip is dangerous, and, also, will she have use of her leg afterward?

Surgeon: All surgery has risks and these things are always hard to predict.

Family:	Well, can you give us typical recovery rates and times?
Surgeon:	Each person is different, but you can rest assured we are doing everything in our power to help.

In this example, everything the surgeon said may be true, but he has not provided any statistics or details to help the family be at ease. Health care professionals can't afford to make promises they can't keep; still, you need to press for information so you can make the best decisions for your health and the well being of your loved ones.

Example

Darlene:	Paul, I really love you, and I think it would be good for our relationship if we started seeing other people.
Paul:	What are you saying? Do you want to break our engagement?
Darlene:	No, nothing like that. I just think it would be healthy for us to date other people.
Paul:	Are you interested in seeing someone else?
Darlene:	No, not at all. I think we'd both just grow more if we were able to experience a variety of relationships.
Paul:	What does that mean?
Darlene:	Well, it means I still love you, but I just think it would be great for our relationship if we saw other people too.

In this situation, Darlene is either confused about what she wants or is sure of what she wants but doesn't know how to tell Paul. He needs to keep pressing for specifics for the sake of his mental health!

Examples: Commercials with Vague Wording

Get your clothes a whiter white and a brighter bright!

Smoke Winters—with cool, smooth flavor!

It's the real thing!

The Hugo Company—we care about people.

By this time, you should be identifying vagueness in language, and, in this case, how advertisers, like politicians, use positive connotations to excite the audience. But, the question is, what are they talking about?

All the preceding examples are meant to show how frustrating it can be to get people to move from the abstract to the concrete so we can really understand what they are saying. Some people are purposefully vague; others just have a hard time expressing themselves or knowing exactly what they want to communicate. Still, critical thinkers need to persist in understanding what is meant by vague words and phrases; then, any decisions about voting, having surgery, buying a product, or continuing a relationship can be made rationally.

EXERCISES

Purpose: To recognize how abstract terms can be misleading and how we can avoid the problems associated with projection. To realize that meanings are in people, not in words.

1. Give an extended example, or several examples, of the use of abstract terms that are not defined by the speaker or writer. You can find these examples in editorials, political speeches, advertisements, or, perhaps, when you converse with friends. List the vague terms or phrases used and tell how different people could interpret these words in different ways. If possible, extend the exercise by asking someone who is using abstract terms to clarify what he or she means by those terms. For further practice, see the discussion questions and suggestions for essay or speech writing after the last article in this chapter.

2. Think of some examples of projection that have occurred in your life or in the life of someone you know. How could the problems associated with projection have been avoided? Consider a time when you misunderstood someone's words or instructions.

Example

I missed an English class and called a friend to get the assignment. She said we had to turn in a copy of a resume that we might use to apply for a job. Then she said, "You also need a cover." I assumed she was using the word *cover* the way I use it, so I bought a report cover. What she really meant was that we were supposed to have a cover letter introducing ourselves to an employer. The cover letter goes with the resume.

I could have avoided these problems by asking what she meant when she mentioned a cover. Or I could have repeated back to her what the assignment was; then she might have caught my error.

3. This exercise should be done in classroom groups. Assume you have been selected as a citizen's advisory committee to the Supreme Court. Your task is to form a clear definition of one (or more) of the following words or phrases: *obscenity, life, cruel and unusual punishment*, or *adult.* Your definition will be used to guide future decisions on issues related to these terms.

In your discussion, try to come to a consensus. Whenever possible, resolve disagreements by presenting evidence to clarify positions. You may also give personal examples to increase the understanding of one another's viewpoints.

After you have used the time allotted (at least 30 minutes), choose a member of your group to present your results to the class as a whole. The spokesperson should discuss:

- The definitions the group agreed upon.
- The difficulties in coming to consensus and why they occurred. Consider especially the values of group members and their different experiences.

Article for Discussion

Read the following as an example of the power of words.

Federal Judge Orders Lawyer Not to Use Her Maiden Name

by Tara Bradley-Steck
Contra Costa Times, July 14, 1988

PITTSBURGH—A federal judge told an attorney he doesn't allow anyone to "use that Ms." in his courtroom, ordered her to use her husband's name or go to jail and found her colleague in contempt for protesting.

"Do what I tell you or you're going to sleep in the county jail tonight. You can't tell me how to run my courtroom," Senior U.S. District Judge Hubert I. Teitelbaum told attorney Barbara Wolvowitz.

The judge told Wolvowitz, whose husband is University of Pittsburgh law professor Jules Lobel, that she must go by the name Mrs. Lobel in his courtroom.

When her co-counsel, Jon Pushinsky, protested, Teitelbaum found him in contempt of court for "officious intermeddling" and gave him a suspended sentence of 30 days in jail.

During a disjointed dialogue Friday that covered about 20 pages of court transcript, Teitelbaum told Wolvowitz that Mrs. Lobel is her legal name "under the laws of the state of Pennsylvania.

"And that's what I want you to be, to call yourself from here on in this courtroom." he said. "That's an intolerable kind of thing."

The judge claimed a married woman must petition Common Pleas Court for permission to use her maiden name. The Pennsylvania Family Law Practice and Procedure Handbook said no legal proceedings are required if a woman chooses to use her maiden name.

Teitelbaum, presiding over a race discrimination suit against PPG Industries Inc., also asked each of the six female jurors on Friday if she used her husband's name or maiden name. All used their husbands' names.

Wolvowitz, 36, said she was "in shock for two days."

"I've practiced for 10 years. I've gotten into arguments with judges but never over something like this. I can't quite understand what happened," said Wolvowitz, who had never previously argued a case before Teitelbaum. "After it was over and the jury left, I had tears in my eyes."

When the trial resumed Monday, Teitelbaum denied Wolvowitz's request for a mistrial, and the attorney again refused to be called Mrs. Lobel.

"What if I call you sweetie?" said Teitelbaum, 73, a former U.S. attorney appointed to the federal bench by President Nixon in 1970.

The judge declared he would refer to Wolvowitz only as "counselor."

Reprinted by permission.

Questions for Discussion

1. What's in a name? What significance do you think that each person gave to the use of the title "Ms." accompanied by a maiden name? In other words, what connotations does the title probably have for each person?
2. Why do think the judge asked each of the six female jurors if she used her husband's name or her maiden name?
3. Analyze the judge's statement, "And that's what I want you to be, to call yourself from here on in this courtroom."

4. What does the abstract term "officious intermeddling" mean in concrete terms?

Ambiguity in Language

Ambiguity in language can also cause problems in communication. A word or expression is ambiguous when it has two or more different meanings. Often, riddles use ambiguity to create a puzzling situation; one common riddle asks you to turn the following drawing into a six by adding just one line.

IX

The answer, reflecting one of the types of sixes, is

SIX

Ambiguity is also the problem in these humorous, but real headlines compiled by Jay Leno:

> "Drought turns coyotes to watermelons."[6]
>
> "Need Plain Clothes Security. Must have shoplifting experience."[7]
>
> "Foreclosure Listings: Entire state of New Jersey available."[8]

On a more serious note, ambiguity in language is confusing and causes numerous communication problems, as in the following example.

In the mid-1960s, FBI director J. Edgar Hoover was reading a typed copy of a letter he had just dictated to his secretary. He didn't like the way she had formatted the letter, so he wrote on the bottom, "Watch the borders," and asked her to re-type it. The secretary did as she was instructed and sent it off to all top agents. For the next two weeks FBI agents were put out on special alert along the Canadian and Mexican borders.[9]

---

6 Jay Leno, *Headlines* (New York: Warner Books, 1989), p. 99.

7 Ibid., p. 148.

8 Ibid., p. 48.

9 Roger von Oech, *A Whack on the Side of the Head* (New York: Warner Books, 1990), p. 114.

Drabble ® by Kevin Fagan
DRABBLE reprinted by permission of UFS, Inc.

Ambiguous language is especially confusing between cultures. Many expressions that are common to speakers of one language group (or subculture) are misunderstood by members of other cultures. For example, when asked if they would like more coffee, some English-speaking people respond, "No, thanks. I'm fine." People who are learning the language can't understand what seems to be a report on the state of one's health as an answer to a question about more coffee.

As in all cases of possible confusion in language, a critical thinker should consider alternative meanings to words and phrases and clarify terms by asking, "What do you mean?"

Doublespeak, Including Weasel Words

We have seen how vagueness and ambiguity in language can be used either unintentionally or deliberately to make issues cloudy. Words can be used to deceive in other ways. In this section, we will look at doublespeak and its subcategory, weasel words.

Doublespeak is "language used to lie or mislead while pretending to tell the truth . . . it is used by the highest elected officials, by bureaucrats in state and local government, by members of industry, academia, and other areas of society in order to deceive, to make the bad seem good, the negative appear positive, the disastrous seem tolerable."[10] If language is the map, as general semanticists like to say, and reality is the territory, then doublespeak is the creation of a map that distorts the territory. Those who hear doublespeak are deceived and misled about the territory because of the map.

---

[10] Position Paper, *National Council of Teachers of English*, 1988.

In his popular book, *Doublespeak,* William Lutz claims that doublespeak is

> a very conscious use of language as a weapon or tool by those in power to achieve their ends at our expense. While some doublespeak is funny, much of it is frightening. We laugh and dismiss doublespeak as empty or meaningless words at our own peril, for, as George Orwell saw so clearly, the great weapon of power, exploitation, manipulation and oppression is language. It is only by being aware of the pervasiveness of doublespeak and its function as a tool of social, economic and political control that we can begin to fight those who would use language against us.[11]

Doublespeak includes the use of **euphemism**, which means the use of a less direct but more acceptable term to describe an event, person, or object. In their daily use, euphemisms are not usually meant to deceive and to distort, but to soften harsh realities. We use euphemisms to explain disease and death to children when we make such statements as, "Aunt Lily isn't feeling well today, so she's in the hospital," or "Grandma passed away." We may use euphemisms to sound better to ourselves or others when we describe ourselves as *slender* (instead of skinny), or *hefty* (instead of fat), or *under a lot of stress* (instead of irritable).

A teacher might use the euphemism "We're going to have a quiz" to announce a 50-item exam, reasoning that people would not panic studying for a "quiz" as much as they would for a "test" and therefore they would do better. Yet, a student might prefer a 10-point "test" to a 50-point "quiz."

Euphemism as doublespeak is common in business and government. In some cases, the euphemisms chosen become another category of doublespeak, which Lutz terms "inflated language." Inflated language is designed to make the commonplace seem extraordinary or to make simple things more complex than they are. Below are some examples compiled by the National Council of Teachers of English.

Fired: dehired, non-renewed, non-retained, selected out

Layoffs: negative employee retention, workforce adjustments, headcount reductions, career alternative enhancement program

---

11   William Lutz, *Doublespeak* (New York: Harper Collins, 1989), pp. xii–xiii.

Pain: discomfort

Death: terminal living, negative patient care outcome (or "That person is no longer a patient at this hospital.")

Classrooms: pupil stations

Poor: economically non-affluent, economically marginalized

Prisoner: client of the correctional system

Lazy: motivationally dispossessed

Doublespeak is a form of personal or corporate denial of painful realities. No company wants to be seen as "firing" employees because that term has negative, cruel connotations. They want to be seen as compassionate, so they use terms that present the company in the best possible light. Many professionals use euphemisms to soften or inflate reality. Psychologists refer to someone who regularly explodes into bursts of anger as a "borderline personality." Real estate agents refer to tiny houses as "darling cottages" or "dollhouses"; they may describe dumps that are falling off of foundations as "needing a little tender loving care."

Doublespeak is used in our personal lives also. If you have children or siblings, you know that a fight is explained differently from each person's viewpoint. A "light tap" to one person ends up being a "big hit" when described by the other. Some women in the business world have complained that when they have made an unpopular decision they are labeled as "aggressive" whereas a favored male counterpart would have been labeled "assertive" or "a strong manager." We may describe a friend of ours who rants and raves at small provocations as "just excitable" or even "dynamic."

EXERCISE

Purpose: To recognize euphemisms and how they are applied.

Think of euphemisms that you've heard or used. Give some euphemisms for the following: selfish, cheap, war, lies, kill. How about for a badly damaged car that someone wants to sell?

Now try an exercise that British philosopher Bertrand Russell created and called "Conjugating Irregular Verbs." Take a personal characteristic or action and express it favorably, neutrally, and unfavorably as follows:

I'm slender.
You're thin.
She's skinny.

I'm frugal.
You're careful with money.
He's cheap.

Complete these conjugations:

1. I have high self-esteem.

2. I'm curious about my neighbors.

3. I like to relax.

4. I'm pleasantly plump.

5. I don't like to stifle my child's creativity.

6. I'm not a perfectionist about cleaning.

7. My car has a lot of character.

Other forms of doublespeak include *jargon,* the use of specialized language to exclude or impress people who don't understand the terminology, and *gobbledygook,* which is vague language used to confuse and overwhelm those who hear it. These forms of doublespeak have been labeled *crazy talk* by professor and semanticist Neil Postman. He defines crazy talk as talk that reflects "bad" purposes.[12] Postman cites Werner Erhard, the founder of the very successful Erhard Seminars Training (a self-help group) as using crazy talk in the following excerpt from an interview:

> Sometimes people get the notion that the purpose of Erhard Seminars Training is to make you better. It is not. I happen to think that you are perfect exactly the way you are. . . . The problem is that people get stuck acting the way they were instead of being the way they are. . . .
>   The purpose of est training is to transform your ability to experience living so that the situations you have been trying to change or have been putting up with clear up just in the process of living.[13]

---

12   Neil Postman, *Crazy Talk, Stupid Talk* (New York: Delacorte Press, 1976), p. 83.

13   Ibid.

Advertisers also use inflated language and gobbledygook to impress consumers. They want to present their products as necessary and in some cases even miraculous, and they have developed the tools to do so in the form of creative doublespeak. According to Carl Wrighter, an advertising copywriter, "Today's advertising industry is the most potent and powerful mass marketing and merchandising instrument ever devised by man."[14] He claims that, even if you think that you're smart enough to see through advertising tricks, you're really not because of the subtle power of **weasel words**.

A weasel word is "a word used in order to evade or retreat from a direct or forthright statement or position" (*Webster's New International Dictionary*).[15] Let's look at how advertisers use these words so that they can make great claims and not have to prove them.

According to Wrighter, the most often used weasel is the word *help* or *helps*. An ad might say, "This cream will help prevent acne." Or "Our new formula helps the pain to go away." "This mouthwash helps stop the germs." Or "This pill helps you feel drowsy so you can sleep." Notice that no one is claiming that the products will prevent acne, make pain disappear, stop germs, or guarantee sleep. They only promise to *help* do those things.

By only promising to help, advertisers relieve the manufacturers of any responsibility for the actual effectiveness of their products. Wrighter says that we don't really hear the word *help*; we only hear the promise (perhaps because we want to believe there is a perfect product for our problem). He also believes that 75 percent of advertising uses the word *help*. If that's true, you should be able to detect this weasel word easily. Watch also for modifications of this word such as "significantly helps" or "greatly improves."

Another prominent weasel word is *like*. The word *like* is used to "romance the product," which means to make you think about something bigger, better, or more interesting than the product and to associate the product with that better thing. You might think of "romancing the product" as creating a faulty analogy.

Wrighter gives several examples of romancing the product. An old Mateus ad claims that drinking their wine is like taking a trip to Portugal. When the ad appears on television, depicting a romantic Portuguese holiday, we forget that we'll be drinking it in our own homes—no beaches, music, or wonderful meals will accompany it like they do in the ad. Other great images from the past include "It cleans

---

14 Carl Wrighter, *I Can Sell You Anything* (New York: Random House, 1972), p. 2.

15 Ibid., p. 23.

like a white tornado" and "It's like a great taste explosion in your mouth." Some products are romanced with a name, like Softique (for tissues) or Beverly Hills (for a perfume). Lipton compares their tea to the experience of a deep massage.

EXERCISE

Purpose: To identify gobbledygook and romancing the product.

An ad for Mercury Sable automobiles featured a silhouette of a dancing couple behind a car.

1. Explain how the following words, which accompanied the ad, were used to romance the product.
2. Point out the vague gobbledygook that is used to describe the "new" changes in the car.

We dressed in silence.
And drove.
When we walked in,
She said something to the piano player.
Next thing, I hear this song we used to love.
She takes my hand. We dance. And something
that was there before, was back. Only stronger.
Mercury Sable.
The new, remarkably sophisticated Sable.
Its body has been totally restyled.
Its interior so thoroughly redesigned
even the controls are easier to read and reach.
It has standard driver and optional passenger air bags.
It rides smoother. Quieter.
And makes driving more of a pleasure.
The car that started it all,
does it again.

Reprinted by permission of Gerry L. Donnelly, Lincoln-Mercury Division, Ford Motor Company, 300 Renaissance Center, Box 43329, Detroit, MI 48243.

Other weasel words cited by Wrighter include:

• *Virtual* or *Virtually:* This word means "almost, but not in fact."

"Virtually foolproof"
"Virtually never needs service"
"Virtually trouble-free"

An ad for a "medication tracking system" reads as follows:

Do you worry when a loved one forgets to take daily medication? Or takes too many pills because he or she loses track of the dosage schedule? You can help by giving Medi-Track™. This caring gift makes it virtually impossible for medication users to lose track of their schedule—no matter where they happen to be.

- *Acts or Works:* This word is another form of *helps* and is often used with the word *help*.
  "Works like magic"
  "Works to help prevent"
  "Acts against. . ."
  "Acts on the cough control center"

- *Can be:* When advertisers say their product *can be* useful they make no definite claim that it *will be* useful. *Can be* simply means that it is possible. Variations are *could be*, *might be*, and *may be*.
  "Shine toothpaste can be of significant value when used in a monitored dental program."

- *Up to: Up to* implies a range from zero to the figure that is given. Consumers tend to hear only the largest number.
  "You may have won up to $500.00."
  "Dude deodorant gives you protection for up to 12 hours."
  "Come to our sale and get up to 50% off."

- *As much as:* Similar to *up to*, *as much as* means that you might get the ultimate benefit described, but you might not.
  "As much as 20 percent greater mileage"
  "Blabble gum gives you as much as an hour more chewing satisfaction than the leading brand."

Also, Wrighter suggests that you be aware of vague terms such as *refreshes, comforts, tackles, fights,* and *comes on.* These are abstract terms with positive connotations that may or may not have a basis in reality when referring to a specific product. Some terms that are commonly used because of their sound but that have no definite meaning include:

Fortified   Flavor and Taste
Style and Good Looks   Different, Special, Exclusive

Sometimes these terms are strung together:

Phitrin: New. Improved. Bigger. Better.

SKILL

Recognize when words are used to deceive and confuse readers and listeners.

Recognizing the problem of misleading commercial claims, the federal government has been making attempts to set clear standards about the meaning of labels given to foods. Consumers have been confused about the meaning of terms such as *fresh, light, low-fat,* and *cholesterol-free.*

New regulations will set guidelines for categories of products, such as yogurt or cheese. Currently, food companies can determine the serving size given on the package. If they make it small enough, then their product can be called lower in fat than a similar product with a larger serving size.

But we as consumers can't rely on government agencies to clarify our thinking about commercial messages. We need to recognize doublespeak in all of its forms and keep in mind William Lutz's admonishment about advertising:

Every word in an ad is there for a reason; no word is wasted. Your job is to figure out exactly what each word is doing in an ad—what each word really means, not what the advertiser wants you to think it means. Remember, the ad is trying to get you to buy a product, so it will put the product in the best possible light, using any device, trick, or means legally allowed. Your only defense against advertising is to develop and use a strong critical reading, listening, and looking ability.[16]

16   William Lutz, *Doublespeak* (New York: HarperCollins, 1989), p. 102

EXERCISE

Purpose: To discover weasel words in persuasive messages.

Analyze some television, radio, or magazine advertising, campaign literature, or junk mail, specifically looking for doublespeak and weasel words. Bring samples to share with your class.

Try to include campaign messages in your search. Look for literature that comes in the mail dealing with upcoming elections.

What particular "weasels" did you find used the most? What effect did the weasel have on the message—i.e., why do you think that the writer of the message used that weasel?

Use the following sample ads to get you started:

Having a party and don't know what to serve? Try Tony's Barbequed Party Wings for that spicy hot partytime action. Our secret sauce has 121 of the world's finest ingredients mixed to virtual perfection and applied with loving care to each piece. So, spice up your next party with Tony's Party Wings; you'll feel like you're flying high with satisfaction.

Is your smile an average dull white in an average dull world? Make the change and brighten your outlook. For that all-day smile, your teeth deserve the best. *Flash* toothpaste with ZX–19 can help whiten and brighten your teeth for up to 8 hours. Stand out from the crowd—join the Flash generation, and change your dull world into a *Flash* world.

Vote for Richmond for school board. She knows about the newest classroom technology and can help make our school district the most progressive in the state. As a parent herself, J. Richmond cares about excellence in education and she shares your concerns. Having J. Richmond on the board is like having a friend attending the meetings for you.

Chapter Highlights

1. Critical thinkers should be aware of the power of words to both clarify and obscure issues.
2. Language has a persuasive impact on people because of connotations, the images associated with words and phrases.

3. Reification occurs when words take on more power than reality.
4. Projection occurs when we neglect to realize that the meaning of words are in people.
5. Four common problems with language are vagueness, ambiguity, doublespeak, and weasel words.

Articles for Discussion

"I didn't have a bad check. . . . I had a problem check."

Dick Cheney, in reference to the check-bouncing scandal of 1992

"I did make a goof—I trusted this bank. I can't just say I'm a victim. I'm embarrassed."

Barbara Boxer, Democratic congresswoman, in reference to the congressional check-bouncing scandal of 1992

No-Fault Syntax

by John Leo
U.S. News and World Report, August 19, 1991

"Obviously, some mistakes were made," said John Sununu, referring to his travel adventures as White House chief of staff. This is a wonderful nonapology, which seizes the blame and casts it firmly into outer space. Having achieved quotability, Sununu rested. But he could easily have gone on, paddling along in the passive voice ("Aisle seats were reserved and filled" or "Haircuts in Hawaii and stamp auctions on Samoa were flown toward") without actually associating himself with any of these mysterious and expensive travel decisions that people keep saying he was somehow involved in. Of course, Sununu could have been protecting the identity of some loyal assistant who misguidedly put the boss on all those planes and limos. It's possible that the aide sent him hurtling along to all those ski slopes and far-off dental appointments without bothering to inform him about it.

Probably not, though. More likely, Sununu was just making exceptional use of the traditional passive voice to fudge things as best he could. President Bush played right along, saying that Sununu had apologized to him, not for screwing up, or for ethically dubious behavior, but for any embarrassment that the travel controversy might have caused. The president said his heart aches for the Sununu family "because they've been through a lot . . . kind of what I refer to as a piling-on syndrome." Sununu and his family are passive here, either bystanders or victims. The active and therefore blamable forces are both abstractions: the travel controversy and the piling-on syndrome.

Demons to Blame

"Mistakes were made." William Schneider, a political analyst for CNN, calls this usage "the past exonerative," a sharp phrase, quoted in William Saffire's language column in the *Sunday New York Times Magazine*. Marion Barry, the embattled ex-mayor of Washington, is a hall-of-fame performer in wielding the past exonerative. When asked why he lied about being "chemically dependent," he replied, "That was the disease talking. I did not purposely do that to you. I was a victim." By combining the three languages of addiction, victimology and political evasion, Barry thus brilliantly positioned himself as the victim of his own mouth. Columnist Charles Krauthammer calls this the "Night of the Living Dead" defense: As in many a scary horror movie, an outside demon invades your body, pours in some gruesome chemicals that you yourself would never ingest and then, to cap it off, uses your very own voice to lie to the press!

Language indicating that one is merely the victim of one's own action is not new, just wildly popular. In the movie "Heartburn," Jack Nicholson told his pregnant wife, Meryl Streep, that the crisis caused by his extra-marital romance "is hard on me, too." Nice touch. Now the past exonerative and other slippery passive usages are rampant (or should that be, are being run rampantly?) thoughout the press. *The Washington Post* reporter fired for plagiarism "had the misfortune to get caught at a moment when the press was focused on the issue of plagiarism" (*The New Republic*). Alcoholism "extracts a disproportionate toll" from minorities (*The New York Times*). Donald Kennedy, who resigned as president of Stanford after a funding scandal, "was caught up in a (post-Trump age) purge" and "paid a high price for failing to meet strict standards" (various educators interviewed by the *Boston Globe*). Actually, he quit because under his leadership, Stanford used more than a million in federal research dollars to pay for flowers, antiques, receptions and yacht depreciation. In the modern manner, Kennedy, like Sununu, took no personal responsibility, generally positioning himself as a scapegoat.

The past exonerative can also be employed to exonerate people accused of success. Ali A. Mazrui, the Afrocentrist professor who dislikes the Western world and all its works and pomps, writes that as a result of the Industrial Revolution, "economic preeminence was bestowed upon the countries of Europe and North America." Like Sununu's mistake-makers, Mazrui's capricious bestowers are unnamed, though it is clear that the bestowel had nothing to do with economic or cultural achievement. With any luck, it just as easily could have happened to Guam or Uganda.

These passive constructions work best if one favors a set of abstractions that can be blamed for pushing people around—society, the privileged, the dominant culture or just social expectations. Writing in the current issue of *Tikkun* magazine, critic Josh Ozersky notes that "like many a higher doctrine before it, 'political correctness' has a strong distaste for the active voice." So do more and more books of social criticism. Naomi Wolf's current book, *The Beauty Myth*, for example, is heavily written in the passive voice. This is because, at root, she is selling a conspiracy theory: Men have created a devastating social juggernaut, the ideal of female beauty, that coerces all women to constantly waste their energies worrying about their appearance.

All writing courses tell students to stick to the active voice as much as possible, partly because the passive voice is the natural home of limp and evasive writing. It is also a terrific screen to conceal choices, responsibility and moral conflicts. Mr. Sununu, could you please recast that for us in the active voice?

Copyright (August 19, 1991), *U.S. News & World Report*.

Questions for Discussion

1. Comment on the author's assertion, "Language indicating that one is merely the victim of one's own action is not new, just wildly popular." How do some of the people discussed in this article use language to paint themselves as victims?

2. Can you think of other examples of people characterizing their actions as understandable because they are the victims of other people, institutions, or society in general? To what extent do terms such as *Adult child of an alcoholic, co-dependent, underclass*, and *chemically dependent* create a sense of victimization, and to what extent do they clarify a state of being?

3. Steven Wolin, researcher and family therapist at George Washington University Medical School, believes that there is much legitimate suffering in families, but that the recovery movement "and its lopsided counsel of damage, has become dangerous. . . . Everywhere we are finding people talking freely about being in the grips of compulsive shopping disorders, sex addictions, food addictions, jogging addictions and unmanageable urges to please other people."[17] In what situations and to what extent can a person claim that their actions are genuinely based on victimization?

17   Tim Larimer, "Dysfunction Junction," *USA Weekend*, May 10, 1992, p. 4.

How much responsibility do we have for our own actions? How can language be used to reflect responsibility, challenge, and opportunity rather than terminal victimization?

Ideas for Writing or Speaking

Respond to one of the following quotes from English novelist George Orwell's *Politics and the English Language*. Take a position on the quote and prove your position using essays; newspaper, magazine, or journal articles; advertisements; books; films; videos; or interviews.

1. "In our time, political speech and writing are largely the defense of the indefensible."
2. "The whole tendency of modern prose is away from concreteness."
3. "The great enemy of clear language is insincerity."
4. "In our age, there is no such thing as 'keeping out of politics.' All issues are political issues, and politics itself is a mass of lies, evasions, folly, hatred, and schizophrenia."
5. "Political language . . . is designed to make lies sound truthful and murder respectable, and to give an appearance of solidity to pure wind."

U.S. Must Stay in World Spotlight

America Has Unique Role, Responsibility in New Era

by Mikhail Gorbachev
New York Times, May 7, 1992

The end of the Cold War was a victory for common sense. It rid the world of the fear of nuclear catastrophe.

It gave us the opportunity to begin radical arms reductions and the dismantling of the giant military-industrial machine.

And now we have the chance to move toward a democratic, free and human world order.

But we are only at the beginning of the road to this goal, and the dangers are great.

The demons of nationalism are coming alive again, and they are putting the stability of the international system to the test.

Even the United States itself is not immune from the dangers of nationalism.

If America is "always right," if her ideas are "the most democratic and just" and because, after all, it is America which takes on the biggest share of the burden for the preservation of order in the world, then the drive will never get under way to create a new world order based on international law, equality and mutual respect, freedom of choice and the balance of interests.

At present, America's position seems paradoxical.

Cardinal changes taking place in the former U.S.S.R.—now enduring difficult times and badly in need of help—have given the United States a much stronger role in the world.

At the same time, many speak about the weakening of America's economy (partly a consequence of the arms race).

They talk about growing global economic and political roles of Western Europe and Japan.

They talk about a decreasing interest among Americans in having their country play a global leadership role.

Following the American press and the public mood, foreign policy is moving to the back ranks of national priorities. Internal problems are taking precedent.

Some of this is understandable.

The burden of the special role of the United States in the world has never been easy. It has demanded material and human losses in two world wars and in their aftermaths.

It is not surprising that many see the end of the Cold War as a victory for the West. It finally made it possible to give domestic affairs a higher priority.

But the United States can neither remove itself from global problems, nor put its trust in the authority of its physical power.

The war in the Persian Gulf and its outcome may argue that America's calling is to be the noble sheriff, able to punish scoundrels in any corner of the planet.

Actually, the Persian Gulf War showed just the opposite: the new role of the United Nations as a mighty instrument in the hands of the world community.

It also showed that the roots of humanity's troubles lie very deep. There are no simple prescriptions to overcome them, no matter how brilliant the prescribing doctor.

What is needed are changes in consciousness, in relations between people, between nations, and in their attitudes toward nature.

A reassessment of values, for instance, opened the road for deep transformations in my country.

I believe that the world awaits from American foreign policy a renewed emphasis on those qualities which made America great—its fidelity to democracy, its love of freedom, its spirit of discovery.

A special role is defined for America by its history, its technical and industrial strength and, of course, by the generosity characteristic of the American people in their readiness to help others.

America must also make a constructive contribution to the effort of the United Nations to strengthen international law and order and to solve global problems.

I am sure such a course would find broad international support.

I am sure, too, that the new democratic Russia will be one of the United States' partners in this effort.

The West, and first of all the United States, needs a strong, integrated, democratic Russia.

It is in America's interest that Russia remains the core of the Eurasian expanse, where the civilizations of West and East, South and North come together and interweave.

Together, the United States and Russia, with the other states of the former U.S.S.R., with the European Community and all the countries of Europe, with the neighbors in the East—Japan and China—with the neighbors in the South—India, Iran and Pakistan—and with the countries of the Middle East—a zone of stability could be created from Vancouver to Vladivostok, from New Delhi to Novaya Zemlya.

It was a great loss when the victors of World War II did not use their triumph for the good of the world. It would be a colossal mistake to miss this chance again.

Questions for Discussion

1. Note how Gorbachev uses language to suggest that events and ideas are active: "It [the end of the Cold War] rid the world of the fear of nuclear catastrophe." "The demons of nationalism are coming alive again." How could these ideas be phrased in the active voice to reflect human decision-making and responsibility?

2. To what extent does Gorbachev clarify his abstract reasoning with concrete examples and proposals? Find some examples of specific proposals. Then, in groups, consider some of the following excerpts from the article and come to a consensus about what, precisely, Gorbachev is saying.

   "What is needed are changes in consciousness, in relations between people, between nations, and in their attitudes toward nature."

"America must also make a constructive contribution to the effort of the United Nations to strengthen international law and order and to solve global problems."

"It is in America's interest that Russia remains the core of the Eurasian expanse, where the civilizations of West and East, South and North come together and interweave."

Ideas for Writing and Speaking

1. Take abstract terms and passages from the article (or use those given in the Questions for Discussion section), and suggest concrete ideas that they represent. If you believe that you know what the author meant, support your belief with reasoning. If you believe that there are different possible interpretations of what the author meant, give several of your interpretations.

2. Write or speak about a proposal for change, using both abstract objectives and concrete proposals. The abstract terms should be used to express the ideals you have in creating your proposal; the concrete explanations are used to let your readers or listeners know exactly what your proposal entails and the real-world impact you expect it to have. For example, you might state that you would like to see increased employment opportunities in the inner cities (abstract objective). Then you can explain exactly how you would go about increasing employment, detailing programs and how the programs would be organized, funded, maintained, and evaluated (concrete proposals).

You may want to use one of the following two formats, which were discussed in Chapter 7. In the first, Monroe's Motivated Sequence, your specific proposal is outlined in the "satisfaction" step. In the second format, your proposal is given under "solvency."

Monroe's Motivated Sequence

1. *Attention:* Get the audience's interest and attention; you can do this with provocative questions, statistics, or a relevant anecdote. End your attention step with your thesis statement (main idea) and a preview of your key ideas.

2.   *Need:* The body of your speech begins with this step, where you show your audience that a serious problem must be addressed.

3.   *Satisfaction:* At this point, you present a solution to the problem that was introduced in the need step.

4.   *Visualization:* This last part of the body of your speech is used to help listeners form a picture of what it would be like if your solution is in place. If there are aspects of the solution that would be of personal benefit to audience members, visualize those benefits in this step.

5.   *Action:* This step is considered the conclusion of the speech and is used to request specific action of the audience members.

Essay or Speech on a Policy

1.   *Introduction:* As in any speech, the introduction to a persuasive speech must put the audience at ease with the topic of the speech, must clearly state the purpose of the speech, and must give some direction about the course of the speech.

2.   *Harms:* The harms section of the speech should answer the question, "How are we hurt by this problem?" Financial losses, personal injuries, and deaths caused by the problem are often detailed in the harms portion.

3.   *Inherency:* The inherency section should answer the question, "Why does the problem exist?" The reasons for the existence of any problem can be categorized as either attitudinal inherency or structural inherency. Attitudinal inherency occurs when the sentiments of the public create a barrier to the solution of the issue or when those sentiments help to perpetuate the cause of difficulty. Structural inherency is a physical barrier that must be overcome in order to solve the problem. Such a barrier could be a law, the lack of trained personnel, or an inefficient system.

4.   *Significance:* The notion of significance addresses the question, "What is the scope of the problem?" Significance is often described by details of the geographic range, quantitative preponderance, or qualitative weight of the problem. More often than not, the significance issue is handled within both the harms and inherency sections.

5.   *Solvency:* This final section is arguably the most important part of the persuasive speech. It answers the question, "What can be done to remedy the problem?" It is important to address two issues within the solvency section. First, be sure to tell your audience how they can help specifically. Second, attempt to give an example of how your solution has worked in the past.

6.   *Conclusion:* The conclusion to the persuasive speech should accomplish two goals: It should initially view how the advocated solution steps will affect the problem and it should secondly make one last appeal to the audience.

Share your essays or speeches with the class. Have members of the class write down your specific proposals as they understand them; also have classmates note the general problems you address. The accuracy of their understanding should give you good information about how well you have communicated your ideas.

Class discussion of essays and speeches should focus on understanding of proposals made, not on agreement or disagreement. Your goal in this assignment is to be clear about what you are advocating, not to reach a classroom consensus or to spark a debate.

More Ideas for Writing or Speaking

1. **Sales Pitch.** Listen to a "hard sell" sales pitch by a professional salesperson. You might go to a car lot or stereo store, or just invite a door-to-door salesperson to speak with you. Then list and analyze the reasons that you are given in favor of buying the product or service. Some questions to answer are as follows:
   a. Were you given valid and well-documented reasons for buying the product or service?
   b. Did the salesperson use deception or mislead or confuse you with vagueness or any of the forms of doublespeak covered in this chapter?
   c. Which arguments were persuasive and which were not? Explain why.
2. **Useless Item Survey.** Find something that you bought and never or rarely used. Then answer the following questions.
   a. What motivated you to buy this item?
   b. Why have you never or rarely used it?

c. Why do you still have it?

d. Have you learned anything useful from this useless purchase?

3. **Ad Campaign.** In the October/November 1991 issue of *Investment Vision,* readers were advised to consider investing in products with ad campaigns that created powerful positive images. They reminded readers that corporations spend $129 billion yearly on ads and that the most effective are those with a clear concept. The best campaigns, they believe, focus on one or two words associated with the product, like *overnight* for Federal Express or *dependable* for Maytag.

Assuming that companies desire positive connotations for their products, study the ad campaigns of several companies.

a. Discuss each image and how it is achieved through the ads, focusing especially on the words.

b. Decide which campaigns are more successful at creating strong, positive connotations. Support your conclusions with reasons.

CHAPTER NINE

Fairmindedness

It's You and Me, Kid, and I'm Not So Sure About You

A critical thinker is aware of egocentrism, sociocentrism, and the role of emotions on our judgment.

A critical thinker listens and responds to opposing viewpoints with empathy and fairmindedness.

This chapter will cover:

◆ Defense mechanisms that cloud our thinking
◆ Ideas that trigger emotional responses
◆ Active listening techniques that foster openmindedness and empathy

Centuries ago, we learned, probably to our disappointment, that the earth, and therefore man, is not the center of the universe. We discovered that the sun did not revolve around the earth; instead our earth, along with the other planets, revolved around the sun.

The fact that we tended to see our earth as predominant reveals the self-centered (not necessarily selfish) nature of our perception of reality. That self-centered tendency did not die out with our ancestors; instead, it has taken on different, more subtle forms. Perhaps a self-centered shortsightedness has contributed to the Western use of a proportion of the earth's resources far outweighing our number of citizens.

Just as our ancestors made corrections to their theories and behaviors when confronted with inescapable facts, we as a culture are changing our ideas and actions in the face of increasingly credible threats to our environment. Instead of living under the assumption that the earth is infinitely supplied with resources, we are focusing on conservation and preservation of our environment as a crucial issue, viewing our resources as precious rather than expendable.

Increasing advances in media technology have enabled us to get a more complete picture of the global interdependence of not only our physical environment but also the world's people. When we see how others live and the problems they face, we can be less ethnocentric. **Ethnocentrism** or **sociocentrism** is the tendency to view one's own race or culture as central, based on the deep-seated belief that one's own group is superior to all others.[1] We can only hold on to ethnocentrism when we can pretend other cultures don't really exist or count. However, with the reality of other cultures coming into our living rooms via television daily, it becomes increasingly difficult to discount their presence and worth.

Egocentrism, the individual version of ethnocentrism, has been defined as a tendency to view everything else in relationship to oneself; one's desires, values, and beliefs (seeming to be self-evidently correct or superior to those of others) are often uncritically used as the norm of all judgment and experience. Egocentrism has been called one of the fundamental impediments to critical thinking.[2]

To be a logical, fair, and less egocentric thinker, we can learn several skills. We can learn:

1. To recognize the basic defense mechanisms we use to distort reality and to deceive ourselves and others.

---

[1]   Richard Paul, *Critical Thinking* (Rohnert Park, CA: Center for Critical Thinking and Moral Critique, 1990), p. 549.
[2]   Ibid., p. 548.

Calvin and Hobbes by Bill Watterson

2. To recognize areas where we, for whatever reasons, have trouble being rational.

3. To understand and have empathy (the ability to share another's feelings and perspective) for someone else's viewpoint.

There is nothing wrong with taking strong, even immovable, stands on issues; we don't want to be so open-minded that we have no beliefs or opinions at all! What is unfair is taking a strong stand without having thought carefully and honestly about all the relevant factors involved in an issue.

How We Defend Our Egos

"Are you thinking or are you just rearranging your prejudices?"

Walter Martin

The best place to start in understanding our weak points in reasoning is to examine human defense mechanisms. Defense mechanisms are "the clever ways we deceive ourselves, protect ourselves, and extract ourselves from uncomfortable situations—they are negative escape hatches that offer us temporary treatments for persistent problems."[3] For our purposes, we will consider some defense mechanisms that interfere with clear thinking.

---

[3] Frank Minirth, M.D., Paul Meier, M.D., and Don Hawkins, ThM., *Worry Free Living* (Nashville: Thomas Nelson Publishers, 1989), p. 78.

Rationalization is a defense mechanism that underlies many others; it is the process of justifying or making sense of things that don't make sense. It's our way of explaining things away that should be brought under examination. When, for whatever reasons, we want to avoid an unpleasant truth or when we want to believe something is true, we can come up with a way to justify our desired belief. Note how we use our minds to distort reality in the following examples.

- Your favorite political candidate is found to have cheated on his taxes. You rationalize your continued support for this person by saying, "He may have cheated on his taxes, but he's made up for it by all the good budget cuts he helped pass."

- You find out that the car you just bought has been criticized by *Consumer Reports* for having a faulty transmission system. You rationalize by saying, "All cars are meant to fall apart in a few years."

- You continue to smoke cigarettes, although considerable evidence supports the fact that cigarettes are a causative factor in several diseases. You tell yourself and others, "I'm not going to worry about every habit I have. I could die tomorrow by slipping on a banana peel, so I might as well enjoy life today."

- Someone you'd like to get to know keeps refusing your requests for a date. You rationalize by saying, "He [or she] must be really busy this year."

- After committing yourself to a strict diet, you have a donut for breakfast. You then eat three more, rationalizing, "I already ruined the diet, so I may as well enjoy today and start again tomorrow."

- A clerk at a supermarket forgets to charge you for some sodas on the bottom of your cart. When you start to load them into your car and realize the mistake, you rationalize by thinking, "Oh, well. They're a big company and will never miss a few dollars."

EXERCISE

Purpose: To understand why people rationalize rather than admit incongruities.

In a small group, take each of the examples of rationalization and discuss why someone might use that rationalization.

1. What need are they trying to meet by rationalizing about that situation?
2. How is rationalization related to the attempt to preserve self-esteem?

As you can see, rationalization can enter every area of our thinking. Leon Festinger, a sociologist, formulated a theory to explain why we use this mechanism so frequently. He said that as humans we are subject to a state of mind called **cognitive dissonance**. This state occurs whenever two ideas (or cognitions) are out of synch and create discomfort in our thinking patterns.

Festinger explained that when we are confronted by two clashing ideas, we try to make them harmonious rather than facing reality and admitting they clash. We explain away inconsistencies rather than face them and deal with them. Interestingly, Festinger believes that the need to resolve mentally inconsistent information is a basic drive, like the need for food; our minds strive to "survive" unpleasant incongruities.

A mentally healthy person is in a state of congruence; that is, the individual's behavior conforms to her beliefs and values. Unfortunately, many of us, instead of striving for true congruence by keeping our behavior in line with our values, will settle for a counterfeit peace of mind through rationalization.

Psychologists and critical thinking advocates tell us that to be emotionally and mentally healthy we need to bring inconsistencies to the surface and deal with them—i.e., to accept reality and work from a reality base. As we keep rationalizing, we become psychologically unhealthy and removed from reality. An example of this removal from reality happened years ago in a small town in Texas.

A particular cult group was told by their leader that they were going to be saved from the impending destruction of earth and airlifted to another planet. They were instructed to stand in a field on a particular night to wait for their spaceship to arrive. When the spaceship did not arrive, the leader said that a delay had occurred so they should continue to wait the following night. When the ship still did not arrive the next night, their leader did not admit to the group that he had been mistaken. Instead, he said that because of their faith the entire world had been saved from the disaster.

This story may seem incredible until you consider the fate of many people who followed a cult leader named Jim Jones to Guyana and their death. When he passed himself off as a man of God and had sexual relations with many of his followers, he rationalized by calling it a form of ritual cleansing. When he humiliated young children for small infractions of his system, Jones (and some of the children's parents) must have rationalized that he had their best interests at heart. Similarly, followers of cult leader David Koresh put irrational confidence in his alleged power to redeem them.

The more we give up our critical thinking abilities, the harder it becomes to face our errors in judgment, and personal and social tragedies can be the result. As people who vote, buy products, influence others, and form relationships, we need to use information to help us learn and make decisions. Rationalization is a form of sloppy thinking we can't afford to use.

A defense mechanism closely related to rationalization is **denial**. Denial is also a state of mind that blocks critical thinking, because it involves the repression of or refusal to recognize any negative or threatening information. Some of us go into denial when we hear we've bounced a check or forgotten to make a payment on a bill. We may tell our creditors they've made a mistake or that they never sent the bill, when in reality we've made a mistake we choose not to face because of fear, pride, or both.

Denial, like other defense mechanisms, comes into play when we experience an emotional reaction to information. In our culture, many of us seem to deny certain warnings from environmentalists, like information about the ozone layer, the fossil fuel supply, or the effects of some pesticides. We may not only deny national problems; we also may rationalize that "you can't worry about every little thing."

Sometimes, denial is normal and helpful to our systems, as when we hear shocking news and give ourselves time, through denial of the facts, to cope with the information.

Betty by Gary Delainey and Gerry Rasmussen
Betty reprinted by permission of USF, Inc.

For example, if you are informed at a doctor's office that you have a life-threatening disease, it may be temporarily helpful for you not to digest this information completely until you are home with supportive family members or in the care of a good counselor. In this case, it might be hard to drive home if you were fully immersed in the truth of your condition.

Denial becomes a problem for critical thinkers when they refuse to acknowledge the truth or the possible truth of an argument presented to them. This problem can be summed up in the cliche "I know what I believe. Don't confuse me with the facts." The facts may be complicated, but the critical thinker needs to sort through them to make a reasonable judgment on an issue, or at least to withhold judgment on a complex issue about which he is uninformed.

SKILL

Recognize defense mechanisms we use to deceive ourselves and others.

In our information-filled society, ideas change as frequently as clothing styles and consumer goods. Knowledge is being expanded, refined, and discovered at a rapid rate. We have to face our current realities and the implications they have for us as citizens.

To avoid the problem of denial, the critical thinker must realize that the rapid rate of new research findings means:

1. Advocates for any issue have to work harder to make a good case for that issue. The research, especially scientific research, you did last year for a report or debate may be outdated when you try to use it again.

2. People are being forced to specialize more in their careers. Doctors, lawyers, teachers, mechanics, journalists, and other professionals are finding it increasingly necessary to focus on a smaller area of expertise; it takes much of their time and energy to be effective in one area.

This shift from generalist to specialist in any given field makes us more reliant on expert testimony about an issue. We as citizens and consumers haven't the time and energy to research thoroughly all claims presented to us; we base our decisions more and more on authoritative testimony that we respect.

Areas Where We Have Trouble Being Rational

Professor Zachary Seech has come up with a wonderful description of the trouble spots in our thinking. He calls them "points of logical vulnerability." We can be vulnerable to a general topic, like politics, or a specific one, such as our sister's choice of a husband.[4]

There are topics about which a person "just cannot be rational." What we mean is that this person has great difficulty in being objective on these topics. He or she finds it difficult, in some cases, to consider the evidence impartially and draw a sensible, justified conclusion. These topics are the **points of logical vulnerability** for that person.[5]

Each person has different "sore spots" in his or her thinking, and this fact further complicates the process of dialogue on a given issue. If you are a rabid fan of a particular team, you may be totally unobjective about how they will do in the next game. If fast food fits your life-style perfectly, you may not be open to any discussion of health problems associated with a steady diet of french fries and cheeseburgers. If you are upset because your roommate is getting married and moving out, you may find yourself disliking his or her new mate.

Points of logical vulnerability are topics affecting us so much on a personal level that we are likely to deny or rationalize any evidence that might disprove our opinions. For example, if you dislike a senator because of his views on the environment and then he supports an environmental bill you also support, you might rationalize that "he's just trying to appease environmentalists; he doesn't really care about the issues."

Conversely, if you like the senator and he does something you consider wrong, you might rationalize that he was forced into making concessions he would not have personally approved. Our points of logical vulnerability cause us to distort or deny information that goes against our deeply held opinions.

EXERCISE

Purpose: To recognize areas of logical vulnerability.

Discover some of your points of logical vulnerability. Think about people whose opinions are not credible for you. Consider political or social issues (capital punishment, drug legalization, euthanasia, affir-

---

4   Zachary Seech, *Logic in Everyday Life* (Belmont, CA: Wadsworth Publishing, 1988), pp. 2–3.

5   Ibid., p. 2.

mative action, or AIDS research policies), or choose an issue about which you frequently argue with other people.

Can you think of any ways in which you might not have been objective in hearing evidence from others about this issue? Do you use denial or rationalization when confronted with your points of logical vulnerability? How could you respond differently?

Example

I don't like a congresswoman in my state. I heard her speak once and thought she was rude in the way she handled a question from the audience. Also, she is against some of the legislation I consider important.

Once in a while, I'll hear her say something that makes sense, but I notice I discount whatever she says; if there's a negative way to look at her comments, I do. I guess I think she has some ulterior motive and don't believe she has any positive contribution to make.

I don't like most of her positions and I'd never vote for her. But I could be more fair and admit that occasionally she does have a good idea and she might have real concern for the people in her district.

Keep in mind the difference between having strong, well-considered convictions about which you are not flexible (like your values) and opinions that have not been thought out, which are based solely on emotions or identification with others who hold those opinions. The latter opinions are probably points of logical vulnerability for you.

Antidotes for Points of Logical Vulnerability

There are several effective ways to confront your points of logical vulnerability. The first approach is to apply certain techniques of rational thought to your opinions; the second is to learn to listen actively and accurately to people with differing opinions.

General semanticists study the relationship between words and behavior. They believe that we can improve our mental health by increasing the accuracy with which we speak, and they have come up with several "cures" for irrational statements.

A classic irrational statement stereotypes a whole group of people based on a limited sample of experience on the part of the speaker. Another term for a stereotypical statement is *sweeping generalization*.

Let's say that Harold has had several bad experiences in his relationships with women: The first woman he wanted to marry left him for another man; the second woman he wanted to marry told him she wasn't ready for a commitment and that she needed "space"; the third woman he wanted to marry left town with no forwarding address. In discussing his problems with his best friend, Harold makes the statement: "All women are cruel and selfish."

Now we can understand how anyone with this record of experience would be upset about his former relationships, but we also can see, as outside observers, that his statement is emotional and would not hold up to critical scrutiny. You can't study three women and then claim all women (about half of the human race) are cruel and selfish.

General semanticists, basing their work on the pioneering writing of Albert Korzypski, have come up with several cures for irrational statements. They would ask Harold to do a few things with his statement, "All women are cruel and selfish."

- Eliminate the word *all* since no one can know every single woman. Change the general term *women* into specifics (woman 1, woman 2, woman 3 become Patty, Suzannah, and Gina).

  Now he has: "Patty, Suzannah, and Gina are cruel and selfish." Not perfect, but more accurate; at least in this case he is not generalizing from three examples to half of the human race.

  Semanticists call this technique *indexing*; you take your general label (women, Catholics, Asians, Americans) and change it to actual people. You also delete the word *all* from your vocabulary when it precedes a general category. One can never know all about any given group.

- Next, a general semanticist would ask Harold to change his vague labels of *cruel* and *selfish* to specific charges: "Patty, Suzannah, and Gina did not marry me, although we were dating and I asked them to marry me. Patty married someone else, Suzannah told me she needed 'space,' and Gina left town without contacting me."

- For accuracy and perspective, our semanticist would also ask Harold to put a date on his statement.

  "Patty, Suzannah, and Gina did not marry me, although we were dating and I asked them to marry me. Patty married someone else, Suzannah told me she needed 'space,' and Gina left town without contacting me. These incidents happened when I was in my late teens and early twenties."

- The final addition to Harold's statement is called the *etc.* because it includes other realities that add balance and fairness to the original statement. Think of a young child who complains with all accuracy, "Joey pushed me!" This statement is clear and unambiguous; yet we don't know what else was going on in the situation. We don't have the total picture or the context in which the event occurred.

  To figure out what was going on, a parent or teacher might ask, "Did you push him too?" It could be that the child who complained was indeed the victim of Joey's aggressiveness, or maybe the complaining child pushed Joey first. Also, it could be that Joey was pushing to get somewhere and was unaware that he had pushed the other child. We can only know what happened in a situation when we get more information.

SKILL

Use rational thinking aids to overcome areas in which you have trouble being rational.

Think about the times you feel really annoyed with someone's behavior. In recounting your irritation to a friend, do you really try to be fair and objective or do you tend to present the details that best support your right to be annoyed?

When general semanticists recommend the use of the *etc.,* they are recognizing the complexity of situations and that we can rarely say all there is to say about the factors that create differences of opinion. They would suggest that Harold add information to his statement to give a more accurate picture of reality:

Patty, Suzannah, and Gina did not marry me, although we were dating and I asked them to marry me. Patty married someone else, Suzannah told me she needed "space" and Gina left town without contacting me. These incidents happened when I was in my late teens and early twenties. I knew Patty was ready to get married, but I didn't ask her until she was involved with someone else; I could have still dated Suzannah as one of the men she was dating, but I wanted to be the only one; I don't know why Gina left town.

If you compare Harold's first statement with this last statement, you might understand why the use of semantic devices improves mental health. A counselor might help Harold arrive at the same kinds of rephrasings. If he continues to see all women as cruel and selfish, he might never try to interact with them again, but if he sees that he has had a few bad experiences, he can learn from his mistakes and continue to grow and develop relationships.

The semantic devices are useful in helping us to change irrational comments we make about people and issues to more truthful and fair-minded statements.

EXERCISE

Purpose: To practice using semantic devices to make statements more accurate and rational.

1. Using the semantic devices, change the following irrational statements into logical statements. You may need to make up details.
   a. Women are terrible drivers. (Note the implied *all* before women.)
   b. Asian students are great in math.
   c. Democrats are bleeding-heart liberals and can't be trusted.
   d. Republicans don't care about the poor and needy.
   e. Most people from ivy-league schools are elitists.
   f. People on welfare don't want to work.

   Can you add a statement that you've heard yourself (or a close friend) say?

2. Listen to yourself for a week and see if you tend to overgeneralize when confronted with your points of logical vulnerability. Try to stop yourself and to use the semantic devices to rephrase your opinions. What is the effect on your emotions and your conversations? You may note that if you try to get other people to be more specific and less prejudicial in their statements, you encounter some hostility. Why might that be?

   Write out several examples of instances in which you or someone else could have used the semantic devices to make more accurate statements.

Actively and Accurately Listening: Developing Empathy

"Some psychologists believe that the ability to listen to another person, to empathize with, and to understand their point of view is one of the highest forms of intelligent behavior."

Edward DeBono, quoted by Arthur L. Costa

Many cultures place a high value on competition, and this competition is not restricted to sporting events—it also comes out in debates and discussions on issues. The desire to win and the enjoyment we find in having the most persuasive argument may limit our ability to be fair to opposing sides of issues.

The most persuasive speaker is one who can understand and address the points brought up by those who don't share his or her opinion. To understand an opposing argument, we must hear what the speaker for the opposition is saying.

Why do we find listening difficult, and why don't politicians listen more fairly in debates? Some of the reasons we don't listen are:

- The thrust of debate is to win; therefore, we tend to listen to the opposition's position only so we can find fault with it. The focus is on victory, not on understanding, especially in public debating forums.

- We are not trained to listen. Some of us have had training in speech, but few have had specific training in effective listening techniques.

- We fear if we really listen to the other person we will lose our train of thought.

- We fear if we really listen to the other person we might agree with him or her and that could be really uncomfortable.

- It requires effort and energy to try to understand the viewpoint of another person.

- For many of us, it is more rewarding to speak about our own ideas than to listen to others.

Listening accurately to an opposing position, however, gives us some clear advantages:

- We can learn what the opposition to our cause or issue believes and we can then address our opponents on specific issues.

- We can grow and adjust our position if new research or reasoning warrants the adjustment.
- When we are seen as secure enough in our position to listen to an opposing argument, our credibility increases.
- Our calm listening is often contagious; as we show our willingness to hear the other side fully, defenses are dropped and our opponents listen to us as well. We have a better chance of explaining our viewpoint and not having it distorted by interruptions.
- In an atmosphere of reduced hostility, areas of agreement can be found.

The Art of Listening Well

Years ago, a southern California psychologist, Carl Rogers, created a listening exercise which has become a staple for counselors and teachers of communications. Rogers' technique is simple and very effective; if done correctly, both sides will come out with a deeper understanding of the other's position.

Understanding does not necessarily mean agreement. We may know exactly what the other's position is and conclude that he is completely off base. The critical thinker is the one who draws conclusions based on understanding of both her and the opponent's position, not solely on an emotional commitment to her original position.

Here is Rogers' listening exercise:

1. Two people with opposing beliefs on an issue sit facing each other.
2. Person A begins with a brief statement about her opinion on an issue.
3. Person B paraphrases—puts person A's opinion in his own words. When person A agrees that person B has understood, then person B states his opinion.
4. Now person A has to paraphrase—restate in her own words what person B has said. When person B is satisfied that person A has understood him, person A can expand on her opinion.
5. This process is continued until both parties feel they have presented their case and that it has been understood. It is helpful to allow each person a few minutes to summarize, as best they can, the complete position of the other person.

6. During the process, both parties attempt to be objective in their summaries of the other person's viewpoint and to avoid sarcasm and ridicule of any points the other person makes.

7. It is also helpful to try to "read between the lines" and understand *why* the other person feels so strongly about his or her position.

SKILL

Listen with empathy to an opposing viewpoint.

Example

Person A:	I believe heroic medical interventions should not be made unless the doctors and nurses have permission of the patient or the patient's family members.
Person B:	So you believe that extending life with technology should not be done unless a patient or his family wants his life extended?
Person A:	That's right.
Person B:	Well, it's my opinion that sometimes there isn't time for a discussion with the patient or the family members about the patient's chances for survival. The medical experts have to act or there is no decision to be made because the patient is dead!
Person A:	So you think that using technology is totally up to the doctors?
Person B:	(clarifying) I didn't mean that. I mean, if the patient is going to die if he's not hooked up to the machines, then he needs to be hooked up first and consulted later.
Person A:	(trying to paraphrase more accurately) So you think in an emergency the doctors should be allowed to treat the patient in any way that will save his life and talk to him or his family members later?

Person B:	That's right. You got it.
Person A:	Well, I don't have a real problem with that. But I believe that if the patient doesn't want to be kept alive through technology, and if he or his family members tell the doctors that, then the doctors have to abide by his wishes and "pull the plug."
Person B:	So, basically, you believe the patient should decide whether he will live or die—or, if he can't decide, then his family should decide for him.
Person A:	(clarifying) That's not exactly it. He may live or die whether he's hooked up to life supports or not. But it's his choice—or his family's choice—whether he will be hooked up.
Person B:	Okay, then it's the patient's choice or, secondly, his family's choice and not the doctor's choice to continue him on life supports.
Person A:	Exactly.
Person B:	I believe it is part of a doctor's job to assess a patient's chances for survival; the patient or the family can get too emotional and decide to let someone die rather than be uncomfortable, and meanwhile, the doctor may know there's a good chance for recovery. Also, doctors are trained to save life at all costs. If we train them to take the patient's advice, then they could let him die just so they could take off early to play golf!
Person A:	That's a lot for me to paraphrase. You believe, if I have it right, that doctors are more objective and less emotional than patients and family members, and they have more of an expert opinion about chances for recovery. And also you think it's dangerous to let patients or family members decide to pull the plug because then doctors don't have to worry about whether the patient could have lived a full life or not.
Person B:	You said it better than I did!

Person A: Well, what I really think is that doctors should give their expert opinion to the patient and the family members. If they then decide, for whatever reason, not to prolong life with technology, then the doctors would have to abide by their decision.

Person B: So you think that the doctor should be an advisor or counselor and give them all the information he can, but the family should have the final power to decide what will be done.

Person A: That's exactly right.

Person B: Well, that sounds fair, but I just believe it's better to go for life, whenever possible. There are many cases of people recovering from comas or serious strokes thanks to life-support systems. If their families had pulled the plug to spare them pain or expense, they would have lost a loved one. Give life a chance.

Person A: You believe we should always choose to use life supports in case the patient does, in some miraculous way, recover.

Person B: (clarifying) Not exactly. Recovery isn't always miraculous; sometimes the doctors can predict a good chance of recovery, and they should go for that chance.

Person A: So you would choose to use life supports until someone is completely beyond hope of recovery?

Person B: Right.

Person A: Well, I have heard of many horror stories of people forced to stay on intravenous machines and respirators when they were completely paralyzed and had no desire to live. There are parents who don't want babies to be subjected to surgery and to spend time hooked up to equipment that hurts them.

Person B: So you believe the patient and his family should decide what the quality of life would be if the patient lived and use that as a basis for deciding whether to pull the plug?

Person A: Yes. Don't you think that's the only basis for a decision?

Person B: I guess I believe that giving it time is more important than rushing into a decision. I feel bad about the pain anyone may feel on life-support equipment. But, to me, going through the pain is worth it if there is a chance for a good life.

Person A: Who decides what a good life is?

Person B: I think you need to paraphrase my last statement first.

Person A: Okay. You believe in giving life a chance, even if it seems desperate. You think that, even if the patient wants to be off the life-support equipment, he needs time. And I guess you believe the doctors are the ones who should decide what kind of time he needs.

Person B: Yes. And the patient may find that a life with limitations is better than no life.

Person A: So you don't think the patient should have the right to say no to life supports?

Person B: I don't think he should have the exclusive rights because I don't think he has all the information he needs to make the decision.

Person A: Well, my position is more simple. It's his body— or his parent's, wife's, or child's body. That gives him the right to decide what will or will not be done in a hospital. I agree it's important to get the doctor's opinion, but after that, his decision should be honored.

Person B: And I agree with you that it's his or her body, but I also think the doctors are more objective and knowledgeable, so they should be allowed to continue treatment if there's a chance for recovery. I guess I can see why some of these cases have to be settled in court. That's not the ideal solution, but it's the best we've come up with so far.

Questions for Discussion

1. The participants in this dialogue did not end by agreeing with much of each other's positions. How, then, is this form of communication useful?
2. Where did you spot inaccurate paraphrases of the other's position? Why do you think these occurred?
3. Often there is a strong emotional component to someone's position. Do you see hints of emotionalism in this dialogue? How does the paraphrasing minimize emotional outbursts or points of logical vulnerability?

EXERCISES

Purpose: To practice active listening.

1. In class, or at home, try discussing an issue with someone who disagrees with you using this listening technique. Be sure to tell the other person the rules and get his or her commitment to abide by them (or you may be in for a good fight!). It may help to have a referee who is familiar with the technique and objective about the issue. Then report on your results by answering the following questions:
   a. Were you able to stay with the paraphrasing process? Why or why not?
   b. Did you and the other person attain greater understanding? If so, give some specific examples of what you learned about each other's positions.
   c. Was the relationship improved in any way?
2. Exchange a persuasive essay paper you have done (perhaps earlier in this course or in another class) with another student's essay; then do the following.
   a. Write a paraphrase of the other's ideas, clearly focusing on thesis statements and evidence used to support the thesis.
   b. Read the other student's paraphrase of your essay; comment on how well he or she understood and expressed your point of view. If there are misunderstandings in each other's viewpoints, try to discover why these occurred. If time permits, explain any problems you encountered with the class.

Precautions About Active Listening

Active listening was first suggested as a technique to be used by professional therapists. Over the years, various workshops have been set up for the purposes of training lay people to use active listening to improve their relationships. These workshops focus on the proper and improper use of the technique.

If you have never been formally trained in active listening, you may find it uncomfortable. However, practice and a basic knowledge of potential problems should enable you to use this very helpful communication tool successfully. Here is a summary of basic precautions in using active listening:

1.   Avoid sarcasm and ridicule of the other person's statements; also don't add negative connotations to what he or she says.

2.   Don't "parrot" the position of the other person; just paraphrase (put in your own words) the ideas you hear.

3.   If you find yourself getting upset, take some time out and assess what it is about this issue that makes it painful for you to be objective. There are some issues we feel so strongly about that there is no room for discussion. These strong feelings are usually connected with a personal experience. For example, if your cousin was killed by someone, you may believe that the death penalty is justified and any arguments against it make no impression when you consider the pain of your cousin and your close family.

Your belief may be based on a value that you hold deeply; if you believe that abortion is the taking of innocent life, then statistics about the teenage pregnancy rate may seem somewhat insignificant.

It is helpful, as a critical thinker, to know the areas in which you hold solid convictions. You can then acknowledge points on an opposing side but make it clear that those points are not strong enough for you to change your mind. The key is to understand both sides of an issue fully and to be open to new information; then you are responsible as a thinker when you, with good conscience, take a strong, even immovable, stand on an issue.

It is unrealistic to assume that you will have many opportunities for this kind of extended dialogue with someone who disagrees with you. The benefit of understanding the paraphrasing technique is that you can use it whenever it seems that something needs to be clarified in a discussion. Your use of this technique gives you credibility and the persuasive power that comes with calmness.

The person who stays cool and calm in a discussion seems secure in his position. The person who blows it by becoming overexcited and unfair to the opposition seems threatened—i.e., logically vulnerable. Shouting, name-calling, interrupting, and other forms of bullying serve only to make the person who uses these tactics seem foolish and unstable.

Your cool, clear mind—don't leave home without it!

Chapter Highlights

1. Our thinking can become less egocentric and more clear and fair when we recognize our defense mechanisms and our areas of logical vulnerability and when we develop specific skills for understanding the viewpoints of others.
2. Rationalization is a defense mechanism in which we try to justify or make sense out of things that are not sensible or justifiable.
3. Denial is a defense mechanism that involves repressing or refusing to recognize threatening information.
4. Points of logical vulnerability are topics about which we have trouble being rational.
5. Thinkers can confront points of logical vulnerability through the use of semantic devices.
6. Active listening, when used properly, can help us to clearly understand the viewpoints of others.

Articles for Discussion

It Happened

To Deny That the Holocaust Occurred Is to Set the Preconditions for Another One

Guest editorial by Richard V. Pierard, professor of history
at Indiana State University
From *Christianity Today,* March 9, 1992

The emergence of David Duke as a political figure has again drawn public attention to the contention that no Jewish Holocaust occurred in World War II. The ex-Klansman has said that Hitler and the Nazis did not systematically and successfully destroy most of Europe's Jews.

For years, Holocaust denial has been a stock-in-trade of shadowy crea-tures on the extreme Right. In recent times, several pseudo-scholars have come forward to argue against the "extermination legend" and "myth of the six million." Through an elaborate process of distortions, half-truths, and falsification of data, these "revisionists" seek to convince the gullible that Hitler did not order the annihilation of the Jews, but instead had this "alien minority" placed in labor camps where they could not subvert the war effort.

Harsh war-time conditions caused the epidemic diseases and malnu-trition in the crowded camps; crematories were necessary to dispose of the remains of the few thousand who died. Cyanide gas was used for delousing and fumigation in order to check the spread of typhus. There were so few Jews left in Europe because most had emigrated to North America or Israel. Pictures of gas chambers and emaciated inmates are fabrications. And so the story goes.

In fact, Holocaust denial is the ultimate Big Lie. The whole process of destruction is so well-attested through eye-witness accounts, official doc-uments, and contemporary press reports that no one in his or her right mind could deny that it happened.

So why is such a monstrous falsehood perpetrated? The answer is twofold. One reason is anti-Semitism—the ongoing hatred of Jews that animates extreme rightist groups in North America, Britain, France, Germany, and elsewhere. The other is the intention to deny Jews the right to a land of their own, where they may live peacefully within secure borders.

Is Holocaust denial merely a Jewish problem? No, it is also an American Christian problem. We must never forget that anti-Semitism has its roots in the theology and practice of the Christian church, from the writings of the church fathers, through the Inquisition, even in the comments of Martin Luther. Moreover, the U.S. government and people did little to help Jews in the years 1933 through 1945. Opinion polls in our "Christian nation" in 1942 found that people disliked Jews more than the German and Japanese enemies, while officials in Washington pooh-poohed the accounts of extermination programs as "atrocity stories."

Evangelicals may try to evade the issue by arguing that the Holocaust was a product of theological liberalism. But we cannot let ourselves off the hook so easily. Robert Ross excellently shows in *So It Was True* (1980) that while our magazines reported the grim details of the Nazi policies, our modest attempts to persuade the U.S. authorities to do something lacked moral passion.

Likewise, conservative free church Christians in Germany supported the Hitler regime just as fervently as most in the official church did. In 1984, the German Baptists even issued a formal statement confessing that they had been taken in by the "ideological seduction" of the time. They had not stood up for truth and righteousness.

The bottom line is that to deny the Holocaust is to set the preconditions for yet another one. It behooves evangelicals to stand up and utter a forthright *no* to the "revisionists" and their fellow travelers. The very credibility of our faith is at stake.

Reprinted by permission of the author.

Questions for Discussion

1. What would cause a person or group of persons to deny the painful history of another group of people? Does ethnocentrism or egocentrism play a role in this denial?
2. What should be the guidelines for any form of "revisionist history"?
3. Why does the author say that "to deny the Holocaust is to set the preconditions for yet another one"?
4. What other historical persecutions have been denied or minimized and for what reasons?

Idea for Writing or Speaking

1. The United States Declaration of Independence claims that "all men are created equal." How would a world in which all people were treated with equal respect and dignity work? Write or speak about what it would take to live in such a world and what that world would look like. If you don't believe that such a world could exist, write about the conditions that make it impossible.

History Texts Often Ignore Racial Minorities, Promote Stereotypes

by Hugh B. Price
Vice President of the Rockefeller Foundation
New York Times, September 23, 1991

"Was Cleopatra black?" That question, posed recently on the cover of *Newsweek*, encapsulates the raging debate over multicultural education in American schools. Mainstream academicians say multi-culturalism mangles history. Aggrieved minorities and women claim that history texts are full of glaring omissions, cultural stereotypes and misrepresentations of their histories.

These accusations ring true to me as an African-American. I grew up in the District of Columbia and am old enough to have attended segregated schools and witnessed the onset of integration. In the newly integrated schools of the 1950s, we were taught one version of the Civil War—the Southern version. Of course, there was another version of the war that we weren't taught. And those contrasting versions clearly were the product of conscious decisions by historians, textbook publishers and school teachers.

I was an adult before I learned that Alexander Pushkin and Alexandre Dumas were partly black. No literary anthologies in my high school or college courses mentioned those facts. This pattern of denial and duplicity helps explain the deep-rooted suspicions among minorities and women about the accuracy of history taught in schools.

Is it even necessary to present all history as settled truth? Where there is sharp disagreement, for example, between traditionalists and Afrocentrists over the ethnicity and contributions of Egypt, why not pose the contrasting positions to students as propositions to be studied? Teach them how to use primary sources, weigh evidence, critique arguments and form their own views.

Those aspects of my early education that did pay homage to African-Americans made a huge impression. We were taught that Ralph Bunche, the American statesman, won the Nobel Prize for bringing peace to the Middle East in the late 1940s; that Dr. Charles Drew discovered blood plasma and saved the lives of many American soldiers in World War II; and, yes, that Jackie Robinson had integrated major-league baseball.

In other words, we learned that blacks were of value to society, whether others thought so or not. It's impossible to overstate the impact of this individual and collective self-confidence on our will to succeed.

We may argue that instilling self-esteem isn't the province of schools, but we delude ourselves if we think there isn't a link between self-esteem and achievement. Or that the nexus between schools and well-functioning families hasn't done this all along for white children. If schools are to succeed for the millions of minority children who lack support at home and in the community, then educators must fill this void in the children's lives.

Multiculturalists also challenge the melting pot metaphor. It is said that most people who have emigrated to the U.S. over the years have arrived expecting to become un-hyphenated Americans. The trouble is that the melting pot still excludes many minorities and women. It took decades of marches and lawsuits to eradicate official segregation. Yet housing and employment discrimination persist.

I wonder whether those who worry that multiculturalism will ruin the melting pot haven't misread American history. Isn't it the opportunity to breathe politically and advance economically that has lured millions of immigrants to our shores? That is the attribute that defines our society, bonds us together and sets our nation apart from others.

Reprinted by permission of the author.

Questions for Discussion or Composition

1. What is the basic disagreement between mainstream academicians and multiculturalists, according to Hugh Price?
2. What in this author's background led him to question the accuracy of history as taught in school? What solution to the teaching of history does he propose?
3. In the author's view, how does self-esteem relate to a multicultural approach to education? Is it the province of schools to instill self-esteem? Why or why not?
4. What is the author's objection to the melting pot metaphor? Using examples, state why you agree or disagree with his viewpoint.
5. What sets our nation apart from others, according to Hugh Price? Do you agree or disagree?

The Cult of Ethnicity—Good and Bad

A Historian Argues That Multiculturalism Threatens the Ideal That Binds America

by Arthur Schlesinger Jr.
Time, July 8, 1991

The history of the world has been in great part the history of the mixing of peoples. Modern communication and transport accelerate mass migrations from one continent to another. Ethnic and racial diversity is more than ever a salient fact of the age.

But what happens when people of different origins, speaking different languages and professing different religions, inhabit the same locality and live under the same political sovereignty? Ethnic and racial conflict—far more than ideological conflict—is the explosive problem of our times.

On every side today ethnicity is breaking up nations. The Soviet Union, India, Yugoslavia, Ethiopia, are all in crisis. Ethnic tensions disturb and divide Sri Lanka, Burma, Indonesia, Iraq, Cyprus, Nigeria, Angola, Lebanon, Guyana, Trinidad—you name it. Even nations as stable and civilized as Britain and France, Belgium and Spain, face growing ethnic troubles. Is there any large multiethnic state that can be made to work?

The answer to that question has been, until recently, the United States. "No other nation," Margaret Thatcher has said, "has so successfully combined people of different races and nations within a single culture." How have Americans succeeded in pulling off this almost unprecedented trick?

We have always been a multiethnic country. Hector St. John de Crevecoeur, who came from France in the 19th century, marveled at the astonishing diversity of the settlers—"a mixture of English, Scotch, Irish, French, Dutch, Germans and Swedes . . . this promiscuous breed." He propounded a famous question: "What then is the American, this new man?" And he gave a famous answer: "Here individuals of all nations are melted into a new race of men." *E pluribus unum.*

The U.S. escaped the divisiveness of a multiethnic society by a brilliant solution: the creation of a brand new national identity. The point of America was not to preserve old cultures but to forge a new *American* culture. "By an intermixture with our people," President George Washington told Vice President John Adams, immigrants will "get assimilated to our customs, measures and laws: in a word, soon become one people." This was the ideal that a century later Israel Zangwill crystallized in the title of his popular 1908 play *The Melting Pot.* And no institution was more potent in molding Crevecoeur's "promiscuous breed" into Washington's "one people" than the American public school.

The new American nationality was inescapably English in language, ideas and institutions. The pot did not melt everybody, not even all the white immigrants; deeply bred racism put black Americans, yellow Americans, red Americans and brown Americans well outside the pale. Still, the infusion of other stocks, even of nonwhite stocks, and the experience of the New World reconfigured the British legacy and made the U.S., as we all know, a very different country from Britain.

In the 20th century, new immigration laws altered the composition of the American people, and a cult of ethnicity erupted both among non-Anglo whites and among nonwhite minorities. This had many healthy consequences. The American culture at last began to give shamefully overdue recognition to the achievements of groups subordinated and spurned during the high noon of Anglo dominance, and it began to acknowledge the great swirling world beyond Europe. Americans acquired a more complex and invigorating sense of their world—and of themselves.

But, pressed too far, the cult of ethnicity has unhealthy consequences. It gives rise, for example, to the conception of the U.S. as a nation composed not of individuals making their own choices but of inviolable ethnic and racial groups. It rejects the historic American goals of assimilation and integration. And, in an excess of zeal, well-intentioned people seek to transform our system of education from a means of creating "one people" into a means of promoting, celebrating and perpetuating separate ethnic origins and identities. The balance is shifting from *unum* to *pluribus.*

That is the issue that lies beyond the hullaballoo over "multiculturalism" and "political correctness," the attack on the "Eurocentric" curriculum and the rise of the notion that history and literature should be taught not as disciplines but as therapies whose function is to raise minority self-esteem. Group separatism crystallizes the differences, magnifies tensions, intensifies hostilities. Europe—the unique source of the liberating ideas of democracy, civil liberties and human rights—is portrayed as the root of all evil, and non-European cultures, their own many crimes deleted, are presented as the means of redemption.

I don't want to sound apocalyptic about these developments. Education is always in ferment, and a good thing too. The situation in our universities, I am confident, will soon right itself. But the impact of separatist pressures on our public schools is more troubling. If a Kleagle of the Ku Klux Klan wanted to use the schools to disable and handicap black Americans, he could hardly come up with anything more effective than the "Afrocentric" curriculum. And if separatist tendencies go unchecked, the result can only be the fragmentation, resegregation, and tribalization of American life.

I remain optimistic. My impression is that the historic forces driving toward "one people" have not lost their power. The eruption of ethnicity is, I believe, a rather superficial enthusiasm stirred by romantic ideologues on the one hand and by unscrupulous con men on the other: self-appointed spokesmen whose claim to represent their minority groups is carelessly accepted by the media. Most American-born members of minority groups, white or nonwhite, see themselves primarily as Americans rather than primarily as members of one or another ethnic group. A notable indicator today is the rate of intermarriage across ethnic lines, across religious lines, even (increasingly) across racial lines. "We Americans," said Theodore Roosevelt, "are children of the crucible."

The growing diversity of the American population makes the quest for unifying ideals and a common culture all the more urgent. In a world savagely rent by ethnic and racial antagonisms, the U.S. must continue as an example of how a highly differentiated society holds itself together.

Questions for Discussion

1. How does Schlesinger believe that the "U.S. escaped the divisiveness of a multiethnic society"? Do you agree with his conclusion?

2. What are the positive and negative consequences to the "cult of ethnicity," according to Schlesinger? Would you add or delete any consequences?

3. Do you believe with Schlesinger that an "Afrocentric curriculum" would disable African-Americans? Why or why not?

4. Schlesinger ends his essay with the statement, "In a world savagely rent by ethnic and racial antagonisms, the U.S. must continue as an example of how a highly differentiated society holds itself together." How, in your opinion, should the U.S. deal with a multiethnic society (in terms of education, opportunities, and customs) so it will be a good example?

Writing or Speaking Assignment

1. Compare the two articles. What issue do they both address? State each of their conclusions and the reasons given for these conclusions. Then write an essay or give a speech in which you explain which author gives a better argument and why.

More Ideas for Writing or Speaking

1. Do an exploratory essay or speech on a current problem. List several of the solutions given for this problem and explore the pros and cons of each solution. Some problems you might explore would be national health care, the creation of a balanced budget, shelters for the homeless, teenage pregnancy, or illegal immigration. You might also want to choose a problem that has emerged on your campus.

   Use this format in preparing your speech or essay:

   a. Clearly define the problem.

   b. Establish criteria for solutions. (For example, consider time and money limits.)

    c. Come up with as many alternative solutions as possible. (If you are working in a group, brainstorm about possibilities.)

    d. When possible alternatives are exhausted, evaluate each alternative against the criteria for solutions.

    e. Choose the best alternative and explain why this alternative is the best.

2. Rent a copy of the classic film *Twelve Angry Men*. This film depicts the various viewpoints and prejudices of a group of jurors who have to determine the guilt or innocence of a man accused of killing his father.

    Before viewing the tape, consider the following excerpt.

> The drive to help juries make the right decisions is drawing some ideas from human-behavior experts who have amassed a wealth of research on how jurors think. Decades ago, judges and lawyers assumed that jurors heard evidence piecemeal and began to analyze it in earnest only during deliberations. But extensive interviews of jurors in recent years have given rise to the theory that they construct evidence into mental "stories" that incorporate interpretations based on their personal experiences. "Jurors used to be viewed as passive objects," says Valerie Hans, a jury researcher at the University of Delaware. "Now we know they are very active in filling in missing evidence and making inferences." The studies are influencing some judges to give jurors more information about the cases they hear.[6]

    After viewing the film, discuss the problems of ethnocentrism and egocentrism that influence the decisions of different jurors and what arguments help them to be fair to the defendant.

3. Choose an issue about which you feel strongly and argue for the position that is opposite to your own real beliefs. Construct a persuasive speech or essay on this position, using one of the formats outlined in Chapter 7. Do thorough research on the stand you are defending, and be as convincing as you can. In the conclusion of your essay or speech, explain whether this exercise caused you to be more or less convinced about your original position on this issue. What changes, if any, did you make in your perspective concerning this issue?

---

[6] Ted Gest with Constance Johnson, "The Justice System: Getting a Fair Trial," *U.S. News and World Report*, May 25, 1992, p. 38.

4. Create a speech or essay on an issue about which you have no strong feelings. Research both sides of the issue and become acquainted with the benefits and shortcomings of each.

   In your discussion of this issue, articulate the conclusions of both sides and the reasons given for each conclusion. Note the strongest and weakest reasons for each side. Point out fallacious reasoning that is used to defend either position. In your conclusion, comment on whether you found either side to be more convincing and why.

CHAPTER TEN

Suggestion in Media

Is What You See What You Get?
Do You Really Want It?

A critical thinker is aware of the presence and power of suggestion in electronic and print media.

"The hand that rules the press, the radio, the screen and the far-spread magazine, rules the country."

Learned Hand, memorial address for Justice Brandeis (December 21, 1942)

Hear Ye! Here's the Smart Way to Listen to a Speech

by Diane Bartley
USA Weekend, February 9–11, 1990

Peggy Noonan is not exactly a household name. But her way with words—"a thousand points of light," "a kinder, gentler nation"—helped one of her bosses make a name for himself.

Now Noonan, who was a speech writer for George Bush and Ronald Reagan, is in the limelight with her Reagan-era memoirs, *What I Saw at the Revolution.*

Noonan, who wrote commentaries for Dan Rather before moving to the White House in 1984, offers these tips for unraveling presidential rhetoric:

Be on the lookout for "daydream time."

Noonan admits "it is hard to follow a political argument for six, seven, or eight minutes at a stretch." Most speeches last roughly 20 minutes. So good speeches include time-outs for the listener to relax and gather energy.

Understand That Nothing is Accidental

Every word was chosen for a reason. A presidential speech is checked and triple-checked for every possible misinterpretation. Assorted top aides read and edit, the president adds his thoughts—and the entire process begins again. Up to 50 people have input.

An example: In a speech for Reagan's reelection, a still-green Noonan used the phrase "I will be frank." It quickly was deleted; it suggested Reagan wasn't always frank.

Don't Be Swayed by Body Movements

They can be deceptive; everyone these days is coached on how to perform before the unforgiving eye of a TV camera.

"At the end of the Reagan era all the presidential candidates looked like local TV news guys," writes Noonan. "They talked with their voices low and cool, not going to the mike but letting the mike go to them."

Don't always blame the president—or the speech writer—for lack of eloquence.

Blame the process, says Noonan. The same editing that is meant to wipe out mistakes also can delete the flavor.

"Think of a bunch of wonderful, clean, shining, perfectly shaped and delicious vegetables," she says. "Then think of one of those old-fashioned metal meat grinders. Imagine the vegetables being forced through and rendered into a smooth, dull, textureless puree."

Reprinted by permission.

Televised arguments, such as the speeches described in the preceding article, can be found on commercials, talk shows, interview programs, segments of news programs, and sometimes even sitcoms and dramas. Arguments that appear in print include advertisements, essays, and editorials.

There are two types of persuasive techniques used by the print and electronic media that every critical thinker should understand. These techniques are called *suggestion* and *subliminal (unconscious) persuasion.*

Suggestion in Daily Life

Suggestion means presenting ideas or images in such a way as to reveal certain ideas or qualities and to conceal others. We use the power of suggestion to create impressions in our personal lives, impressions that help us to look or seem better in some way than we actually are.

You might stuff any debris under the seat of your car if you are unexpectedly asked to drive an attractive person home, so that the car (and you) look neater than you actually are. Women (and some men) use suggestion when they wear make-up to look older, younger, or prettier. Balding men might wear hats or comb their remaining hair so it looks thicker than it is. Most of us choose clothing that makes us look better by concealing flaws.

People use the power of suggestion in the professional world also—like when a real estate agent tells a client to bake something sweet for an open house so the house will smell inviting and warm—or when salesclerks are told to look busy, even when there is no real work to do—or when a car salesperson asks you to sit inside a car and feel comfortable, hoping that the suggestion of ownership and the smell and feel of a new car will induce you to buy.

EXERCISE

Purpose: To discover and analyze examples of suggestion in personal and professional contexts.

1. For the brave and honest only: Think of five ways you use the power of suggestion in your life to create an impression on a boss, friend, mate, teacher, parent, or in general. Or, observe or interview someone else about how they arrange their world to create impressions.

2. Interview a professional, telling him or her about the concept of suggestion and asking in what ways it is used in his or her business. Examples are asking a manager of a supermarket if certain products are arranged at kid level to appeal to children and if items at the checkout counter are chosen for a particular reason. Or ask stereo salespersons or department store managers how their stores are arranged to give the desired impression to customers.

   Another approach to this exercise is to begin by analyzing the layout of a store or office (supermarket, department store, stereo store, bank, doctor's office, or toy store). Come to some conclusions about why the room is laid out in that particular way; support your conclusions with reasons. After you have made some assumptions about the layout, interview the manager of the store or office to find out if the layout is meant to influence customers in any way.

Televised Suggestion

> *"The media does set the agenda about what will and will not get discussed."*
>
> Sherry Bebitch Jaffe, Center for Politics and Policy, Claremont Graduate School, addressing the Society for Professional Journalists (September 1992)

Television producers, directors, editors, and advertisers have always used the power of suggestion. The following guidelines will help you view television with an understanding of the subtle, but consciously detectable, use of suggestion.

For news programs and talk shows, be aware of:

1. The selection of issues.

2. The use of time.

3. Selection of guest and panel members.

4. What is included or excluded on a set.

5. The nonverbal element of clothing.

6. Use of language.

7. Use of camera angles and cuts.

8. Camera distance and framing.

THE SELECTION OF ISSUES

Hundreds of global and national issues could be covered on any given day. The average network and local newscast is 24 minutes long, including sports and weather (with 6 minutes of commercials). Many stories are written but not aired because of these time limitations. So the selection of which stories are important and the decision about the order in which they will be presented gives network news editors enormous power. The very fact that a story is on the morning or evening news makes it seem important to us; we never really know what issues are not being covered.

Mike Wallace, host of CBS' popular "60 Minutes" (an investigative reporting program), stated that on news-related programs, the reporter's interest often decides whether a story is profiled. In other words, both reporters (by choosing stories) and editors (by deciding which stories are aired) have the power to decide what is worthy of coverage and what is not.

Another important factor in determining the content of programming is called *numbers* or *ratings*. The shows that get the largest audiences (decided by independent research companies, such as Nielsen) also get the largest share of advertising revenue. In effect, if a program wants to stay on the air, it has to attract a large audience. (For more information on the Nielsen ratings, see the article at the end of Chapter 4.)

One method used to attract viewers is called **sensationalism**. More exciting stories are chosen over less exciting but perhaps more newsworthy ones, and the most bizarre, visually interesting, or sensational elements of these stories are featured. For example, a local station might focus in on the day's fires and auto accidents, showing all the gory details, and bypass stories on upcoming legislation or elections.

The apparent success of sensational coverage of the news is one factor behind the claim that the primary purpose of television news is

"THAT'S 73% WHO ARE DISGUSTED BY TABLOID JOURNALISM BUT CAN'T TALK TO US WHILE 'CURRENT AFFAIR' IS ON."

Dunagin's People by Ralph Dunagin
Reprinted with special permission of North American Syndicate

to entertain rather than to inform. Whatever the objectives of the media, we as critical thinkers can choose to view news broadcasts with discernment rather than to passively absorb the program as we would a situation comedy.

THE TIME FACTOR

Two elements of time can influence listeners. One is the time placement of a story. A story given prime (early) coverage on a newscast will seem very important to the audience. On network news, when the worldwide events of the day are given only 24 minutes, any item rating coverage also attains instant credibility with viewers.

Phil Donahue spoke to Dan Rather about the power of network news and asked him why CBS used some of its precious evening broadcast time to cover a frog who could jump 30 feet. Rather laughed and said that when a frog can jump 30 feet, that is news! He skirted the question gracefully, but the issue remains: What is worthy of national broadcast in a limited time-frame, and, more importantly, who decides?

David Brinkley addressed the question of who decides what to broadcast at a meeting of the Radio-Television News Directors Association. He commented on the fact that most Americans don't read newspapers to be informed, choosing to watch television news instead. "All they know about public policy," he said, "is what we tell them."[1]

The quantity of time is also a factor on television and radio, especially on talk shows featuring guests who discuss different sides of the same issue. When one guest is given more time than another to make his or her points, that guest has a greater chance of influencing the audience.

In addition, we begin to feel better acquainted with the person who is given more time; the factor of familiarity may unconsciously persuade us to feel closer to that person's position, especially on a topic that is new to us.

EXERCISES

Purpose: To compare the effect of different selection and ordering of news stories.

1. Watch the evening news on several stations, either local or national, for one or two nights. You may have to switch back and forth from one channel to another if the coverage is simultaneous (unless you can hook up two sets in the same room or have a classmate watch a different station). Then, consider the following elements.

   Note the selection of issues, the order of the stories shown, and the time given to each story. If different stories were covered, which station covered the more important story, in your opinion? Note also any "slant" given to a story by the comments or facial expressions of the anchorpersons. Did some stations feature more sensational stories or more in-depth coverage of stories than others?

   You may not notice any different selection of issues on the commercial networks; try comparing a commercial network with public television's or C-SPAN's coverage. Are there any major differences?

[1] Marlin Maddoux, *Free Speech or Propaganda?* (Nashville: Thomas Nelson Publishers, 1990), p. 73.

After compiling your research, answer this question: If you were an editor on one of the broadcasts, what changes would you make in the coverage of the news? Which stories would you give more, less, or no coverage? Which stories would get top priority on your network?

2. In class groups, assume you are the program editors for a local edition of the evening news. Look at the story topics below and put them in order from most to least important. The most important will be covered at the top of the program and the least important may be cut in the interest of time.

To make your task easier, set some criteria before you order the stories. Possible criteria include informational value, usefulness to the local populace, and relevance to the largest number of people. In essence, you are to decide what the people in your audience should know. Think about other important criteria and then list your criteria in order of the most to least important.

   a. There is an update on hopeful signs in Mideast peace talks.
   b. A murder-suicide occurred at a downtown hotel.
   c. Polls on an upcoming campaign show the frontrunner falling behind.
   d. There is a serious drought in a neighboring country.
   e. A death-row inmate has been executed, and there was a protest involving 300 people.
   f. Someone has written a book claiming that a famous star, thought dead for 20 years, is alive and well.
   g. A major freeway accident is causing hour-long delays in the evening commute.
   h. A local daycare center has been charged with child abuse.
   i. A new drug for treating AIDS, which has been used with some good results in France, has been banned indefinitely, pending Food and Drug Administration approval.
   j. There is massive starvation in another country, and relief efforts are hindered by a lack of funds.

SELECTION OF GUEST AND PANEL MEMBERS

When you watch a debate or talk show on an issue, notice the credentials of the persons being interviewed. On programs where the producer or editor is either not careful or biased, one side may be represented by attractive, articulate spokespersons and the other by intensely emotional, unattractive people. Are the persons selected really in leadership positions in the causes they represent and are they respected by their colleagues? Does the professional on the panel (usually a doctor, psychologist, or lawyer) represent only one side of the controversy and therefore lend credibility only to that side?

Be fair by keeping in mind the principle that if a controversy rages for a long time, that usually means reasonable people are disagreeing about important definitions or principles. Don't judge an issue by an abrasive spokesperson who may not represent the norm of persons who support his or her side. The producer may have chosen a more colorful and interesting, but much less representative, person to discuss either side.

Related to the selection of panel members or others who are chosen to be interviewed about an issue is the treatment of the spokesperson(s) by the interviewer. Note whether the interviewer is equally positive (or negative) in his or her interrogation of the guests. Sometimes a biased interviewer will direct positive, easily answered questions to one guest and more negative, probing questions to a guest who represents the other side of the issue.

WHAT'S INCLUDED OR EXCLUDED ON A TELEVISED SET

When an interview is set up, you should note the environment in which it is set. For example, on a commercial for encyclopedias, we might be impressed by a "teacher" who is surrounded with books and diplomas.

The director of a commercial can create an academic background that may have nothing to do with anyone's credentials. The actress who introduces herself as a teacher on an encyclopedia commercial doesn't have to be a teacher. Advertisers know that the impression of authority—created by a setting of a doctor's office, a classroom, or a law library—can have a positive impact on our response to the commercial message.

EXERCISE

Purpose: To understand the altering of settings to create impressions on viewers.

Analyze the setting of a place that you frequent—it could be your classroom, the business you work for, a store, a restaurant, or your home. What impression does the room convey? If you put a camera in different places in the same room, what different impressions would be created? Do the people in charge of this environment consciously set it up the way it is? If so, what is their purpose?

Analyze the set of a commercial or television program—why do you think it looks the way it does? How have the set designers "framed" the environment? What impression does it convey?

THE NONVERBAL ELEMENT OF CLOTHING, WHICH INCLUDES MAKE-UP AND ACCESSORIES

How someone is dressed is an important factor in creating a suggestion of their character and appropriateness for a given role. For example, both the Republican and Democratic parties have "schools" for their candidates in which training is given on campaign techniques; part of this training covers proper dress in various situations. Spouses are also encouraged to attend sessions on how to dress themselves and how to help their mates dress to create the right impressions. Even small details such as appropriate length and color of socks are covered in these workshops.

Clothing style is an essential element of advertising as well. Actors who are portraying teachers, doctors, or other professionals are dressed to fit the part.

Several years ago, John Molloy wrote the best-selling books *Dress for Success* (for men) and *The Woman's Dress for Success Book* about his extensive studies on how styles and colors create impressions. His books are filled with research about how changing the look or color of one's clothes, jewelry, accessories, and hair-style has helped individuals do better on job interviews, with sales calls, or in other difficult communication situations. Many advertisers, candidates, or spokespersons are familiar with Molloy's techniques and use them to create positive suggestions on their audiences.

EXERCISE

Purpose: To understand personal image-engineering for the larger purpose of viewing in a more discerning way political candidates, salespersons, or actors promoting products.

1. Stop and write down everything you are wearing that is visible to others. Include make-up, jewelry, and accessories and consider your choice of colors. What impression are you trying to convey to others with your "look"? If you generally dress while you're half-asleep, stop and think about how someone else might judge you based on your clothing.

   You can extend this exercise to the classroom by having a few classmates write down the impression they get from your appearance. Compare their answers with the impression you'd like to make. How did you do as an image engineer?

2. Note how the actors in some commercials are dressed; what impression are they trying to create? If you have access to a televised trial, or even to the program "People's Court," you can note the appearance of the plaintiffs and defendants and draw conclusions about why they are dressed as they are. How does their image affect their credibility? How might a different image give viewers a different impression?

USE OF LANGUAGE

Setting and appearance send messages nonverbally; the use of a reporter's language also can slant our perception of an issue. Some years ago, when a terrorist bombing would occur, news reporters would say, "Such and such a group takes *credit* for the bombing." Other reporters and the public took offense at the word *credit*, which has a positive connotation. The late Eric Severeid, a respected commentator, did a segment on the harm done by such words. Because of these protests, the commonly accepted statement is now "Such and such a group claimed *responsibility* for the bombing."

One media critic gave this example of the slanting of facts by the choice of words:

I might say "I've been a journalist for thirty years." Now a newspaper could pick that up and report: "Charles Wiley said he has been a journalist for thirty years." That's fact. Just straight reporting. Or the reporter could say, "Marlin's guest *admitted* he's been a journalist for thirty years." Or he can say, "He has *conceded* he's been a journalist for thirty years." Or he could go to the final step and say, "Wiley *confessed* he's been a journalist for thirty years." You see how one word changes the whole meaning.[2]

SKILL

Recognize the techniques of suggestion used by electronic media.

CAMERA ANGLE AND CUTS

Sometimes, directors tell camerapersons to shoot a person from below; this angle gives the speaker more authority as if the viewers are "looking up to" the individual. Some networks were accused of using this angle to enhance the image of Oliver North when he spoke about the Iran-Contra affair.[3] Commercials use this technique to command attention and respect for a particular actor who is telling us to buy something, or to show how large and impressive an authority figure looks to a "common" person. One recent commercial used this technique to illustrate how big a parent looks to a toddler.

Conversely, when the camera angle is above the speaker, the impression is that the viewers are looking down on the speaker; in this case, the speaker may look insignificant or even shifty.

The ability to use cuts (switching from one camera to another) to create positive or negative impressions about a speaker during a debate or talk show, or even in a news report, gives television directors great power. For example, a director can cut to a shot of an audience member's reaction to a speaker, thereby giving the impression of approval or disapproval of what the speaker has said. Also, during convention coverage, directors can cut to one audience member who appears bored with a candidate and thus unfairly represent the majority of audience members. Conversely, C-SPAN has used wide-angle cuts to show the audience that while a congressperson or senator is making an impassioned speech, the chairs in the room are empty.

---

2   Ibid., p. 54.

3   John Splaine, "Critically Viewing the Social Studies: A New Literacy," *Louisiana Social Studies Journal*, Volume XVI, Number 1, Fall, 1989, p. 16.

Cuts in editing are used to select a short segment of a longer interview for broadcast. Sometimes, these cuts distort the statements that have been made by taking them out of context. The *sound bite* is a brief selection of a longer speech, usually heard out of context; both politicians and editors use sound bites to create impressions on viewers.

CAMERA DISTANCE AND FRAMING

Directors of programs may deliberately or unconsciously use camera shots to influence audiences. Close-ups control our emotions by adding an element of intimacy. We feel closer to a person and identify more readily with the person's viewpoint when we can see him or her as, literally, close to us. We may believe that the speaker is telling us the truth because he appears to be looking us in the eye. In fact, the speaker is looking at the camera or at the interviewer and only appears to be making eye contact with us. Conversely, educator John Splaine writes, "A camera angle from the side will suggest that a pictured person, who is responding to an incriminating question, might not be telling the truth."[4]

A wide-angle shot can make us feel distant from an individual. We feel uncomfortable with someone who seems far away from us, and that may translate into a lack of trust for his or her position on a given issue. When a scene is shot from a helicopter, the people below are seen as far away and alien, sometimes appearing more like ants than human beings.

In addition, **framing**—the deliberate or unconscious use of camera shots to influence audiences—can make a critical difference. One loud demonstrator shown close up at a rally can create a distorted image if there are hundreds of other people protesting quietly. During the coverage of the chaos in Los Angeles following the verdict of the Rodney King trial in the spring of 1992, television viewers saw two Korean men standing in front of their businesses pointing handguns; a Korean community leader criticized the reporters for leaving out the rest of the scene, which consisted of groups of looters heading for the stores. By showing only the two men with handguns, viewers were given a false impression and the storeowners were literally "framed."

Critical thinkers need to be vigilant in their awareness of the subtle impressions that can be created electronically.

[4] Ibid.

EXERCISE

Purpose: To find examples of suggestive techniques used by broadcast media.

Watch a news or interview program and analyze the suggestive elements we've mentioned in this section: the selection of issues, the use of time, the selection of guest and panel members, what is included or excluded on a set, the nonverbal element of clothing, the use of language, the use of camera angles and cuts, and camera distance and framing. Is there anything about the presentation of the material that creates suggestions? If so, what do you think might be the motive of the producers, directors, or editors in charge of the broadcast?

Watch (or tape if possible) several commercials. Using the list of techniques as a guide, isolate the ways in which the advertisers are trying to persuade you to buy their product or use their service.

Suggestion in Print Media

"Four hostile newspapers are more to be feared than a thousand bayonets."

Napoleon I, *Maxims* (1804–1815)

The broadcast media, television, and radio, are subject to what is called the **fairness doctrine**, which means that if broadcasters allow air time for one side of an issue, they must allow time for other points of view as well. Because of the fairness doctrine, a talk show cannot allow people to speak against capital punishment and then refuse to air a program with panelists who favor capital punishment. Within that provision, however, broadcasters can choose which guests appear and can manipulate programs using the techniques detailed in the previous section.

The print media, however, are not under the same governmental pressure to be fair. In noting the need for some kind of fairness doctrine for the press, media scholar Ben Bagdikian stated that "most daily newspapers have not faced up to the fact that they are monopoly institutions and therefore have an obligation to speak for the entire community and to be sensitive to every segment of it."[5]

5   Ben Bagdikian, *The Media Monopoly* (Boston: Beacon Press, 1973).

Different newspapers and magazines often have reputations for being conservative or liberal. They may feature columnists who largely subscribe to the publisher's political and social viewpoints. As critical thinkers, we can be responsible readers when we consider the following:

1. Use of headlines.
2. Balance of reporting on an issue.
3. Fairness in editorial essays and letters.
4. Photo composition.

USE OF HEADLINES

Most readers know that the sensational headlines featured on papers found in supermarket check-out lines are not credible. When we read a headline proclaiming that a famous star has "8 new babies," we can assume that her cat had a litter of kittens or another equally silly explanation for this amazing news. Few of us believe that a 13 year old really did elope with a two-headed alien. Justifiably, these tabloids have little credibility and should not be used as resource material for your term papers!

Less sensational headlines can also distort information and mislead readers in subtle ways. Headlines in respectable newspapers and magazines are important because many readers are scanners—that means that they skim the paper, reading headlines, and then go back to read only the articles of interest to them.

A headline that is scanned and recorded in the memory of a reader can give a distorted picture of information without actually being false. For example, let's say a reporter did a detailed story about an anti-nuclear protest that was held at a local power plant. The story covers the issues brought up by the demonstrators and the responses made by the plant spokesperson.

An editor who did not approve of this protest could use the headline, "No one arrested at power plant demonstration." Bringing in the idea of arrest by stating that there were no arrests is a subtle way of implying there might have been arrests, i.e., that the protesters were not peaceful.

Another example of an irresponsible and misleading headline was given in Chapter 4. The headline read, "Family Members, Not Strangers, Abduct Most Children." This headline could lead casual skimmers of the paper to the conclusion that child abduction by strangers is not a serious problem.

Still, the article itself points out that although the majority of abductions are done by family members, as many as 4,600 children were abducted by strangers, and there were approximately 100,000 attempted abductions that year. The reporter did an admirable job of explaining the statistical research in this area; however, the editor may have seriously limited the effectiveness of the article with a headline implying something different from what the article reported.

Consider also the titles given to editorials written by readers of a newspaper or magazine. Sometimes these titles are representative of the position of the person who wrote the editorial, but sometimes they are used to distort or ridicule the position of the writer. In this way, an editorial page may appear balanced, but in reality is not.

BALANCE OF REPORTING ON AN ISSUE

Whereas network news and interview programs have a shortage of *time*, newspapers and newsmagazines have limited *space*. The editor decides which stories are important enough to cover and on what page. Generally, if a story is on the front page it is perceived by readers as more important than a story placed farther back in the paper.

EXERCISE

Purpose: To note that news coverage varies depending on the source and to consider different priorities held by various sources.

1. Compare your local newspaper, a large city newspaper, and a national paper. What stories are covered on the first few pages? Why do you think different stories are featured by the various papers?

2. Choose an issue that is getting wide press coverage. Find articles on this issue in several different newspapers or magazines. Compare the coverage in each one, and then write an essay in which you address the following questions.
   a. What elements of coverage framed the story in different ways? Analyze the summary of the story given in the first one or two paragraphs, the quotes selected from the persons interviewed, the amount of coverage given to both sides of the issue, and the use of headlines and photographs.
   b. Which source reported the issue most fairly, in your view? Give examples to support your position.

FAIRNESS IN EDITORIAL ESSAYS AND LETTERS

Some newspapers and magazines get a reputation for being primarily liberal or conservative because of the stands taken by their editorial commentators. In addition, local newspapers often print their suggestions as to how readers should vote in an upcoming election. It is important for critical thinkers to realize that reporting is not always objective and fair and that the editorial pages are set aside to reflect the *opinions* of readers and essayists.

Notice if the essays on the editorial page seem to favor one political viewpoint over another. In addition, examine the letters to the editor. They should reflect differing, rather than homogeneous, opinions on the same issue.

SKILL

Recognize the use of suggestion in print media.

PHOTO COMPOSITION

If a picture is worth a thousand words, then photojournalists have a strong communicative advantage. They can influence our perceptions of people or events with the photographs they print.

Most of us would agree that outright lies using photographs are unethical; for example, when photographers for *TV Guide* used image processing to create a cover featuring the head of Oprah Winfrey with the body of Ann-Margaret, readers and fellow journalists alike were disapproving. We don't like to be deceived by our technology.

But more subtle forms of manipulation can occur through photo composition. A responsible photographer could take a wide-angle shot of a rally, thus giving the viewer a sense of the general scene. A less scrupulous, or less careful, photographer could shoot instead a few unruly persons, which would discredit the general group of peaceful participants. Conversely, he or she could focus the camera on a fight between one police officer and one participant, which would give an impression of police brutality. In addition, captions beneath photographs can influence our perceptions of a person or event.

Newspapers and newsmagazines should treat photographs as documentary information that helps us get the general feel of an event.

When you sense that a photograph is making an editorial statement, stop and consider what viewpoint is being suggested through the picture.

EXERCISE

Purpose: To gain awareness of misleading headlines and how they distort information; to find examples of imbalanced reporting and editorializing and of slanted photojournalism.

1. Look for examples of headlines that distort the meanings of stories. Bring the headlines to class for discussion, or write a paper in which you explain the following.
   a. How does the headline distort the information in the story?
   b. Why do you think that headline was chosen?
   c. What would be a more appropriate headline for this story? Why do you think it was not chosen?
2. Look for examples of imbalanced reporting or editorializing or use of misleading photographs. Bring the stories, photographs, or editorial essays to class or write a paper in which you explain the following.
   a. How is the story, photograph, or editorial biased?
   b. How could bias have been prevented? What would be a more fair representation of the information?

Subliminal Persuasion

It takes an educated or very discerning person to be aware of the many methods used to persuade viewers to think or act in a certain way. The old saying "Let the buyer beware" means that when we are subjected to various pitches by advertisers and politicians, we should have the power to say no to their claims and to resist being persuaded against our will. Increasing our awareness of the persuasive techniques used by print and electronic media gives us more power as thinkers, voters, and consumers.

What if, however, we are being persuaded to think and act against our will by messages geared to affect us in ways our conscious minds cannot detect? This happens when we are exposed to *subliminal persuasion*.

For our purposes, we will consider two types of subliminal (unconscious) persuasion:

1.   Information that is tangential to the main message given. This information can be perceived if we are made aware of it, but this perception usually requires training.

2.   Information that cannot be registered by the conscious mind, despite training. This information takes the form of photographs altered under high magnification and messages embedded in film, audio tracks, and videotape, which are meant to be picked up by the unconscious mind.

The existence of this second form of subliminal persuasion is controversial; many respected scholars dismiss it as the stuff urban legends are made of; others believe it is done frequently, yet usually denied by commercial artists and technicians. Among those scholars who do believe that this form of subliminal persuasion exists, there is disagreement as to its effectiveness.

PERSUASION WE CAN DETECT

Information that can be perceived if we know what to look for can be considered a form of suggestion. Copywriters and graphic designers can use subtle phrasing and combinations of colors and formats to attract us to certain products.

Television advertisers get our attention with loud music or words and frequent camera cuts. You may have noticed that you can do homework during a television program, except when the commercials come on; they seem to grab your attention. This process happens to children, too. The next time you are watching television with a young child, notice how alert the child becomes during almost any commercial. We respond to loud, fast-paced programming with frequent camera changes. Even public television programs like "Sesame Street" use this technique of 15–30 second spots to keep attention levels high. Commercials shown on programs airing after midnight are particularly loud; people who fall asleep in front of a television set may be startled awake by the blaring of a commercial message (invariably advising late-night viewers to get a life by using their product or service). No advertiser wants to play to a sleeping audience.

In addition to using the initial attention-getting devices, advertisers (and political media coordinators) are keenly interested in holding attention, even for just a few seconds more than their competitors.

To hold attention they have to "grab" the audience in some way, and many utilize the psychological principles of Gestalt theory.

The Gestalt Principle

Our minds strive toward congruence and completion of information. If a message strikes us as incomplete, we will fill in the missing details ourselves. Consider the following Gestalt techniques that are commonly used but seldom questioned by the consumers of the message (us).

1. *Questions or Slogans That the Consumer Is Taught to Answer.*
Years ago, Winston cigarettes used a simple jingle: "Winston tastes good like a cigarette should. Winston tastes good like a [clap, clap] cigarette should." For a long time, television and radio listeners heard this jingle sung in a joyful manner.

Then one day, the jingle proceeded as follows: "Winston tastes good like a cigarette should. Winston tastes good like a [clap, clap]." Listeners who had heard the jingle before could hardly help completing the song in their minds, thus joining in with the advertisers to laud the praises of this cigarette. They had been trained over time to know the ending of the commercial, and when the standard ending was left out, they filled it in.

We are generally taught as children that it is rude not to answer a question asked of us, and this carries over into adulthood. Assertiveness trainers sometimes spend much time and energy teaching clients that they don't need to answer every question they are asked.

Advertisers capitalize on our early training by asking us questions, knowing we probably will instinctively formulate answers in our minds. Here are some examples:

> Aren't you hungry for King Burgers now?
>
> Why do you think they call it Up Close?
>
> Doesn't your child deserve a gift of love?

2. *Images That Don't Make Sense.*
Again, our minds try to make sense out of things that are together but don't seem to go together. Leon Festinger's theory of cognitive dissonance states that the need for congruence (consonance, harmony) is not only a human need but a *drive,* just as powerful as our drive for food and water. We are motivated by this drive and so we take action when things don't make sense: We try to make sense out of them.

For example, you may be disturbed by a couple who don't seem suited for each other; their presence together may cause you to try to figure out what they see in each other. Even children love challenges called "What is wrong with this picture?"

Advertisers capitalize on our fascination with the incongruent by sometimes putting things together that don't seem to go together. They know that if we are puzzled we will give more attention to or spend more time on the ad, even if we aren't aware of doing so. They also know that if we become familiar with a product's brand name (because we've given more time and attention to its claims) then we are more likely to buy the product.

Benson and Hedges had a series of print ads showing two scenes of people interacting; there was no clear indication of what was going on between these people or why they were together. Often, the people were shown laughing, but the readers were not told what they were laughing about.

Sometimes incongruous scenes are combined with sexual insinuations, making them doubly fascinating to viewers. For example, a few years ago Jantzen swim suits carried an ad showing a man and a woman who had just emerged from swimming and were sitting on the beach. Only their bodies were visible and the female was wearing the male suit as the bottom half of her suit while the male was wearing the female bottom suit as his swimsuit. The patterns were similar, but different enough to be detected.

PERSUASION WE CAN'T DETECT

Information that cannot be perceived by the conscious mind (but that is registered unconsciously) despite training is the more controversial form of subliminal persuasion.

You may remember hearing about the merchandising trick drive-in movies allegedly used to play on customers. During a movie, they would insert one frame (remember that movies are shown on a frame-by-frame basis) of delicious looking hot-buttered popcorn within the movie. It was said that this frame, shown beneath the level of the viewers' conscious awareness, was correlated with an increase in popcorn sales at intermission time.

Graphic artists who use subliminal persuasion assume the following.

* Brand name recognition is a key to selling a product.
* A product will be remembered if the advertisement for the product holds the attention of the viewer in as many ways as

possible, including the use of loud or catchy music, colors, movements, and fascinating images.

- Among the fascinating images that hold attention the most are suggestions of sex and death.

Advertisers have used these principles in a variety of ways: One toothpaste ad showed a cute, smiling baby; the word *sex* had been airbrushed (invisibly to the naked eye, but not to a microscope) on his arm. An ad for a popular cigarette had the word *cancer* outlined on the gloves of a hockey player.

Words and other subliminal images can be discovered through magnification; yet, most of us don't have the time to devote to researching and scrutinizing every ad we see. So what can a critical thinker do to be more aware of suggestion and subtle persuasion and to act responsibly?

SKILL

Be aware of the use of subliminal persuasion.

As a critical thinker, you can:

- Understand the ways subliminal persuasion operates.
- Become aware of your attention span when you are listening to or viewing an advertisement. Are you drawn to a particular image, but can't explain why?
- When making decisions as a consumer, consider why you are buying a particular brand. Do you really believe this brand is the best or is it just a name you recognize? Read labels to see if the ingredients in your brand really differ from less expensive brands.
- When making decisions as a voter, be clear on the reasons you are supporting a particular candidate or proposition. Have you bought into a slogan or into someone's claims without thinking? Do you clearly understand the issues and the various conclusions about the issues?

The key to walking through the mines of print and electronic persuasion is to be armed with facts and logical reasoning about your decisions as a citizen and a consumer. Critical thinkers avoid basing their judgments on the consciously or unconsciously applied manipulations of campaign managers and advertisers. A good offense is your best defense.

EXERCISE

Purpose: To be able to detect subliminal persuasion in advertisements.

Find examples of television commercials or advertisements in magazines or newspapers that employ one or more of the forms of subliminal persuasion discussed in this chapter. Share your findings with class members. This is an exercise in which many heads are better than one because of the different perceptual abilities people have. One person may discover a musical trick used in a television commercial; another may detect subtle images in a print ad.

EXERCISE

Purpose: To gain a deeper understanding of subliminal persuasion.

Read more about it! This chapter gives you a basic understanding of the principles of suggestion and persuasion. Many books and articles, such as the *Newsweek* article later in this chapter, have been written on the subject. If you find these subjects interesting, do further research on them, including interviews with reporters or instructors of journalism and broadcasting.

You may want to focus your research on the controversial questions associated with subliminal persuasion: Does it currently exist? If so, what are the influences on audiences? Share your research findings with your class.

Chapter Highlights

1. The power of suggestion is used by professionals to create impressions about products, ideas, or candidates.
2. To be more critical of televised suggestion, viewers should be aware of the selection of issues, the use of time, the selection of

guest and panel members, the set, the clothing of television personalities, and the use of language, camera angles, camera cuts, camera distance, and framing.

3. To be more critical of suggestion in print media, readers should be aware of the use of headlines, the balance of reporting on an issue, the degree of fairness in editorial essays and letters, and photo composition.

4. One form of subliminal persuasion involves information meant to affect people on an unconscious level. Messages of this kind can be detected with training.

5. A second form of subliminal persuasion, whose existence and effect are not agreed upon by experts, involves information that cannot be registered by the conscious mind, regardless of training.

Articles for Discussion

Sound Too Good to Be True?

Behind the Boom in Subliminal Tapes

by Kevin Krajick
Newsweek, July 30, 1990

Rob Gregory wanted to do better at his job selling used factory-ventilation systems in Kansas City. So three years ago he bought a "subliminal" audiotape called "Unconditional Love." All Gregory heard was "some synthesized music and weird gongs." But buried beneath the sounds, supposedly, were inaudible messages subconsciously persuading him to feel better about other people. It worked, he says. His sales went up because "people sense if you really care." Encouraged, he bought another tape, this one called "Stop Hair Loss." He says he soon stopped losing his hair. Now Gregory, 30, owns 15 different improvement tapes—none of whose "hidden" messages he can hear. "Subliminals are both practical and spiritual," he says. "They're a smorgasbord for human potential."

Sound too good to be true? Not to the millions of people snapping up subliminal tapes that promise to help them shed weight or regain faith in God. Sales have doubled since 1985, and this year cassettes are expected to bring in $50 million, mostly from middle-class buyers under 45. Once sold only through the mail by small New Age firms, subliminals are now found in chain bookstores. At least 20 publishers, including Bantam, Simon and Schuster and Random House, have jumped into the business. "The whole idea that a $9.95 tape can change your life and you don't have to do anything seems so absurd," says Harriet Pironti, a spokesperson for Random House. "But it's the American way."

The tapes are said to work because their "messages" bypass conscious defense mechanisms. One hears only music or relaxing sounds; underneath, encouraging words are "embedded" at decibel levels perceived only subconsciously. Some manufacturers even speed up messages to a blur or run them through electronic filters to disguise them further. An audible voice at the start of "How To Be Popular," one of more than 170 titles from Potentials Unlimited of Grand Rapids, Mich., says, "The messages will enter your subconscious . . . so that changes will take place in your life as they should; without effort, without thought, without strain." Ocean waves and aimless harp music well up, the voice vanishes; results are guaranteed in 30 days.

The top sellers are cassettes to lose weight or quit smoking; from there, the world is at your earlobes. Single and lonely? Get "How To Attract Love." Or maybe it's time for "Divorce—Yes." For other vital concerns, there is "Agoraphobia," "Freedom From Acne," "Winning at the Track" and "I Am a Genius." Credence Cassettes of Kansas City, Mo., offers tapes designed to "correct and heal . . . concepts of God that are negative, distorted or even hostile." Inmates at Utah's South Point Prison use one called "Pedophilia" to quell criminal impulses; Texas Rangers pitchers use custom-made cassettes to increase confidence. Kids' tapes, such as "I am a Great Reader," are popular, says Patricia Mounteer, owner of Mind Mint, a Salt Lake City self-help store. "Prenatal mothers play it to the fetus and the kids come out more intelligent and walk sooner," she claims. "Positive Thoughts for Children" offers the sounds of a seashore and, somewhere in there, the assurance: "I am loved."

One needs no scientific credentials to make tapes. Potentials Unlimited president and chief "hypnotherapist" Barrie Konicov, 51, whose soothing voice is heard on his firm's cassettes, sold aluminum hair curlers, fire alarms and life insurance (his license was yanked in 1973 for forgery) before discovering self-help tapes in 1977. A federal judge once summed up Konicov's qualifications as a degree in marketing and "approximately three weekend seminars on hypnosis." Potentials Unlimited sells a million tapes a year, mostly through chains like Barnes and Noble.

Subliminal cassettes generate ridicule as well as riches. They're "worthless trash," says Brooklyn College psychology professor Arthur Reber. "People want to make their lives better by some kind of magical pseudoscience." Most psychologists, while acknowledging that experiments show people can sometimes process sounds or sights so slight they can't be consciously perceived, say there's no evidence such stimuli change lives. Even the advertising industry, which flirted with the tantalizing idea of subliminal manipulation in the 1950's, has long since abandoned the concept as ineffective.

In some cases, the tapes may be no more than a placebo. In three recent studies at the University of Washington and the University of California, San Jose, volunteers went home with popular tapes designed to improve their memory or self-esteem. After a month, tests detected no measurable improvement. Yet many subjects believed they'd made progress. "Any time you get off your butt to improve yourself, you'll probably see results," says Eric Eich, a psychology professor at the University of British Columbia who is leading a study of subliminals for the National Research Council. "If you just spent money on a tape, you'll claim it helped."

Unproven Products

Placebos used as medical cures are not necessarily innocuous, however. "People might use unproven products like this and not get professional help," says Robert Reyna, a Texas assistant attorney general investigating several companies. In 1984 a federal judge ordered Potentials Unlimited to erase copies of 31 different cassettes claiming relief for ailments ranging from high blood pressure to warts. (Potentials still markets many of the same titles with slightly reworded claims.) Since last July the federal Food and Drug Administration has warned at least two other firms to stop implying that their tapes can address illnesses such as arthritis, cancer and AIDS.

Undeterred by criticism, the tape makers are constantly striving to open new technological frontiers. Next month Valley of the Sun Publishers of Malibu, Calif., will begin marketing a range of ultra-high frequency "Silent Subliminals" that, in addition to the inaudible subliminal message, have no audible background sound whatsoever. "You won't hear anything at all," says Valley of the Sun's Sharon Boyd. "It'll be like a dog whistle going straight into your brain." . . .

Questions for Discussion

1. Do you believe that subliminal messages (positive or negative) work on the unconscious mind? How might companies that sell subliminal tapes research the effects of these messages? Try to design a controlled study (see Chapter 5) that could shed light on the effectiveness of subliminal tapes.

2. Advertisers assess the effectiveness of subliminal messages by the sales of the advertised product. The writer of this article says that the advertising industry has abandoned the concept of subliminal manipulation. What evidence does he offer to support this statement?
3. Do you believe subliminal messages can be dangerous? Why or why not?
4. Valley of the Sun publishers say that their new "Silent Subliminals" will have no sound at all. Given that consumers would not know if they were buying blank tapes, should the Food and Drug Administration monitor this product? If not, why not? If so, on what basis should it be regulated?

Identity Crises: Stereotypes Stifle Self-Development

by Joseph Giordano
Media & Values, Winter 1987

There is hardly an ethnic group in American society that doesn't feel maligned by the media. Although analysis of the media's limited viewpoint often focuses on racial minorities, white ethnics and national minorities also resent stereotyped, negative or unbalanced portrayals.

What the media that perpetrate them choose to ignore is the extent to which ethnic consciousness shapes individual identity. Mass media practitioners, particularly, find it easy to forget their viewers' history as children and grandchildren of immigrants. They fail to realize how this immigrant heritage becomes a shaper of values and attitudes that are transmitted through generations and continue as vital forces in their descendents' lives.

This tendency reflects our new understanding of the role this history plays in identity. In fact, research in the field of mental health confirms a deep psychological need for a sense of peoplehood, for historical continuity. Our ethnicity often plays a major role in determining how we feel about ourselves, how we work, how we play, how we celebrate holidays and rituals, how we feel about life, death, and illness.

As a reflector of society's values, the media have a tremendous impact on the shaping of our personal and group identities. Radio, television, films, newspapers, magazines and comics can convey the rich textures of a pluralistic society or they can, directly or indirectly (by omission and distortion), alter our perceptions of other ethnic groups and reinforce our defensiveness and ambivalence about our own cultural backgrounds. As an Italian-American, I've realized this myself when comparing the ethnic invisibility of '50s television with modern shows that concentrate on Mafia hit men and multiple biographies of Mussolini. Having squirmed as I watched some of these portrayals, I can empathize with Arabs who resent being characterized as villainous sheikhs, Jews seen as mendacious moguls or even the current vogue for matching a Russian accent with a kind of oafish villainy. Although such stereotypes may or may not serve political ends, they share the cartoonlike isolation of a few traits that ignore the humanity and variety of a group's members.

What is the impact of ethnic stereotypes on TV and in film on how people feel about themselves and how they perceive other ethnic groups?

Although research in this area is limited, what is available suggests that TV and film's portrayal of ethnics does have a deleterious effect on perceptions of self and others. In my own clinical work, I have found that minority children and adults will often internalize negative stereotypes about their own group. Other studies have shown that ethnic stereotypes on television and in the movies can contribute to prejudice against a particular group—especially when the person is not acquainted with any member of that group.

For example, in one study of television fiction, both white and black children indicated fairly high levels of acceptance that what they were viewing was like "real life," including stereotypes about their own ethnic groups.

Teaching Prejudice

In studies of youngsters who commit hate acts—desecration of religious institutions, racial and anti-Semitic incidents—many youngsters apprehended reported they got the idea of performing vandalism from news coverage of similar acts (the copy cat syndrome). They saw media coverage as conferring recognition and prestige, temporarily raising their low self-esteem.

Add to TV fiction and news the rash of "truly tasteless" joke books, radio call-in shows that invite bigoted calls from listeners, late-night TV hosts and comedians who denigrate ethnic groups, and the impact on peoples' perceptions is considerable. While the media cannot be blamed for creating the bigotry, their insensitive reporting and encouragement of inflammatory comments establishes a societal norm that gives license to such attitudes and behavior.

An important cause of distorted and damaging TV stereotypes is the tendency of some media executives to view ethnic culture as an "immigrant phenomenon," a transitional phase in the process of Americanization rather than a continuing influence on people's language, religious lives, arts, politics, food preferences and so on. Except for a colorful parade here and a human-interest story there, even ethnic news is sometimes suspect—"Parochial" or "divisive," an encouragement to the nation's "balkanization."

The media often fail to see that for many Americans, ethnic and religious traditions are still powerful influences. At times, these traditions conflict with surrounding values, but they are also sources of strength and understanding. How they work in second-, third-, and fourth-generation families can provide a rich store of story ideas and authentic characterizations for writers, directors, and actors.

Becoming Real

What, then, do ethnic Americans want? Just accurate portrayals of our lives. "Feedback" to us of a sense of pride in who we are. Appreciation of our special sadnesses, joys, achievements, faults, humor, the diversity of our lifestyles and the common experiences that bind all Americans together as human beings.

And what can ethnic groups do to make the media more culturally sensitive? To begin with, go beyond complaining and work more closely with media executives and the creative community. Applaud the industry when it presents high-quality, culturally authentic programs. Urge media people to use such resources on the ethnic experience as good novels, plays, short stories, magazine articles, newspaper stories.

Of course, some stereotyping is unavoidable in a simplified media like television and ethnic groups should understand that. But the media should also stop relying on these old negative caricatures. When ethnic groups ask for a balanced presentation in programs that reach millions of Americans, they are certainly not trying to censor the media. They only want to be shown as they are—not better, but surely not worse.

Reprinted by permission of the publisher.

Questions for Discussion

1. The author states, "Radio, television, films, newspapers, magazines and comics can convey the rich textures of a pluralistic society or they can, directly or indirectly (by omission and distortion), alter our perceptions of other ethnic groups and reinforce our defensiveness and ambivalence about our own cultural backgrounds." To what extent has the media affected your view of your own ethnic group (and we all belong to an ethnic group), and to what extent has it shaped your view of other groups?
2. When we see films from the past, we may notice stereotypes of ethnic groups and women promoted by the filmmakers of that time.

Can you think of examples of portrayals in older films that would be considered insulting? Are there portrayals of groups in current films that might be considered insulting to future generations?

3. Comment on the author's statement, "In studies of youngsters who commit hate acts—desecration of religious institutions, racial and anti-Semitic incidents—many youngsters apprehended reported they got the idea of performing vandalism from news coverage of similar acts (the copy cat syndrome). They saw media coverage as conferring recognition and prestige, temporarily raising their low self-esteem." If media coverage of violent acts against minority groups tends to motivate similar crimes, should there be any restrictions placed on the reporting of these crimes? Why or why not?

Ideas for Writing or Speaking

1. The author states, "An important cause of distorted and damaging TV stereotypes is the tendency of some media executives to view ethnic culture as an 'immigrant phenomenon,' a transitional phase in the process of Americanization rather than a continuing influence on people's language, religious lives, arts, politics, food preferences and so on." Should the media strive to emphasize our similarities, differences, or both? Provide reasons for your answer.

2. In discussing ethnic and religious traditions, the author notes that "At times, these traditions conflict with surrounding values, but they are also sources of strength and understanding. How they work in second-, third-, and fourth-generation families can provide a rich store of story ideas and authentic characterizations for writers, directors, and actors." Write a proposal for a television program or a feature-length film centered around a tradition that provides strength and cultural understanding to an individual or group. How could a program like this be used to increase cultural understanding in a pluralistic society?

More Ideas for Writing or Speaking

1. Respond to one of the following quotes from *Amusing Ourselves to Death* by Neil Postman. Support your thesis statement with evidence from radio, television, advertising, newspapers, magazines, journals, or books.

Indeed, we may have reached the point where cosmetics has replaced ideology as the field of expertise over which a politician must have competent control.[6]

The shape of a man's body is largely irrelevant to the shape of his ideas when he is addressing a public in writing or on the radio or, for that matter, in smoke signals. But it is quite relevant on television.[7]

The photograph presents the world as object; language, the world as idea.[8]

2. Analyze one of the more successful television programs and draw some specific conclusions about why it is successful. Support your conclusions with reasons. Consider the images the program projects about the people it represents.

    Another approach to this assignment would be to contrast programs that are popular now with shows (or films) that were popular in the past. Write about the different cultural, economic, or historical elements influencing these shows or films; it would be interesting to take programs from different decades for this assignment. Some questions to think about as you watch these programs are: What was acceptable in the past but is in some way politically incorrect now? What is acceptable now that would have been considered unacceptable in the past?

3. Discuss the influence of television programs on culture. To what extent does television *reflect* cultural norms and to what extent does it *create* them? Given your answer, what considerations, if any, should television producers make before approving new projects?

4. "You can tell the ideals of a nation by its advertisements."[9] What does our current advertising say about our culture's ideals? Consider values, roles of men and women, the view of the elderly, the importance of technology, and the use of time and space. Support your position with at least six examples from both print and electronic media.

5. Some critics have accused television news as functioning primarily as a form of entertainment. Watch several news programs and respond to these critics. To what extent do you agree or disagree with them and why? Give specific examples to support your answer.

---

6 Neil Postman, *Amusing Ourselves to Death* (New York: Viking Press, 1985), p. 4.

7 Ibid., p. 7.

8 Ibid., p. 72.

9 Norman Douglas, *South Wind* (London: Martin Secker & Warburg, 1917), p. 64.

6. Collect your junk mail for two or three weeks without opening it. Then analyze it by answering these questions:
   a. How did you recognize it as junk mail?
   b. What techniques does the sender use to entice you to open the envelope?
   c. Once opened, what techniques are used to prompt you to read farther than the first line?
   d. Are these techniques effective? Consider graphic design, placement of key words, how you are addressed, special offers, enticements, and deadlines.

7. Write an essay or speech about your viewpoint on the following quote by Senator John Danforth, R-Missouri, taken from the "MacNeil-Lehrer Newshour," May 8, 1992.

   If what we are talking about is the basic value system of this country, . . . then I really believe that a lot of the problem and a lot of the solution has to do with the medium of television and with the movies. What people see when they turn on the TV is violence. What they see is sex. What they see is total disrespect for family and for authority, and what they see is stereotypes. And this is, in my opinion, a very large part of the problem. The medium of television right now is disgusting. So are many of the movies that people see. And I think that one way to start on this problem is to have a summit meeting perhaps called by the President which brings together people who are leaders of broadcast, the broadcast networks, people who are leaders of cable television, of the motion picture industry, and ask them what responsibility they have for this country, other than squeezing every last dime they can out of it.

Glossary

Ad hominem
A Latin term meaning "to the man" or attacking the person. Ad hominem occurs when a person is attacked on a personal quality that is irrelevant to the issue.

Ad populum fallacy
A fallacy that consists of a false appeal to the authority of "everyone." A course of action should be taken or an idea should be supported because "everyone" is doing it or believes it.

Ambiguity
A communication problem caused when a word or expression has two or more different meanings.

Appeal to tradition
A fallacy that occurs when a belief or action is supported simply because it conforms to traditional ideas or practices.

Assumption
A belief, usually taken for granted, that is based on the experience, observations, or desires of an individual or group.

Begging the question
A fallacy that occurs when a speaker or writer assumes what needs to be proven.

Characteristic of interest
The information that a researcher seeks about a given population.

Cognitive dissonance
A theory that states that the need for congruence (consonance, harmony) is not only a human need but a drive, just as powerful as our drive for food and water. We are motivated by this drive and so we take action when things don't make sense: We try to make sense out of them.

Conclusion
A position taken about an issue; also called a claim or an opinion.

Connotation
All the images—positive, negative, or neutral—that are associated with any given denotation. The connotations of words include their emotional meanings. Both concrete and abstract words have connotations that are different for different individuals.

Control
The process of weeding out extraneous factors that could affect the outcome of a study.

Controlled studies
Research involving specific methods for comparing groups of subjects; these methods can be duplicated by other researchers.

Critical thinker
Someone who uses careful and objective reasoning to evaluate claims and make decisions.

Data
The observations made and information collected by the researcher as he or she completes a study.

Deductive reasoning
The process of reasoning from premises which, if valid and true, lead with certainty to a conclusion.

Denial
A state of mind that blocks critical thinking, and involves the repression of or refusal to recognize any negative or threatening information.

Denotation
The specific object or act that a word points to or refers to. Abstract terms have no specific denotation.

Doublespeak

Language used to lie or mislead while pretending to tell the truth. Doublespeak includes the use of *euphemism,* which means the use of a more acceptable term to describe an event, person, or object.

Egocentrism

The individual version of ethnocentrism, which has been defined as a tendency to view everything else in relationship to oneself; one's desires, values, and beliefs seem to be self-evidently correct or superior to those of others.

Enthymeme

A syllogism with a key part or parts implied rather than directly stated.

Ethics

Standards of conduct reflecting what we consider to be right or wrong behavior.

Ethnocentrism (sociocentrism)

The tendency to view one's own race or culture as central, based on the deep-seated belief that one's own group is superior to all others.

Ethos

One's credibility or reputation as a speaker.

Experimental group

A group of subjects from the sample who are exposed to a variable created by the researcher.

Expert

An individual who has education, significant experience, or both in a given area.

Fairness doctrine

A policy by which broadcasters must allow equal air time for all sides of an issue.

Fallacies

Errors in reasoning. Fallacies can be seen as (1) reasons that seem logical but don't necessarily support the conclusion, or (2) statements that distract listeners from the real issue.

False cause (also called **Post Hoc** or **Post Hoc Ergo Proctor Hoc**)
A fallacy that occurs when there is no real proof that one event caused another event; there is only evidence that one event came after another event.

False dilemma (either-or fallacy)
An error in reasoning that occurs when one polarizes a situation by presenting only two alternatives, at two extremes of the spectrum of possibilities.

Faulty analogies
The process of comparing one situation or idea to another and disregarding significant differences that make this comparison invalid.

Framing
The deliberate or unconscious use of camera shots to influence audiences.

General semanticists
Individuals who study the effects of words on people.

Gestalt principle
A principle that states that our minds strive toward congruence and completion of information. If a message strikes us as incomplete, we will fill in the missing details ourselves.

Hasty conclusions
The process of making inferences on a small sample of information.

Hypothesis
A speculation about what will be discovered from the research.

Ideal value
A value considered to be right and good.

Induction
The process of looking at known facts or research and making inferences about possible conclusions.

Issue
A question or controversial subject.

Logos
Logical organization and credible content in a speech.

Monroe's Motivated Sequence

A five-step method of organizing speeches.

Necessary condition

A condition (state of affairs, thing, process, etc.) that must be present if a particular effect is present. Equivalently, if the necessary condition is absent, then the effect cannot occur.

Opinion leaders

People who are well informed, usually through the media, about specific information and issues.

Pathos

The use of emotional appeal to support conclusions.

Points of logical vulnerability

Topics about which a person has difficulty being rational or objective.

Post hoc

See *False cause*.

Projection

The process of assuming that what another person means is what we would mean if we had used the same words.

Protocol

The design of a controlled research study.

Prejudicial enthymeme

A generalization about a person or group of persons made without adequate evidence.

Rationalization

A defense mechanism that underlies many others; it is our way of justifying or making sense of things that don't make sense and explaining things away that should be brought under examination.

Real value

A value considered to be right and good and acted upon in one's life.

Reasoning by analogy

Comparing one idea or plan to another for the purpose of supporting a conclusion. When we reason by analogy, we assume that since an idea, process, or event is similar in one way to another idea, process, or event that it is also similar in another significant way.

Reasons

Statements that provide support for conclusions.

Red herring fallacy

A fallacy in which misleading reasons are offered to support conclusions.

Reification

A process that occurs when words themselves become more powerful and real than objective reality.

Sample

Members of the target population who are studied by a researcher.

Self-fulfilling prophecy

The process whereby expectations based on inferences become true realities.

Semantic differential

A tool that allows semanticists to assess the cultural connotations of a word.

Semanticists

Individuals who study the meaning of words.

Sensationalism

A method used to attract viewers by presenting more exciting stories over less exciting but perhaps more newsworthy ones; the most bizarre, visually interesting, or *sensational* elements of these stories are featured.

Slippery slope

A fallacy that occurs when the consequences of a single act are predicted and not substantiated by evidence.

Statistical evidence

Data collected by specific methods that have been found to be reliable.

Subjects

People or animals studied to get information about a target population.

Sufficient condition

A condition (state of affairs, thing, process, etc.) that automatically leads to the production of another event. If the condition is present, then the effect will definitely occur. The sufficient condition creates the effect.

Suggestion

Presenting ideas or images in such a way as to reveal certain ideas or qualities and to conceal others.

Target population

The group about which a researcher wishes to generalize.

Vagueness

A problem that arises with the use of abstract words. A word or phrase is vague when its meaning is unclear.

Values

Beliefs, ideas, persons, or things that are held in high regard.

Value assumptions

Beliefs held by individuals that form the basis of their opinions on issues.

Weasel word

A word used to evade or retreat from a direct or forthright statement or position.

Index